MORE THAN WORDS

MORE THAN WORDS

The SCIENCE *of* DEEPENING
LOVE *and* CONNECTION
in ANY RELATIONSHIP

JOHN HOWARD, LMFT

SIMON ELEMENT

New York London Toronto Sydney New Delhi

SIMON
ELEMENT

An Imprint of Simon & Schuster, Inc.
1230 Avenue of the Americas
New York, NY 10020

First Simon Element trade paperback edition February 2023

SIMON ELEMENT is a trademark of Simon & Schuster, Inc.

For information about special discounts for bulk purchases, please contact Simon &
Schuster Special Sales at 1-866-506-1949 or business@simonandschuster.com.

The Simon & Schuster Speakers Bureau can bring authors to your live event.
For more information or to book an event, contact the Simon & Schuster Speakers
Bureau at 1-866-248-3049 or visit our website at www.simonspeakers.com.

Manufactured in the United States of America

10 9 8 7 6 5 4 3 2 1

Library of Congress Cataloging-in-Publication Data is available.

ISBN 978-1-9821-8232-8
ISBN 978-1-9821-8234-2 (pbk)
ISBN 978-1-9821-8233-5 (ebook)

This book is dedicated to my kids, because the world turns on teaching humans how to love and care for one another.

Your task is not to seek for love, but merely to seek and find all the barriers within yourself that you have built against it.

—Rumi

Contents

Foreword

John Howard's wonderful debut book, *More Than Words*, is about human connection and communication—two essentials required for surviving and thriving in our lives with others. Allow me a few moments to add my two cents to this comprehensive manual on getting along and becoming intimate in adult romantic relationships.

Our need to connect as human beings begins in the womb and continues throughout life. Our earliest means of connecting, beyond the fetal umbilical connection we have with our mothers, is our postnatal connection fastened to a primary caregiver with whom we connect nonverbally. We join through face-to-face, skin-to-skin interaction with another who seeks and finds us, again and again through an imperfect process of attunement, misattunement, and reattunement. It's a kind of mind reading as led by our caregiver who is present, interested, and attentive.

Through repeated close-up nonverbal interactions, we develop an increasingly complex connection to the outside world—the caregiver's vocal prosody, facial expressions, smell, taste, and touch. Our experience-dependent brain is lit up by these continuous exchanges between caregiver and self, constantly matching up and aligning as if synchronizing two nervous systems. Our sense of self and not-self emerges through an experience of external regulation by the caregiver, facilitating the rapid development of our own basic regulatory functions, such as thermoregulation, autonomic nervous system regulation, sleep-wake regulation, stress regulation, as well as the setting up of other vital neurobiological systems. External regulation (one-direction only) soon gives way to co-regulation (two-directions), in which our infant self interactively regulates our caregiver's nervous system, like partners flowing together in unison. Thus begins the blissful collaboration and synchrony in union we continue to seek as teens and adults—to be simultaneously separate and at one with someone else.

As we continue to develop relationships throughout life, we seek to be found, again and again, by another human being—to match up, attune, and align as if synchronizing two nervous systems. That is our natural drive as human animals, and it is as vital to our existence as is our need for air, water, and food. We are not solitary like the bear, the wolverine, or the leopard. Rather, we are herd animals that tend to pair-bond—sometimes frequently. We need other people. We need to interact with other people—a lot, actually—although some need to interact more than others. Too much solitude makes us batty.

The brain's hardware for language and speech is present at birth. However, language and speech development begin at about six months, with our first words appearing around twelve months or so. Our capacity for verbal conversation is one of our finest evolutionary achievements, along with our unique ability to imagine and invent things that don't yet exist, to predict future outcomes, to manipulate our environment, and to organize and plan ahead.

And while our ability to communicate verbally is a social and organizational boon to our species, it is also one of our downfalls. Words can easily be misused, be misunderstood, be taken as threats, and be used to distance ourselves from others.

Consider going to a foreign land where you do not speak the language. You fall back on nonverbal cues, gestures, pictures, symbols, and other behaviors to get your message across. Though energy expending and fatiguing, you get the job done. Now, you start to speak just a little bit of this still-foreign language, and what happens? Perhaps you experience more misunderstandings than when you relied simply on nonverbals. Soon you are better at speaking the language, and then perhaps you become fluent. You may believe there are fewer misunderstandings, but you might be wrong. Speaking fluently in any language can be hazardous. Why? Because our modern languages contain nuances and multiple meanings depending on context, perception, state of mind, various levels of attention, vocal tone, facial expression, gestures, postures, and atmospheric noise levels.

I could go on.

We think we're being clear with our speech, but we don't really know. We think we understand what's being said, but we can't be sure. In fact, we might find that we are misunderstanding each other much of the time. While this is often no big deal, it can sometimes be disastrous. When we are under stress, in distress, distracted, or in a hurry, our verbal and nonverbal communication can lead to big problems, misunderstandings, hurt feelings, and threat reactions.

What are the reasons for this vulnerability in human communication? For one, all human beings scan for threat cues in the environment as part of the survival instinct. Threat perception increases with stress and distress. Threat readiness amplifies with the memory of previous injury. Threat perception intensifies with environmental sensory cues such as unexpected or inundating sounds, visuals, movements, smells, as well as discomforting internal sensations. When we perceive threat from inside or from outside of ourselves, we act swiftly because our survival instincts demand immediate self-preservation.

Most of us mean no harm most of the time. The harm we inflict on those we love is less intentional than we might believe in a stressful moment. Rather, the speed at which we interact is much faster than thought and tends to be reflexive, automatic, memory-based, and frankly, self-centered. Good communication and connection require full presence and attention to our partner and consideration of self and other at the same time. This is especially so when we are less than relaxed, happy, and feeling safe.

If you are like most people, you might believe you're fine with communication and connection. But what about when you or your partner aren't feeling good, aren't feeling understood, or aren't feeling safe or secure? How good are you then?

Under even minor levels of stress, we mostly think of ourselves, our own interests and concerns. While that is a normal part of being human, thinking only of oneself when attached to another person can lead to perceived threat in the mind of the other. For instance, as I speak to you about my wants, concerns, and hurt feelings, do I keep you in mind at the same time? Do I make certain you know that I'm keeping your interests and concerns in mind—even if I'm the target of your distress? If I don't, why should you believe I care? If my speech or actions do not take into account who you are and how you are likely to react to my chosen words, vocal tone, facial expressions, and gestures, why should you believe I am safe and friendly? If I fail to maintain eye contact with you as I talk, how can I make necessary immediate adjustments if I should misattune, misunderstand, or misread the moment?

Communication and connection with another human being is fragile business. It's not something to take casually, for granted, or in haste, and it's not a time for cutting corners. It's a bit like being on a tightwire together. Really fun and cool when concentrated and in the flow and really dangerous if either of you is inattentive, reckless, and out of sync.

As you read Howard's book, pay close attention to the information and advice he provides. Use it to practice with your partner. Use it to become better, more skillful and sensitive than most average human beings will likely ever be. Use it because our relationships are the key to our happiness and well-being.

—Stan Tatkin, PsyD, cofounder of the PACT Institute
and author of *Wired for Love*, *Your Brain on Love*, and *We Do*

Acknowledgments

I'd like to thank my wife, Dr. Charlotte Howard, who was incredibly patient and supportive of me as I wrote this book, and who has been a tremendous catalyst of my relationship growth. My teachers and therapists have generously steered my personal and professional development, helping me to heal traumas from the past, illuminate some of my blind spots, and learn how to be more caring toward myself. I'd like to thank my children, who were also patient and understanding as I took time to write, and who I hope will one day grow up to read this book and apply some of its principles in their relationship lives. I learned much of the material in this book from Dr. Stan Tatkin, my mentor in the relationship space, whose brilliant mind continues to inspire many relationship professionals to integrate neuroscience and the art of love. I also have much gratitude for my spiritual teachers who have helped me grow in directions I could not have pointed myself toward.

I'd like to thank my colleagues and team members at PRESENCE for their dedication in helping to build the world's first wellness center integrating mental, physical, and relationship health based in the latest science. My personal editor, Jennifer Gandin Le, deserves much credit for helping to shape the book as I wrote it and acting as a sounding board for some of its elements. Thank you to my agent, David Fugate, for representing me—always chill, yet always on the ball. Special acknowledgment goes to the incredibly talented Ronnie Alvarado, my editor at Simon Element, who made this project a reality: she saw what this book could be from the beginning and helped bring a much-needed, inclusive relationship resource into the world. Thank you to the entire publishing team at Simon & Schuster, including art director Patrick Sullivan for the epic cover art.

My advance readers and colleagues generously gave of their time to help improve this material: Dr. Tori Olds, my sister Daphne Howard Myers, and Juliane Taylor Shore. My parents catch some heat in this book but have also supported me personally and professionally and deserve much thanks, appreciation, and credit. Without them, I would not be who I am today. It is a humbling honor to work with my clients past and present: their growth inspires me and gives me faith in these concepts by seeing them work in real-life settings. And I'd like to thank my friends who inspired me to think big, reach for greater heights, and make an impact on the world.

I'd like to thank the academic researchers, clinicians, and theorists whose ideas and work make up the science of the book, including luminaries in the field of interpersonal neurobiology such as Drs. Daniel J. Siegel, Pat Ogden, Allan N. Schore, Diana Fosha, Bonnie Badenoch, Louis Cozolino, and others. This book incorporates the important work of Stephen W. Porges, Jaak Panksepp, Peter A. Levine, Sue Johnson, Antonio R. Damasio, Robert M. Sapolsky, Don R. Catherall, Ellyn Bader, John M. Gottman, Bessel A. van der Kolk, and many others referenced throughout the text. Special appreciation goes to trailblazers who have highlighted the importance of diversity inclusion in social resources such as Resmaa Menakem, Jack Drescher, Kimberlé Williams Crenshaw, and Tristan Taormino. Thank you for the important work you all do to deepen love and connection in our world.

Introduction

*The human mind is a relational and embodied process that
regulates the flow of energy and information.*

—Dr. Dan Siegel

Connection is in. Communication is out.

Yes, communication has been the darling of pop psychology since research in the 1970s put it front and center as a key factor in healthy relationships.
The theory was that good communication would facilitate connection.

But twenty-first-century neuroscience has transformed our understanding of
what builds and sustains fulfilling relationships. Connection is what we're really
looking for, and it facilitates communication, not the other way around. The reason for that is simple: our nervous system is most concerned with survival, and
connection speaks a security language to that system that helps it relax and open
up.[1] When our bodies feel safe, we let down our guard, and we can be playful,
vulnerable, and bond with others. We can open our minds to new ideas. We can
learn and grow. When the nervous system doesn't feel safe, however, words just
can't make up the difference. We try to talk, but a disconnected feeling persists,
and it influences the words we hear. Communication continues to feel labored,
resentments are not truly repaired, and the feeling of love can't fully return. This
book will teach you powerful ways to connect that speak security directly to the
nervous system and help you deepen love and trust in any relationship.

Even though humans are wired to connect to others, most of us struggle
in relationships. At one point in my life, I wondered if having a relationship was

worth it at all. It seemed to be loaded with stress, friction, responsibility, and no guarantee that it will go well. But relationships can also convey love, connection, and support. While we exhibit great diversity, humans are also much alike in some ways: we have brains and nervous systems that desire safety, trust, connection, peace, love, and emotional support in our relationships. When we learn how to satisfy these deeper needs, communication improves and our relationships feel supportive and fulfilling. When our relationships don't go well, the resulting stress impacts our health and well-being in negative ways.[2] It's worth investing in how to deepen connection and create more secure relationships in your life.

> Communication has been sold as the golden ticket to improve relationships, but experts now understand that dialogue is a poor way to address problems of connection—and *most relationship issues are problems of connection.* We may argue about the dishes, but what we really want to know is, *Do I matter to you?*

Connection is everything. While we may argue about petty things in our relationships, what we really want to know is, *Do you love me?*, *Do you care?*, and *Am I a priority to you?* Words alone can't answer those questions. Most of human communication is nonverbal and nonconscious,[3,4] taking place through signals such as facial expressions, tone of voice, and body language, which the brain can read to gauge friendliness and through that judge whether we should open to connection with someone.[5] As much as 90 percent of the information that travels back and forth between people in human interactions is outside of conscious awareness, yet it communicates key connecting information to others' nervous systems.[6]

Understanding how to speak in terms of attachment to the nervous system gives you relationship superpowers. You can harness the 90 percent that is outside of conscious awareness and speak directly to the parts of the brain and body that measure connection.[7] I call these tools the Language of the Nervous System, as they help you convey trust and security that facilitate closeness and bonding. Once you learn and practice this language, you'll be able to shape your bonds more intentionally toward the love and stability you seek.

If you are partnered, this book will give you a road map to deeper connection, and if you are not, it still provides you with valuable advice you can use to help you better date and prepare for fulfilling future partnerships. While this book is written primarily for committed romantic partners, it has valuable advice to deepen any relationship—with your kids, co-workers, friends, and family members. This science also has the power to help heal our communities and provide a valuable path of personal growth, helping you mature and develop wholeness as a person.

One of the biggest issues we all face in our relationships is that we receive very little education and training on how to have awesome, connected bonds with others. Imagine if we spent as much time on relationship skills as we spent memorizing Algebra II equations! The lack of support for relationship skills in our education mirrors what often happens at home—a dearth of examples of how to lead healthy, connected, emotionally supportive lives. I started noticing this gap in the fourth grade. Reeling from the loss of my primary caregiver and without anyone close to talk to, I started wondering why we don't spend more time learning how to love and care for each other.

In 2013, I created Ready Set Love®, the world's first neuroscience-based online course for couples, and referred to it as "the class you never got on how to have a healthy, connected relationship." I felt strongly that everyone should have such a tutorial, since relationship skills make such a big difference in our lives. We know that the health of our relationships affects everything from our happiness to our physical health, from our stress levels and well-being to our sense of success in life. Considering relationships are one of the most complex and challenging things we take on in life, the chance that we might be really good at them without much training or practice is, unfortunately, very low. It's a wonder we don't support ourselves better as a society to have close, connected relationships.

Consider other difficult, complex things we take on in life. How often are we good at them without specialized education and training? We spend hours practicing instruments, languages, and sports, because our brains need that support to develop competency. Our society has misplaced its priorities, allotting too much focus in school to obscure topics few will use in life and not enough attention toward the universal need for relationship skills. Whenever I speak, I ask people if anyone received a class on how to have a healthy, connected relationship. To date, no one has said that they did, although some have mentioned carrying around an egg for a couple days and trying to keep it from breaking as a simplified exercise in caring for a newborn. Yep, that's it.

As a result, we're often not prepared to have the kinds of relationships we desire. We want love, connection, good communication, ease, calm, romance, and fun, but instead we often get into petty arguments, we feel disconnected, annoyed by differences, and sometimes our relationships fail. Hurtful experiences in relationships then create their own trauma, grief, and loss that further complicate our ability to have healthy partnerships.

We also need to develop the specific skills that help each unique relationship feel connected, which have to be discovered in every partnership by working together and testing your methods until you know what works. Modern neuroscience has given us secrets for how to improve relationships based on how the brain relates to others, including a special one to develop the connecting habits we need: practice.[8] Yes, you read that right—just like any other skill, our relationships need time and energy put into them in the form of practicing. In fact, leading approaches to couples therapy utilize practice as a primary learning strategy, leaving the old approach of just conversing about problems behind.[9,10] Rather than just talking about issues, science has shown that practice can reshape poor relationship habits by assisting the parts of the brain responsible for connecting behaviors to learn new tricks.[11] That skill then shows itself in greater relationship satisfaction.[12]

The Brilliance of Practice

Practice is a common tool for improvement in sports, music, and other endeavors because it targets procedural memory, the memory behind automatic behavior. Since many of our relationship tendencies come from the automatic system, practicing new connecting skills is important to developing better habits that bring you closer together.[13] My daughter, for example, is a dancer. After a recent competition, she told me how when she gets onstage, she just performs without thinking about each move, and that's because she rehearses her routines until they are ingrained deep in her muscle memory. When she's in front of an audience and under pressure, she can just flow based on the procedural memory she has developed. Most relationship behaviors come from that same automated place. Many of our actions and reactions, facial expressions, tone of voice, body language, and knee-jerk responses come out before we really think carefully about them, and that's how we are designed to be—interactions happen at a fast rate of speed. Practice helps us build natural connecting skills, so we can trust that our bodies remember the moves that engender security with others. Surprisingly, practice has not been commonly used as a strategy to improve relationships, but it works, and instills hope as you build skill and collaborate with others to deepen your abilities.

Learning to connect more deeply helps you to bridge differences with others and serves as a potent path of personal growth.[14] According to neuroscience experts, the complexity, challenges, and closeness of our relationship lives offer extensive growth opportunities to us as individuals.[15,16] By embracing the natural diversity present in our relationships and focusing on connecting in the moment, we can improve the security of our bonds and make use of them as a powerful avenue for personal growth.

Relational neuroscience has helped us understand that if you work together, supporting each other to retrain automatic tendencies, you can each change habits more quickly and effectively than you can on your own. The relational space is the best training ground, because it surfaces emotional wounds, automatic tendencies, and issues, challenges us to develop new skills, brings the resources of two nervous systems together, and can offer support in the change process.

When we train the procedural system, our natural and automatic relationship behaviors become more secure and connecting. Friendliness and goodwill come through our faces, in our tone, and in our body language. Deliberate practice with others gives you a fun and effective way to improve skills that brings you together and shares the responsibility for growth, getting you to a sense of confidence and competency faster than talking about your issues alone.

I have used the power of these concepts for years with clients as a couples therapist and seen tremendous results in how they reduce conflict and deepen love between partners. I have also incorporated them in my own partnership and relationships and have seen much improvement as a result. While much of the information about how to use these powerful ideas and tools is still housed in academic minds and publications and discussed at professional conferences, *More Than Words* puts these valuable concepts in your hands so you can use them to deepen your relationships and to grow as an individual.

This book will teach you effective approaches from the new science for how to deepen connection in your relationships, and the methods used by the world's top couples therapists to enhance trust, security, and love with others. It will also give you a dynamic road map for how to deepen your personal growth as an individual through relationship life. When connection is compromised, everything is a problem, but when you have a strong sense of connection, it imparts goodwill that smooths over relationship errors. You don't need fancy communication to have meaningful, bonding interactions with others. *More Than Words* is a modern guidebook for how to implement science-based strategies to achieve deeper love with those you care about most.

The Science of Connection

Within the last fifteen to twenty years, new research in the fields of neuroscience and psychology has shown that connection is measured more by primitive security centers in the brain than by the frontal lobes that process language and thinking.[17] The neuroscience research on relationships has also helped us understand that most of our behaviors in relationships are automatic—driven by the procedural memory system that propels performance in any domain where quick, native skill is needed.[18] Because our reactions with others often move too quickly to premeditate, human emotions and facial expressions often occur pre-thought and many of these habits are shaped in childhood, when much of the brain's social systems is built.[19] The good news about knowing how automatic we are in relationships is that we can bring compassion and understanding to patterns that do not serve connection, and create a shared purpose around improving those habits. We may be angry at our partners for their faults, but the real question is, *What helps our partnerships get better?*

The short answer begins with nervous system safety and developing a shared culture of responsibility and practice around improvement. As you will see in the chapters that follow, however, there are many approaches to connecting more deeply with others, all illuminated by modern science. This book relies on the scientific fields of interpersonal neurobiology, affective neuroscience, attachment theory, affect regulation theory, trauma healing, somatic psychology, primatology, experiential psychotherapy, emotion-focused psychology, psychobiology, and research on how the brain learns. I also build on my many years of experience working with hundreds of couples, utilizing the new science and testing what works, and trading notes with other leading couples therapists to determine what is most effective at creating positive change.

This book emphasizes how much of connection occurs through primitive aspects of the nervous system but also how deliberate practice that involves our bodies, feelings, and repetition can help reshape automatic habits. The new science has shown that improving relationship skills takes practice—not just talk.[20] Practice helps to retrain implicit patterns and provides a fun way to improve relationships skills. *More Than Words* will help you deepen your connection with others, retrain disconnecting tendencies, and sharpen your skills so that you can have more meaningful relationships.

Working to improve connection in your relationships is one of the best ways to increase your *psychological flexibility* and *emotional resilience*, two key markers of mental health and of optimized psychology.[21] One aspect of psychological flexibility is the ability to see the world from more than one perspective. Relationships ask us to look at the world around us and to develop a relational mindset that is complex, resilient, and embracing of diversity. This ability matures the mind, helps people be less rigid and judgmental, and often makes us smarter.[22]

Psychological flexibility is an important determinant of mental health and behavioral effectiveness.[23] Rather than basing actions on the myriad of thoughts and feelings in any given moment, this flexibility helps you stay connected to your core sense of who you are and how you want to be with others.[24] Emotional resilience is the ability to recover from hurt feelings or after suffering a setback. It's our dedication to keep going when we feel fragile or emotionally wounded, as well as our ability to handle stressful experiences and to mobilize the robustness of our nervous systems to find our way back to balance. It is a key ability that allows us to surf the emotional waves of life and of relationships without becoming destabilized[25] and tends to strengthen and improve as we practice engaging emotion and extending compassion to ourselves and to others.[26]

Connection Is More Important than Communication

We often persist in trying *to communicate in order to connect, rather than connecting to facilitate smooth communication.* This misalignment is one reason why many modern relationships fail.

While verbal communication in the form of language usually imparts information, it is a poor mediator of connection, as it makes the frontal lobes—a very resource-intensive part of the brain—work hard to interpret language and meaning.[27] Which means that processing verbal communication can be tiring, and so when we want to bond in a more relaxing way, primitive connecting cues help us avoid the pitfalls of language and debates or technical conversations that highlight our differences of thought with others. Understanding the role of verbal communication and when to connect through other means helps establish a greater sense of security at your core.

After all, connection is the feeling we are going for when we couple up. None of us thinks, *I'd like to find a partner I can regularly exchange information with!* Sure, we appreciate good communication, but what we really want is a *feeling*—feelings of love, trust, connection, romantic attraction, reliability, and security. Good communication is well and good, but feeling connected is essential. We form relationships for many reasons: lust, financial stability, love, friendship, romantic chemistry, a common lifestyle, or to start a family together, but according to modern neuroscience, what the brain primarily seeks in a partnership is a sense of greater safety and security in the world.[28] That intrinsic sense of security serves as the foundation for all the other dimensions of relationship life.

So what's the difference between communication and connection? Communication is talking about things, whereas connection is creating an emotional bond in the moment. When you're in a purely intellectual back-and-forth with others, you can try to get on the same page and connect through ideas and words, but it's often inefficient and cumbersome and can highlight differences in your approach. If we connect more by reaching out, touching, offering a friendly smile, or saying something loving, we are reminded of what really matters in our relationships—feeling loved and supported, and knowing that someone cares. We all have logistical details that need to be discussed throughout daily life, but if you establish connection first, your interactions stay focused on the primary task of your union—to love and care for each other.

Why Connection?

Let's talk dishwashers. Many people argue about how to load the dishwasher, or similarly silly things, and it's because our anxieties and need to feel secure get wrapped up in small daily activities and decisions. (Personally, I like bowls at the top, without them overlapping too much so I know they're getting clean. My wife doesn't mind crowding up the machine and just tossing everything in there.) But let's be honest, little things like this don't matter compared to love, and we need to notice when we feel anxious about such things. On those days when you're mired in seemingly petty arguments and each of you feels controlled or unappreciated by the other, or when you're in a back-and-forth on a minor issue, words don't typically help to untangle those annoying debates. Our conversations are already a little too heady and highlight our differences. What we really need is connection to remind ourselves of what matters. With communication, you might trade perspectives and engage in some debate and disagreement as to the *right* way to do things. With connection, you return to the feeling of closeness that defines your purpose for being together.

Connection allows you to get away from silly back-and-forth conversation in moments like that and signal love and friendliness. When that occurs, you stop arguing about the dishwasher. In fact, you might end up making love on the dishwasher and forget to load it altogether! Let all the dishes be dirty!! Love is in the air!! Prioritizing connection reminds us that the core task in relationship is to care about each other, not be "right" or have everything the way we want. When love is the focus, your communication becomes more efficient. Connection solves what communication can't because it breaks through emotionally.[29]

Connection allows us to relax with others and derive the social and health benefits of a stable relationship. When you feel connected, it's because you feel secure enough to let your guard down and trust that others have your back. Connection overcomes judgment of faults and differences in what Dr. John Gottman calls Positive Sentiment Override (PSO),[30] just like how we tend to love and support our children even when they mess up. Connection is trust in the security of your relationship and how confident you feel that you have the emotional support of your partner. Connection promotes reliability, consistency, consideration, thoughtfulness, and kindness with others.

Connection and Health

Connection is a basic human need that most people require to thrive, much in the same way that we need food and shelter to thrive. A growing body of research has begun to highlight the critical link between healthy relationships and physical and mental health.[31] Healthy relationships increase emotional resilience and self-confidence.[32] Harvard's Grant Study, one of the longest longitudinal studies in the world, found that the quality of our close relationships impacts longevity, immune system health, and fulfillment more than any other health factors.[33] Having strong social relationships has been shown to be equal to diet and exercise as a key factor affecting wellness, inflammation, hypertension, and improving our overall physical health.[34]

Stressful and dysfunctional relationships, on the other hand, can have the opposite effect, increasing susceptibility to disease, unhappiness, decreased lifespan, and contributing significantly to *allostatic load*, the cumulative impact of stress that degrades cell tissue, DNA, and cellular function.[35,36] Harvard's *Living Better, Living Longer*, a compilation of recent health research, examined data from more than 309,000 people and found that a lack of strong relationships increases the risk of premature death from all causes by 50 percent.[37] Social isolation and loneliness, which can be felt even in committed relationships when connection is lacking, has been shown to be a risk factor to health and longevity equal to smoking fifteen cigarettes a day, being an alcoholic, or being obese.[38]

The future of health care is integrating physical and mental health with having close, caring relationships. These three primary domains of health intersect with one another in important ways, which is why relationships benefit when we take care of ourselves mentally and physically and why our mental and physical health often improve as we have more connected relationships.[39] We can no longer afford to ignore the important dimension of the quality of our relationships in our lives or focus solely on physical or mental agility while neglecting our ability to connect with others. Not only does learning to connect impart clear physical and mental benefits; it makes life more meaningful, more fun, and helps us develop a more equitable and collaborative society.

Connecting in a Busy World

The pace and nature of modern life can make it challenging to connect deeply with others. Most of us are busy, and when we're not we have other outlets that demand our attention. As such, many people report feeling lonely, despite having frequent access to text, email, the internet, and social media, all of which is supposed to connect us but can leave us feeling isolated in our feelings from others. While modern technology has evolved quickly, our nervous systems are still the result of hundreds of thousands of years of evolution, and our connecting mechanisms still look for the primitive cues they were developed to measure.[40] We need human-to-human physical and emotional contact to feel connected, even in the technological age.

One of the most obvious examples of our need for in-person connection has been the experience of children during the coronavirus pandemic. When kids were required to engage with school and their classmates online, mental health issues in children skyrocketed.[41] Despite their familiarity with technology and the ability to connect easily with others via Zoom and other video tools, children sequestered at home began to show signs of depression, low self-esteem, irritability, and suicidality.[42] As kids began to return to in-person classes and to engage in person with their peers at school, mental health issues for kids seemed to improve.[43] Many families I have spoken with reported a huge difference in their kids' mental health as children resumed in-person activities with their peers and friends.

Even when we're with others, distractions to emotional connection abound. A few years ago, I walked into a trendy New York City bar and thought, *Imagine all the cool people here to talk to, how exciting it will be to learn about what they're building and working on in the world!* I was then dismayed to see that literally every person sitting at the bar had their head down and was interacting with their phone rather than talking with another person. Sure, I could have interrupted, but it goes to show how easy it is to get sucked into technology and how we sometimes de-prioritize in-person connection, even when it's available.

Of course, connection also takes emotional courage. To not feel lonely, we have to open up, be vulnerable, share, cry, celebrate wins with others, and let others into our real experience of life. As a society focused on independence, intellectual communication, and productivity, we're often uncomfortable with emotional intimacy and slowing down enough to share our experience with others. Shame, one of the most difficult emotions to tolerate, is one reason why we keep many things to ourselves, including our struggles, fears, mistakes, and needs. We may also feel weak or embarrassed in reaching out to others for emotional connection and support, or worry that others won't care for us well. No amount of technology or time spent together can make up for the difficult process of opening up and sharing our tender emotional experience with others.

Opening up and seeking to create strong emotional bonds is helpful not only for committed partners but also when seeking a primary relationship. Dating these days often begins as a technological exercise of navigating apps and texting with others, which doesn't lend itself to creating strong connections. People are often connecting digitally with many others and can be flaky when it comes to responding or maintaining connection. Even when people meet in person, they're often on their best behavior, trying to impress. To go deeper and make a meaningful connection, it helps to be vulnerable and get real, which also helps evaluate the emotional skills of your prospective partner. People who can share emotions and show some vulnerability generally develop close bonds more quickly. When you are less comfortable with emotional intimacy, you may not know your partner as well until many months in. Opening up makes you more memorable to others, encourages (and tests) empathy, and establishes good, caring habits at the outset of a relationship, all valuable in the dating process.

Feeling disconnected from others or isolated is fairly common in the modern world. Millennials and Gen Zers report feeling the loneliest, despite being "digital natives" and having abundant access to communication technologies such as social media, texting, and video apps.[44] Those who are technologically oriented are sometimes more familiar with communicating through such tools and may be less comfortable with direct, human-to-human bonding and intimacy. Technology that is supposed to connect us can leave us feeling alone, or with more superficial relationships. Even married partners score highly on loneliness scales, as many people don't feel comfortable opening up to their partners to share their true feelings or don't have a culture of connection.[45] Scores of partners feel stretched for time to tend to their relationship due to work, parenting, and other factors, but even when they have time together, they may not use it in the service of connection. While we easily meet the needs of countless other tasks, tending to our relationships often doesn't make the daily to-do list.

Attachment

Attachment research started in the 1960s observing how infants develop secure bonds with parents and caregivers.[46] In the 1980s, the research was extended to adults, and important parallels were found between those early experiences in childhood and people's patterns in adult relationships, revealing that the brain treats adult partnerships as attachment bonds.[47] That research helps explain the genesis of our automatic and wired-in tendencies and now connects to neuroscience.[48,49] *Attachment theory*—the result of that research—is helpful for decoding relationship dynamics and exploring our individual styles that get set up in childhood.[50] Learning about my attachment style was one of the most valuable insights I gained from studying relationship science and it made a huge difference in my awareness and level of connecting skill.

Attachment research helps us understand that love is not just a feeling, but part of the attachment behavioral system in mammals that facilitates bonding and survival.[51] It illuminates how the human nervous system uses the same process as most other mammals do when it comes to creating secure bonds via physical proximity, touch, tone, eye contact, and responsiveness.[52] And attachment theory helps explain why connection matters more than communication, and the connecting power of nonverbal signals as a critical bonding tool between humans.[53]

"Secure attachment" refers to relationships in which people pay attention to one another's experience and shift interactions in real time to care for one another. It is a healthy interdependence between partners that celebrates need and connection. Further, secure relationships exhibit *mutuality* ("good for you and good for me" interactions), and tracking of emotional states by partners to offer support as needed.[54] Partners who engage in such secure behaviors can develop strong, enjoyable, fulfilling relationships that last. Secure attachment also requires consistency in connecting behaviors that foster trust and allow reliable bonds to form, and can heal traumas by creating a safe space for mental and emotional wounds to surface while offering nurture and care to those parts.[55]

The attachment tendencies we develop in our families growing up are often subconsciously expressed in how we relate to ourselves and others as adults.[56] Those who experienced challenging relationships in childhood, yet found a way to exhibit more secure tendencies through healthy adult bonds, achieve what is known as *earned security*. While there are several pathways to earned security such as counseling, developing a better understanding of one's childhood, and processing traumas, having healthy relationships is considered the most effective way to heal past relational traumas and their resulting tendencies.[57]

The Neuroscience Era

From fields as diverse as education, athletics, medicine, and psychology, modern neuroscience has changed the game across disciplines and revised previous understandings and best practices. The intersection of how mind, body, brain, and nervous system interact in relationships is clearer than ever. Such research is busting many long-held myths about partnership and connection, changing popular ideas about relationships, and causing leading institutes to update their materials. Neuroscience studies help us understand what creates stress between people, what allows the brain to relax and trust, and what creates guardedness and suspicion. Brain science helps us understand what generates love and bonding so we can be more effective at creating secure, fulfilling relationships.

Modern science ties relationship habits to developmental patterns in childhood, explains the automatic strategies we use to seek calm and relief, and explores mental resilience from a psychological and a neurological perspective, considering how both the software of the mind and the hardware of the brain affect relationships. Our understanding of how to heal from traumas has evolved, based on our expanded understanding of the neurochemistry of psychological damage and the role that relationships play in eliciting traumatic triggers and in healing them. In addition, greater awareness exists about the impact of racialized trauma and oppression on populations and individuals, how those experiences impact the nervous system, and how those forces shape the experience of connecting to others.[58]

We live in an exciting new era of relationship improvement. Ideas we once had in the field of psychology and in pop culture about relationship health are giving way to more exact science about how connection works and what happens in the nervous system and in our brains when humans interact. Psychology has always been considered a "soft science" because of the assumptions it has had to make about how the mind works. Now soft and hard science are blending together due to new technology that can measure some of those assumptions, such as PET scans and functional MRIs.[59] With greater quantitative research on what happens in the brain and mind during human interactions, we can be more definitive about what improves connection. This research has given us a better sense of what bonds people to each other, how the brain interprets connection, and what creates the conditions for optimal trust and safety.

> The new science of connection has tremendous ability to help us be more effective in our relationships, form deeper connections, and heal individual issues and past traumas through an increased sense of security in ourselves, with others, and in the world. Having deeper, more connected relationships is a path toward individual healing, healing to your relationship, and even to the community at large.

One of the biggest takeaways from the neuroscience of relationships is that under stress, the frontal lobes of the brain tend to go offline and we rely on more primitive strategies of interaction.[60] All the fancy concepts we have learned about how to interact in a healthy manner tend to go out the window, and we are left with implicit, procedural tactics: habits that are wired deep into our core and often are the result of childhood impressions during the critical years that the brain builds much of its attachment infrastructure.[61] To compensate for that tendency, it is important to train our nervous systems and implicit wiring to act more securely under stress. That is easier said than done, but once we know not just *what to improve*, but *how* we can improve, our efforts become more successful and efficient.

Modern neuroscience has helped us understand that the brain has a hierarchy of needs, and that it seeks to satisfy its most important questions first before it moves on to other matters. Because the human nervous system is built primarily to keep us safe and to help us survive, the brain's initial question marks around others have to do with security. If you can satisfy those internal questions cleanly and convincingly, the brain moves on, opening itself up to play, intimacy, romance, witty banter, and more.[62] But if the brain's initial safety concerns are left unanswered, then there's always a crack in the relationship's foundation and all other tasks become harder.

Using neuroscience, you can learn how to create a stronger sense of security with others more quickly and deeply, allowing you to move on to more complex aspects of relationship. With that, interactions can become relaxing and fun, because the subconscious stress of worrying about security considerations such as *Can I rely on you?* and *Will you leave me?* are answered. Without us realizing it, when we're with others our subconscious is constantly analyzing security information, gathering and calculating that data in the background.[63] Because the nervous system runs an ongoing program of establishing security, we need habits and skills that can answer those subconscious questions, consistently and naturally in the moment.

When the brain feels connected and secure, you are far less likely to get into the petty arguments with others that are the result of disconnection and insecurity, and which often cause friction. As you read this book, you can start using its techniques today to avoid those conflicts, increase intimacy and emotional connection in your closest relationships, and sustain that feeling of connection most of the time.

What Defines Relationship Health?

Only recently has relationship health begun to be defined in scientific terms. For a long time, religious, cultural, and governmental norms dominated the definition, sometimes excluding same-sex, non-monogamous, or non-married couples from the club. The definition of what constitutes a valid, healthy relationship has often been politicized and found itself at the crossroads of changing cultural forces. For example, interracial marriage was banned in the United States until

1967.[64] Further, too often such cultural agendas have also held that the healthiest relationship is a monogamous marriage between a man and a woman. Modern science disagrees, however, and today relationship experts use more fact-based criteria and measurements to assess relationship health.

To establish a good working definition of relationship health, it is helpful to understand a little of the history of its politics and culture in the Western world. Here's the quick take: the sexual revolution of the 1960s ushered in a new era in Western society that was more willing to upend traditional relational frameworks. Sex became less taboo, open relationships more normalized, LGBTQ+ individuals began to receive more public acceptance, and women in particular felt more empowered to take charge in relationships and ask for what makes them feel good. That questioning of traditional relationship life also led to a countermovement to shore up the traditional view of marriage.[65] Religious and other institutions poured money into research to define relationship health according to more traditional cultural values, funding academic chair positions at universities and engaging in public education campaigns.[66] Such efforts continue today, even by governmental entities. As recently as 2004, the US House and Senate attempted to pass the Federal Marriage Amendment (FMA), which would have legally defined marriage as a union of one man and one woman.[67]

While the 1970s built on the legacy of the 1960s cultural revolution and saw advancements for women, LGBTQ+ individuals, and minorities, conservative institutions were still hard at work seeking to tie relationship life to more traditional norms and exalting the heterosexual, monogamous marriage as the most valid—and healthy—type of relationship.[68]

Despite the persistence of traditionalists to define relationship health according to cultural and religious norms, scientific efforts to understand health between primary partners began in the 1970s, and built on previous research in the areas of attachment, family therapy, and individual psychology. Trailblazers such as Drs. Ellyn Bader and John Gottman began to gather data and analyze satisfaction in primary partner relationships in more scientific terms. While some of the efforts developed would be colored by the religious or cultural influences of the people involved, or by the white normative standards of the academic and scientific communities, ultimately the path was being laid for a more diverse, accepting, and scientific assessment of what constitutes a healthy relationship.

By 2015—when the United States finally legalized same-sex marriage in all fifty states—the field of relationship improvement had begun to wrest definitions of relationship health away from traditionally minded institutions and engage in an important scientific correction to balance out their influence. The work to celebrate healthy relationships of all types continues today as science-based experts promote relationship resources and self-help that welcomes all individuals seeking loving and secure relationships, in whichever form they choose.

This book builds on that modern work and uses a definition of relationship health developed by Dr. Stan Tatkin called secure functioning. "Secure functioning" refers to the health of people's interactions—do they relate to each other in a secure manner? Do interactions feel good to both partners? Do they pay attention to each other to know when to shift to ease upset and stress? Healthy relationships elicit security rather than fear and look out for all partners in real time. They use emotional connection to create a trusted bond and are attuned and responsive. Because this definition looks at nervous system safety and what the brain does in partner interactions, it is a more cross-cultural way of measuring relationship health than using social norms.

To really understand secure functioning, though, we must comprehend what a healthy relationship really is. In this book, a healthy relationship is understood as one in which people care for each other well in the process of interacting and which makes room for individuality while tending to security needs. Secure-functioning relationships exhibit mutuality, caring for the needs of all parties simultaneously. In such a bond, partners are present with each other in the moment, paying attention to shifting emotional experience and responding sensitively with support.

Secure functioning is a science-based understanding of relationship health that is broadly relevant across cultures, sexual orientations, and relationship preferences.[69] It is important that any definition of relationship health be embracing of diverse partnerships such as same-sex, non-married, biracial, and non-monogamous couples. Work by leading thinkers Jack Drescher, Resmaa Menakem, Tristan Taormino, and others has highlighted the importance of using a definition of relationship health that is inclusive of diverse populations and accounts for social traumas that impact individuals and couples.[70,71,72] Race, religion, sexual orientation, culture, and relationship orientation have no intrinsic impact on the ability of people to function securely, outside of known impacts due to systemic oppression. Even partners who choose to not define their relationship and commitment, preferring to keep identity structures and relationship attachments flexible, can function securely. It's all measured by how people treat each other, not if they fit into a pre-approved cultural box.

A New Era of Science and Inclusion

Social norms have changed since many relationship self-help classics were written. Modern readers don't want to hear about relationship roles defined by sex or gender, or to be held to a culturally normative standard that is decades old. With that, it is critical to include same-sex couples in relationship resources and to avoid simple stereotypes. Today's partners navigate their own relational culture, identity, preferences, commitment structure, and division of labor based on their individual and shared worldview and don't want outdated, nonscientific views that tell them how to do it.

The neuroscience era has coincided with social changes, including an increased acceptance of diverse unions, a relaxing of relationship norms, an evolving distribution of domestic and parental roles that are no longer assigned simply by gender, and greater awareness of unequal power dynamics between partners. Social issues such as patriarchy, toxic masculinity, racism, classism, and oppression are more often discussed, including in the context of how they may shape primary relationships. Many today seek greater equality for oppressed and marginalized individuals, and therapists like myself seek more inclusivity and diversity in science and self-help resources. This book aims to promote that new era of relationship improvement—one based in the latest science, neuroscience, and helping to dismantle outdated tropes about relationship life.

We do a disservice to all relationships when we rely on non-science-based ideas or stereotypes in our evaluation of what constitutes a healthy, connected relationship. Relationship resources that use concepts, language, and examples that apply to all seeking love and connection are more scientifically sound than those that are only inclusive of specific groups and identities, and have the additional benefit of helping our society become more equal and compassionate. The methods in these pages follow in that vein and work toward facilitating connection that relies on the hard-wiring built into the human brain and nervous system and are effective across different types of relationships with diverse and unique individuals.[73]

Historically, much emphasis has been placed on marriage as the gold standard of committed relationship. But that understanding is misconstrued at best. The truth is that many partners prefer to remain unmarried for a variety of reasons. Some individuals' second or third non-married committed relationships are healthier than their first marriages. Those in nontraditional relationships, including nonmonogamous, asexual, polyamorous, or open orientations, deserve respect as able to form healthy unions like everyone else. Even now, widespread cultural bias often treats nontraditional relationships as less secure or satisfying, even though they involve consenting adults and often exhibit greater self-awareness, maturity, and relationship skill among partners. Nontraditional relationship lifestyles are common among young people,[74] another reason why it is important to address the full variety of relationship structures that they and others may pursue in improvement and support resources. Non-monogamy is not a sign of an unhealthy relationship, or a sign of trauma in the individuals who pursue such lifestyles.[75] These can be healthy, secure, fulfilling relationships, but they do require a great deal of self-awareness, communication, and tracking of emotional process to be successful.

Relationship self-help has often adopted a white, heteronormative lens that many don't relate to anymore and many never did. The BIPOC community come into relationships with their individual experiences and unique traumas related to racial prejudice in society and may also be treated differently as couples relative to white individuals.[76] Multiracial couples get little attention in research literature but have additional social stigmas and personal stressors to navigate, such as judgmental perceptions by some in society, their own family members, or in their respective communities. In all these aspects, it is important to acknowledge and be aware of the cultural environment in which relationships exist and to include working toward greater equality, recognition, and fairness across diverse populations as part of promoting relationship security and health.

It almost goes without saying that the promotion of traditional definitions of relationship health causes many to feel less-than, judged, ashamed, and excluded. I appeal professionally and personally to all relationship experts, professionals, academics, and therapists to be more inclusive in their work and hope the science and framework in this book will support a shift toward greater inclusion of diverse populations in relationship self-help. Our world is a better place when we feel connected, when there is less loneliness, isolation, and trauma, and when all people feel welcomed to pursue the diversity of relationship structures and lifestyles that feel authentic to them.

Why Listen to Me? A Personal Story

So why should you take my word on any of this? I am a licensed marriage and family therapist who has worked with hundreds of couples over ten years, helping them heal and strengthen their relationships. I was one of twelve couples therapists in the world selected to form the founding core faculty of PACT®, a leading training institute for neuroscience-based couples therapy.[77,78] In 2013 I founded Ready Set Love®, an online relationship training program for couples,[79] and in 2018 I began hosting a popular podcast on the science of relationships. I have trained many therapists around the world in new neuroscience-based techniques, helping them achieve greater, faster results in their work. I have presented on the neuroscience of couples therapy at a leading psychological conference and developed a modern couples and family therapy curriculum for the Dell Medical School in Austin, Texas. I am a professor of couples and family therapy and counseling private practice and have also brought this new science into companies, designing and leading a relationship wellness program for Google, Inc.

On a more personal level, I care about understanding and promoting love and connection between people because my entire life has been a journey from disconnection and trauma to learning how to connect deeply with others, and it hasn't been easy. As a Cuban-American kid growing up in New York, I didn't live with my parents and often felt lonely and neglected. My Cuban grandmother raised me but didn't play with me, and I didn't have regular friends or playmates. My family didn't talk about emotions, hug, or say, "I love you." Spanish is my first language, and the language barrier in English-speaking classrooms initially made it difficult for me to feel connected or form friendships with classmates. For most of elementary school, I didn't have friends, felt isolated and often sad.

I also had bad anxiety and needed to have certain objects with me to feel secure. In the third grade, after someone realized I hadn't been able to see well for two years, I started wearing these really thick, Coke-bottle glasses. Between the glasses and my rigid, organizing tendencies, like slicking my hair and wearing starched shirts, I was definitely the class nerd, with all the feelings of social isolation that came with that.

My grandmother, who had been my primary caregiver, died when I was eight, and my family thought it best not to talk about it. I wasn't invited to visit her in the hospital or attend the funeral, and I didn't have an outlet to process my grief or even really understand what had happened. The trauma of that loss sent me into a tailspin, and I had trouble focusing in school. I had to repeat the fourth grade, and while I had made some friends for the first time that year, they moved on without me, which left me crying myself to sleep many nights feeling alone and unsupported.

At thirteen, I met my first girlfriend and fell madly in love as teenagers tend to do, but also in part because I hadn't felt that others were interested in me before then. When that relationship ended in a painful heartbreak, I was again left without anyone I felt I could talk to, so I promised to never love again, closed my heart, and didn't smile for two years. During that time I started getting in trouble on the streets of New York, playing hooky from school, hanging out with the wrong crowd, and eventually left home at fifteen. I bounced around from place to place, attended five high schools in four years, spent a year in South America, and moved too often to ever really make close friends.

After high school, I spent some time trying to find myself and a deeper sense of what life is really about. I was homeless for a period of time, begging for change on the street, eating out of dumpsters, sleeping out in the cold, and brushing my teeth with pine needles. I spent time living in the woods by myself, wandering, and trying to make sense out of life. My relationships in that phase were superficial and transient—even the good ones didn't last. Eventually, I had to face a deep loneliness in myself, recognize that my heart was closed, start healing from past trauma, and learn what it means to be in relationship.

I wasn't even sure relationship was a good idea at first. I had been burned too many times and didn't see the value of risking the emotional pain, taking on the stress of a partnership and the weight of responsibility to someone else. I had learned how to navigate the world alone, so being independent had some appeal, but I was also disconnected and intrigued by some of the relationships that started to present themselves. When your heart lacks love, something feels off, even if you've learned to deal with it.

After much contemplation, I decided to give it a go and open myself up to relationship, but I still had to learn how to function in a healthy and connected manner, which I was really bad at. My relationship skills were poor, and I frustrated many partners. I've come a long way since then, and I'm intimately familiar with the journey from being isolated, disconnected, and having bad habits to forming deep, loving, and fulfilling relationships that last. So while this book gives you the latest science-based tips for how to improve your relationships, it also offers what I've learned along the way about how to obtain and develop the skills needed for a healthy and secure life with others.

You may be similar to me in that you may have trauma in your background. You may have been neglected or experienced a lack of emotional support at home growing up. You may be carrying attachment wounds from childhood. Maybe you've had some tough, painful relationship experiences that have left you wounded and isolated. Perhaps you didn't see positive examples of loving adult partners in your childhood, or your previous marriage was traumatic. And maybe you haven't had much practice developing connecting behaviors that create closeness. That's where I began, and I can relate to all those issues.

The good news is that those issues can be overcome. Attachment research shows us that the brain and mind can learn new tricks when it comes to connecting skills and ability. Earned security moves us closer to healing our minds, brains, and nervous systems from dysfunctional patterns to healthy new ones.[80] You can become an expert connector, regardless of your background.

What made the greatest difference for me was learning about the new science of relationships and implementing those ideas in my life—the same ones I'm going to teach you in the chapters that follow. I learned that I needed to rehearse relationship skills before they would feel natural. I learned that practicing by myself or in my own mind was not enough to create meaningful change, and that I needed to challenge myself in real relationships to build the skills necessary to connect. Sometimes we think awareness alone can improve our relationship skills, but change often requires uncomfortable action just beyond our native skill set, like lifting those weights at the gym that look a little outside your range at first, but then you get used to them. Being willing to work outside your comfort zone and practice new habits in real relationships is the training ground for these connecting skills.

As I implemented what I was learning from the new science of relationships, I got feedback from those I was connecting with, which helped me refine the practice of skills I was engaged in. By making myself practice unfamiliar but more secure habits, my relationships began to improve. I started to heal many of my past traumas by forging deeper connections with others and my life took a positive turn. Neuroscience has shown that our sense of self comes in large part from the quality of our relationships, because the brain internalizes how it is treated by others.[81] Feeling safe with others allows us to open emotional wounds and receive care right where we need it. Healing past traumas, especially the tender ones from early childhood, is most effectively done in the confines of a secure relationship, which at times elicits our wounds but also has the power to heal them.

After growing up lonely and frustrated by my connection to others, I felt I had to learn how to have healthy relationships from scratch. My passion for my work comes from the pain, despair, and lack of support I felt as a kid. I often longed to feel connected, cared for, and understood, and I can relate to those who long for the same. The principles in this book are what helped me get there. If I was able to learn how to have healthy, satisfying relationships and develop the skills to fulfill that desire, I believe you can as well.

How to Use This Book

This is a practical book. In it, I distill the modern science about how to improve connection to its most important components, giving you tools you can easily implement into your life that make a difference in your relationships right away. The concepts in this book represent the leading science on how to improve close relationships, as well as my many years of testing them with hundreds of couples, helping them move from disconnection to security and happiness. The approach of focusing on connection and the process of interaction rather than on communication or on solving specific problems constitutes the leading edge for how to address issues of disconnection in relationships. It represents the most effective and efficient way to improve as a couple and develop a fulfilling, long-term relationship. This book will give you the concepts and strategies I have seen create the most positive impact with my clients.

The framework for improvement is relatively simple, but implementing it takes dedication and effort. Too many individuals put up with so-so or dysfunctional relationships, hoping time will heal their issues. Your investment in focusing on relationship improvement now, however, can pay huge dividends to your overall satisfaction and give you better habits going forward.

As you read this book, I encourage you to keep this framework of improvement in mind. The first step in improving your relationships is to set an intention to grow along positively defined goals. If you're in a committed relationship, you might set those goals together. You might consider creating your own little book club and reading this book at the same time so you can discuss each chapter as you go. Partners who take a shared interest in learning and growing together give themselves valuable support to deepen connection. Define what specific issues or behaviors you want to work on to move toward those goals and share the responsibility of improvement as a team. Create opportunities for the deliberate practice of those problem patterns so that you can develop better skills for those situations, and get partner feedback. And finally, seek help if you get stuck, feel you are going backward, or just want additional support.

You can still apply the concepts in the book, however, if you read it without your partner. You can practice the methods and discuss some of them with your partner. Sometimes one individual needs to get the ball rolling on growth and then the other will eventually follow. You can make a difference to your relationship by implementing these ideas, and your partner can experience their benefits and perhaps grow more interested in them in time.

If you're single, these tools will help you have healthier friendship and family relationships and develop closer connections with others. If you're dating, this book is valuable in that it will help you date more efficiently and choose partners wisely in a way that promotes relationship security and satisfaction. This book will help you prepare for a healthy, dynamic, and fulfilling partnership and set healthy habits from the get-go. You can use the concepts in this book in any of your current relationships, benefiting from the practice and deepening your skills for developing close relationships.

The relationship science embedded in these pages changed my life and I think it can change yours. You'll learn a lot about yourself and about how relationships actually work. Although it focuses primarily on adult romantic partnership, the information in this book is based on how the brain and nervous system act in human relationships, so you'll learn powerful concepts that can positively shape any interaction and bond. As you learn this material, your relationship life can improve dramatically, with your partner, kids, family members, and friends, which can also boost your enjoyment of life and self-confidence as an individual.

Relationship is a journey of personal growth, one that reveals as much about us as it does about our ability to have fulfilling shared lives with others. Through relationship, we can hone individual qualities that help us be more successful humans, deepen our sense of purpose and meaning, and go beyond ourselves to learn how to live for something greater that makes our own lives more meaningful and fulfilling in the process.

Having healthier relationships can change your life and the lives of your loved ones for the better and help impart greater equality and fairness into the societies we live in. Having better relationships teaches us how to be more caring, respectful, empathic human beings and conveys a sense of peace in ourselves, in our homes, and in our communities. Becoming a person who can connect well with others helps heal the world around you by embracing diversity, bridging differences, and placing our societal interactions on more secure footing. **Let's get started!**

Notes

1. Stephen W. Porges, "Making the World Safe for Our Children: Down-Regulating Defence and Up-Regulating Social Engagement to 'Optimise' the Human Experience," *Children Australia* 40, no. 2 (June 2015): 114.

2. Thomas G. Guilliams and Lena Edwards, "Chronic Stress and the HPA Axis," *The Standard* 9, no. 2 (2010): 1–12.

3. Judee K. Burgoon, Laura K. Guerrero, and Valerie Manusov, *Nonverbal Communication* (New York: Routledge, 2016).

4. Marco Tamietto and Beatrice de Gelder, "Neural Bases of the Non-conscious Perception of Emotional Signals," *Nature Reviews Neuroscience* 11, no. 10 (October 2010): 697–709.

5. Allan N. Schore, "Attachment and the Regulation of the Right Brain," *Attachment & Human Development* 2, no. 1 (April 2000): 23–47.

6. Allan N. Schore, "Playing on the Right Side of the Brain: An Interview with Allan N. Schore," *American Journal of Play* 9, no. 2 (Winter 2017): 105–142.

7. Allan N. Schore, "The Right Brain Implicit Self Lies at the Core of Psychoanalysis," *Psychoanalytic Dialogues* 21, no. 1 (February 2011): 75–100.

8. Mona DeKoven Fishbane, *Loving with the Brain in Mind: Neurobiology and Couple Therapy*, Norton Series on Interpersonal Neurobiology (New York: W. W. Norton, 2013).

9. Sondra Goldstein and Susan Thau, "Integrating Attachment Theory and Neuroscience in Couple Therapy," *International Journal of Applied Psychoanalytic Studies* 1, no. 3 (September 2004): 214–223.

10. B. J. Atkinson, *Emotional Intelligence in Couples Therapy: Advances from Neurobiology and the Science of Intimate Relationships* (New York: W. W. Norton, 2005).

11. Stan Tatkin, "A Psychobiological Approach to Couple Therapy: Integrating Attachment and Personality Theory as Interchangeable Structural Components," *Psychologist-Psychoanalyst: Division 39 of the American Psychological Association* 29, no. 3 (2009): 7–15.

12. Francine Lapides, "The Implicit Realm in Couples Therapy: Improving Right Hemisphere Affect-Regulating Capabilities," *Clinical Social Work Journal* 39, no. 2 (May 2010): 161–169.

13. Marion F. Solomon and Stan Tatkin, *Love and War in Intimate Relationships: Connection, Disconnection, and Mutual Regulation in Couple Therapy*, Norton Series on Interpersonal Neurobiology (New York: W. W. Norton, 2011).

14. David S. Lee, Oscar Ybarra, Richard Gonzalez, and Phoebe Ellsworth, "I-through-We: How Supportive Social Relationships Facilitate Personal Growth," *Personality and Social Psychology Bulletin* 44, no. 1 (January 2018): 37–48.

15. Daniel J. Siegel, *The Developing Mind: How Relationships and the Brain Interact to Shape Who We Are* (New York: Guilford, 2020).

16. Marion F. Solomon and Daniel J. Siegel, eds., *How People Change: Relationships and Neuroplasticity in Psychotherapy*, Norton Series on Interpersonal Neurobiology (New York: W. W. Norton, 2017).

17. Stephen W. Porges, "Social Engagement and Attachment: A Phylogenetic Perspective," *Annals of the New York Academy of Sciences* 1008 (2003): 31–47.

18. Louis J. Cozolino, *The Neuroscience of Human Relationships: Attachment and the Developing Social Brain*, Norton Series on Interpersonal Neurobiology (New York: W. W. Norton, 2014).

19. Joseph LeDoux, *The Emotional Brain: The Mysterious Underpinnings of Emotional Life* (New York: Simon & Schuster, 2015).

20. Solomon and Tatkin, *Love and War in Intimate Relationships*.

21. Todd B. Kashdan and Jonathan Rottenberg, "Psychological Flexibility as a Fundamental Aspect of Health," *Clinical Psychology Review* 30, no. 7 (2010): 865–878, https://doi.org/10.1016/j.cpr.2010.03.001.

22. David West and Scott Dellana, "Diversity of Ability and Cognitive Style for Group Decision Processes, *Information Sciences* 179, no. 5 (February 2009): 542–558.

23. Frank W. Bond, J. Lloyd, and N. Guenole, "The Work-Related Acceptance and Action Questionnaire: Initial Psychometric Findings and Their Implications for Measuring Psychological Flexibility in Specific Contexts," *Journal of Occupational and Organizational Psychology* 86, no. 3 (September 2013): 331–347, https://doi.org/10.1111/joop.12001.

24. Frank W. Bond, Steven C. Hayes, and Dermot Barnes-Holmes, "Psychological Flexibility, ACT, and Organizational Behavior," *Journal of Organizational Behavior Management* 26 (2006):1–2, 25–54, https://doi.org/10.1300/J075v26n01_02.

25. Steven M. Southwick, George A. Bonanno, Ann S. Masten, Catherine Panter-Brick, and Rachel Yehuda, "Resilience Definitions, Theory, and Challenges: Interdisciplinary Perspectives," *European Journal of Psychotraumatology* 5 (October 2014), 10.3402/ejpt.v5.25338. https://doi.org/10.3402/ejpt.v5.25338.

26. Kristin D. Neff, "Self-Compassion, Self-Esteem, and Well-Being," *Social and Personality Psychology Compass* 5, no. 1 (January 2011): 1–12.

27. David Rock, *Your Brain at Work, Revised and Updated: Strategies for Overcoming Distraction, Regaining Focus, and Working Smarter All Day Long* (New York: Harper Business, 2020).

28. Cozolino, *The Neuroscience of Human Relationships.*

29. A. R. Damasio, "The Somatic Marker Hypothesis and the Possible Functions of the Prefrontal Cortex," *Philosophical Transactions of the Royal Society of London, Series B: Biological Sciences* 351 (October 1996): 1413–1420.

30. Vagdevi Meunier and Wayne Baker, "Positive Couple Relationships: The Evidence for Long-Lasting Relationship Satisfaction and Happiness," in *Positive Relationships*, ed. S. Roffey (Berlin: Springer, Dordrecht, 2012), 73–89.

31. Debra Umberson and Jennifer Karas Montez, "Social Relationships and Health: A Flashpoint for Health Policy," *Journal of Health and Social Behavior* 51 (Suppl.) (2010): S54–S66, https://doi.org/10.1177/0022146510383501.

32. Linda M. Hartling, PhD, "Strengthening Resilience in a Risky World: It's All about Relationships," *Women & Therapy* 31 (2008): 2–4, 51–70, https://doi.org/10.1080/02703140802145870.

33. George E. Vaillant, Charles C. McArthur, and Arlie Bock, "Grant Study of Adult Development, 1938–2000," Harvard Dataverse V4 (2010), https://hdl.handle.net/1902.1/00290.

34. Yang Claire Yang, Courtney Boen, Karen Gerken, Ting Li, Kristen Schorpp, and Kathleen Mullan Harris, "Social Relationships and Physiological Determinants of Longevity across the Human Lifespan," *Proceedings of the National Academy of Sciences* (January 2016), http://www.pnas.org.content/early/2016/01/02/1511085112.

35. Kathryn P. Brooks, Tara Gruenewald, Arun Karlamangla, Peifung Hu, Brandon Koretz, and Teresa E. Seeman, "Social Relationships and Allostatic Load in the MIDUS Study," *Health Psychology* 33, no. 11 (November 2014): 1373–1381.

36. Bruce S. McEwen and Peter J. Gianaros, "Central Role of the Brain in Stress and Adaptation: Links to Socioeconomic Status, Health, and Disease," *Annals of the New York Academy of Sciences* 1186 (February 2010): 190–222.

37. Editors of Harvard Health Publishing in Consultation with Robert Schreiber, MD, *Living Better, Living Longer* (Boston: Harvard Health, 2017), 1–50.

38. Julianne Holt-Lunstad, Timothy B. Smith, Mark Baker, Tyler Harris, and David Stephenson, "Loneliness and Social Isolation as Risk Factors for Mortality: A Meta-analytic Review," *Perspectives on Psychological Science* 10, no. 2 (March 2015): 227–237, https://doi.org/10.1177/1745691614568352.

39. Bethany E. Kok, Kimberly A. Coffey, Michael A. Cohn, Lahnna I. Catalino, Tanya Vacharkulksemsuk, Sara B. Algoe, Mary Brantley, and Barbara L. Fredrickson, "How Positive Emotions Build Physical Health: Perceived Positive Social Connections Account for the Upward Spiral between Positive Emotions and Vagal Tone," *Psychological Science* 24, no. 7 (July 2013): 1123–1132.

40. Stephen W. Porges, *The Polyvagal Theory: Neurophysiological Foundations of Emotions, Attachment, Communication, and Self-Regulation* (New York: W. W. Norton, 2011).

41. Debora Marques de Miranda, Bruno da Silva Athanasio, Ana Cecília de Sena Oliveira, and Ana Cristina Simoes Silva, "How Is COVID-19 Pandemic Impacting Mental Health of Children and Adolescents?," *International Journal of Disaster Risk Reduction* 51 (December 2020): 101845.

42. Nazish Imran, Muhammad Zeshan, and Zainab Pervaiz, "Mental Health Considerations for Children & Adolescents in COVID-19 Pandemic," *Pakistan Journal of Medical Sciences* 36, no. COVID19-S4 (May 2020): S67.

43. Jörg M. Fegert, Benedetto Vitiello, Paul L. Plener, and Vera Clemens, "Challenges and Burden of the Coronavirus 2019 (COVID-19) Pandemic for Child and Adolescent Mental Health: A Narrative Review to Highlight Clinical and Research Needs in the Acute Phase and the Long Return to Normality," *Child and Adolescent Psychiatry and Mental Health* 14 (May 2020): 1–11.

44. Susie Demarinis, "Loneliness at Epidemic Levels in America," *Explore* 16, no. 5 (September–October 2020): 278–279, https://doi.org/10.1016/j.explore.2020.06.008.

45. Liana DesHarnais Bruce, Joshua S. Wu, Stuart L. Lustig, Daniel W. Russell, and Douglas A. Nemecek, "Loneliness in the United States: A 2018 National Panel Survey of Demographic, Structural, Cognitive, and Behavioral Characteristics," *American Journal of Health Promotion* 33, no. 8 (June 2019): 1123–1133.

46. Inge Bretherton, "The Origins of Attachment Theory: John Bowlby and Mary Ainsworth," *Developmental Psychology* 28, no. 5 (1992): 759.

47. Cindy Hazan and Phillip Shaver, "Romantic Love Conceptualized as an Attachment Process," *Journal of Personality and Social Psychology* 52, no. 3 (March 1987): 511.

48. Stan Tatkin, *Wired for Love: How Understanding Your Partner's Brain and Attachment Style Can Help You Defuse Conflict and Build a Secure Relationship* (Oakland: New Harbinger, 2012).

49. J. R. Shapiro and J. S. Applegate, "Cognitive Neuroscience, Neurobiology and Affect Regulation: Implications for Clinical Social Work," *Clinical Social Work Journal* 28, no 9–3 (March 2000) https://doi.org/10.1023/A:1005139123963.

50. Amir Levine and Rachel Heller, *Attached: The New Science of Adult Attachment and How It Can Help You Find—and Keep—Love* (London: Penguin, 2010).

51. Mario Mikulincer and Phillip R. Shaver, "The Attachment Behavioral System in Adulthood: Activation, Psychodynamics, and Interpersonal Processes," in *Advances in Experimental Social Psychology*, vol. 35, ed. M. P. Zanna (New York: Academic Press, 2003), 53–152.

52. Daniel J. Siegel, "Toward an Interpersonal Neurobiology of the Developing Mind: Attachment Relationships, 'Mindsight,' and Neural Integration," *Infant Mental Health Journal: Official Publication of the World Association for Infant Mental Health* 22, no. 1–2 (2001): 67–94.

53. Schore, "Attachment and the Regulation of the Right Brain," 23–47.

54. Pat Sable, "What Is Adult Attachment?," *Clinical Social Work Journal* 36, no. 1 (March 2008): 21–30.

55. Diana Fosha, *The Transforming Power of Affect: A Model for Accelerated Change* (New York: Basic Books, 2000).

56. Peter Fonagy and Mary Target, "Attachment and Reflective Function: Their Role in Self-Organization," *Development and Psychopathology* 9, no. 4 (1997): 679–700.

57. Erik Hesse, "The Adult Attachment Interview: Protocol, Method of Analysis, and Selected Empirical Studies: 1985–2015," in *Handbook of Attachment: Theory, Research, and Clinical Applications*, 3rd ed., ed. J. Cassidy and P. R. Shaver (New York: Guilford, 2016), 553–597.

58. Janet E. Helms, Nicolas Guerda, and Carlton E. Green, "Racism and Ethnoviolence as Trauma: Enhancing Professional and Research Training," *Traumatology* 18, no. 1 (2012): 65–74.

59. Dan Siegel, *Pocket Guide to Interpersonal Neurobiology: An Integrative Handbook of the Mind* (New York: W. W. Norton, 2012).

60. Amy F. T. Arnsten, "Stress Signalling Pathways That Impair Prefrontal Cortex Structure and Function," *Nature Reviews Neuroscience* 10, no. 6 (June 2009): 410–422, https://doi.org/10.1038/nrn2648.

61. Amy F. T. Arnsten, Murray A. Raskind, Fletcher B. Taylor, and Daniel F. Connor, "The Effects of Stress Exposure on Prefrontal Cortex: Translating Basic Research into Successful Treatments for Post-traumatic Stress Disorder," *Neurobiology of Stress* 1, no. 1 (2015): 89–99.

62. Porges, *The Polyvagal Theory*.

63. Louis J. Cozolino and Erin N. Santos, "Why We Need Therapy—and Why It Works: A Neuroscientific Perspective," *Smith College Studies in Social Work* 84, no. 2–3 (August 2014): 157–177.

64. Zhenchao Qian and Daniel T. Lichter, "Changing Patterns of Interracial Marriage in a Multiracial Society," *Journal of Marriage and Family* 73, no. 5 (October 2011): 1065–1084.

65. Melanie Heath, *One Marriage under God: The Campaign to Promote Marriage in America*, vol. 16 (New York: NYU Press, 2012).

66. Joseph Locke and Ben Wright, "The Politics of Love, Sex and Gender," in *American Yawp: A Massively Collaborative Open U.S. History Textbook* (Stanford: Stanford University Press, 2014 [2020–2021 updates]), http://www.americanyawp.com/.

67. Frederick Liu and Stephen Macedo, "The Federal Marriage Amendment and the Strange Evolution of the Conservative Case against Gay Marriage," *PS: Political Science and Politics* 38, no. 2 (2005): 211–215.

68. Darren E. Sherkat, Melissa Powell-Williams, Gregory Maddox, and Kylan Mattias De Vries, "Religion, Politics, and Support for Same-Sex Marriage in the United States, 1988–2008," *Social Science Research* 40, no. 1 (January 2011): 167–180.

69. Judi Mesman, Marinus H. Van Ijzendoorn, and Abraham Sagi-Schwartz, "Cross-cultural Patterns of Attachment," *Handbook of Attachment: Theory, Research, and Clinical Applications* (2016): 852–877.

70. Jack Drescher and Kenneth J. Zucker, *Ex-gay Research: Analyzing the Spitzer Study and Its Relation to Science, Religion, Politics, and Culture* (New York: Routledge, 2013).

71. Resmaa Menakem, *My Grandmother's Hands: Racialized Trauma and the Pathway to Mending Our Hearts and Bodies* (Las Vegas: Central Recovery Press, 2017).

72. Tristan Taormino, *Opening Up: A Guide to Creating and Sustaining Open Relationships* (San Francisco: Cleis Press, 2008).

73. Fatma Gökçe Özkarar-Gradwohl, "Cross-cultural Affective Neuroscience," *Frontiers in Psychology* 10 (2019): 794.

74. Amy C. Moors, Amanda N. Gesselman, and Justin R. Garcia, "Desire, Familiarity, and Engagement in Polyamory: Results from a National Sample of Single Adults in the United States," *Frontiers in Psychology* 12 (March 2021): 811.

75. Geri Weitzman, Joy Davidson, R. A. Phillips, James R. Fleckenstein, and C. Morotti-Meeker, "What Psychology Professionals Should Know about Polyamory," *National Coalition on Sexual Freedom* 7 (2009): 1–28.

76. Menakem, *My Grandmother's Hands*.

77. "PACT®" refers to a Psychobiological Approach to Couple Therapy and was developed by Dr. Stan Tatkin.

78. Stan Tatkin, "How Couples Change. A Psychobiological Approach to Couple Therapy (PACT)," in Solomon and Siegel, eds., *How People Change*, 320.

79. Ready Set Love® is a twelve-week, science-based relationship improvement program, www.readysetlove.com.

80. J. L. Pearson, D. A. Cohn, P. A. Cowan, and C. P. Cowan, "Earned- and Continuous-Security in Adult Attachment: Relation to Depressive Symptomatology and Parenting Style," *Development and Psychopathology* 6, no. 2 (March 1994): 359–373.

81. Allan N. Schore, *Affect Regulation and the Origin of the Self: The Neurobiology of Emotional Development* (New York: Routledge, 2016).

1.

Connection versus Communication

The body, not the thinking brain, is where we experience most of our pain, pleasure, and joy, and where we process most of what happens to us. It is also where we do most of our healing, including our emotional and psychological healing. And it is where we experience resilience and a sense of flow.

—Resmaa Menakem

Relationship Is about Connection

While most people point to communication as the key ingredient in healthy relationships, the truth is that it's really connection that makes all the difference. Research on the intersection between the brain and relationships has shown that what we seek most in close relationships is a sense of safety and security with others.[1] Connecting cues such as touch, proximity, eye contact, and tone of voice can create a sense of closeness more effectively than words. Underneath our issues of the day, our arguments about kids, money, cleanliness, schedules, or sex, are the brain's priorities: *Do you love me? Do you care? Do I matter to you?* We often use the issues of the day as placeholders for our sense of connection, because it can be difficult to identify those underlying feelings or awkward to talk about not feeling cared for, prioritized, or loved. In moments when we feel disconnected, we use the kitchen being dirty again as the focus of our frustration.

Does that mean we don't have legitimate preferences around parenting, money, or cleanliness, or that we shouldn't be talking about those things? No, it simply means that when we feel connected, we can have productive, loving, and kind conversations about those things rather than fights or arguments. When you're connected, you trust that others care and have your back and you can get through difficult and sensitive conversations without having the perfect words. We can navigate our differences and the daily issues of life without debates that leave us feeling isolated and unsupported, on edge in conversations, or anxious. People put a lot of energy into resolving specific incidents or issues that come up, but if you get lost litigating specific issues and don't pay more attention to your sense of connection, you end up on a never-ending hamster wheel of irritating interactions and a lack of understanding about why you feel disconnected. You keep hoping communication will resolve those differences, but it never does.

Underneath those annoying squabbles are vital, deeper questions coming from the security system in the brain. What is taking place in these moments is "neuroception," a term coined by Dr. Stephen Porges of Indiana University to describe how the nervous system continually scans for security information via primitive circuits, out of conscious awareness, to make determinations about who feels safe enough to connect with.[2] When you focus instead on those underlying questions and address the root of the sense of disconnection, you can put the subconscious at ease and free up the mind to handle differences with greater maturity and support.

Connection is a gut feeling, a sense of trust and safety in the nervous system that says it's okay to relax and let down your guard with someone. When you're connected, you can be yourself, and rely on the strength and resilience of the relationship to handle errors, which occur constantly even when you don't mean them to. Verbal communication tends to stress the mind; it can require much energy and interpretation to get on the same page. On the other hand, connection deactivates the threat response between people and elicits oxytocin, en-

> Generally, when partners feel connected, they can navigate the issues of life with care and relative ease, and when they don't, everything is an issue.

dorphins, and neurotransmitters that increase the feeling of bonding and contentment. When connected, you feel emotionally cared for by others and trusting of their empathy and support.

There's a neurobiological reason for this: the parts of the brain and nervous system that measure connection don't interface much with the frontal lobes that handle higher-level functions like verbal communication. The separation between these discrete systems in the brain helps explain why words of affirmation don't always settle upset feelings and why talking about issues doesn't always change deep-seated habits. Our relationships benefit when we learn how to use each system for the role it's best suited for—our thinking minds to solve problems, and our connecting mechanisms to create a secure bond.

The Security System
and the Biology of Connection

We all want to feel connected. What we don't notice sometimes is how much the physical nature of our bodies and brains plays a role in that. Our nervous systems need to be relaxed around others in order to open up and be playful, and our bodies need to be well cared for to handle the emotional tasks of relationship life. The body, brain, and nervous system form an incredibly complex system of electrical and chemical communication that determines how we feel. Think of the human mind as the operating system that runs on the hardware of the body, brain, and nervous system. Sometimes the software program of the mind (our concepts, beliefs, intent, memory, and focus) is "buggy," to use a software term, and interferes with developing strong, close connections with others. And sometimes our hardware—neurological wiring, capability, depression, stress, health problems, and developmental deficits—is not as optimized for social function as we might like. Learning to connect better recruits both software and hardware to improve their ability and serve the needs of connection by increasing demand for those abilities and so developing new automatic skill into the body.

Humans are wired for survival more than love, so knowing how to put others at ease and not elicit defensive reactions is an important key to forming bonds. And because we make mistakes and will inevitably trigger others at times, it is also important to know how to clean up errors and hurts and reestablish security with others' nervous systems. To do this, it helps to understand how the human security system works.

Most of us are familiar with fight-or-flight, also known as the *threat response*, our body's physiological reaction to a perceived threat or danger. It's how our *autonomic nervous system* reacts quickly (and largely unconsciously) to keep us out of harm's way. For the sake of speed and efficiency, fight-or-flight signals are fairly binary: safe or unsafe. They don't tell the brain much more than that. Some of these signals sponsor direct action, such as moving a hand away from a hot stove, and some reach the *amygdala*—a group of small centers in the brain involved in threat response—which codes them with emotion.

The amygdala is an important player in the human survival system: it gathers inputs directly from sensory stimuli and sends corresponding signals throughout the body.[3] Because it is a fast, primitive system, it is also somewhat inaccurate and can lump things together that don't belong or perceive threats where there are none. The amygdala allows emotional information to be distributed prior to thought, which, although error-prone, can be useful and provides a fast and initial measure of safety in connection.[4] It is important that our connecting signals be obviously friendly in order to not trigger the amygdala or cause it to make errors, coding our signals incorrectly and sending threat responses throughout the subconscious and nervous system.

Thanks in part to research by Dr. Porges, we know that the *vagus nerve* plays a huge role in managing our threat responses.[5] The vagus is the body's longest cranial nerve, running all the way from the brain down through the neck, heart, and abdomen and delivering important information to the brain about the body's experience.[6] It lets the brain know how we "feel" based on security measures of our environment. Our "gut sense" and what we "feel in our hearts" are not just metaphors—they describe the real physical process of neurons in those parts of the body communicating with the brain via the vagus nerve.[7] The vagus also sends signals back to the body in return, regulating heart rate, muscle tension, respiratory rate, blood pressure, and more. In addition, it connects our hearts and our faces, allowing what our hearts feel to be communicated to nerves on the face that modulate expression. This face-heart connection allows us to take in information from someone's facial expression and feel it in our hearts, regulating or dysregulating our nervous system based on what we see.[8] So, by having an obviously friendly expression, kind eyes, and smiling, you can send a signal directly to another's heart and gut that you are a safe person they can trust to open up with.

When the amygdala receives sensory inputs about a perceived threat, it sends a danger signal to the *hypothalamus*, the body's command center housed in the brain. The hypothalamus activates our physiological response via the sympathetic nervous system, causing adrenaline to be pumped throughout the body, which in turn raises blood pressure, heightens our senses, and moves blood flow to our muscles. This prepares us for action and survival but tends to make it difficult for us to relax and connect with others.[9]

When our threat response system kicks in, our connecting systems often kick off—our body prioritizes physical safety over social engagement. The fight-or-flight reaction tends to sideline our social circuits, causing us to get heated, combative, or defensive, protecting us as if survival were at stake. Unfortunately, these primitive systems don't distinguish well between an actual predator and an argument over salad dressing—the adrenals can dump adrenaline into the system either way, especially if we don't feel connected. The key is recognizing when these threat responses become active in our bodies and reestablishing calm so they don't generate disconnecting behaviors we may regret later. This can be done using individual calming strategies, but it can be even more effective at times to seek soothing from others.

If safety and security are not established and the brain and body continue to feel under threat, a second threat response might be initiated via the hypothalamic-pituitary-adrenal (HPA) axis, which directs the adrenals to release cortisol into the body. Cortisol is a stress hormone that takes longer to produce than adrenaline but has a more sustained effect. Having too much cortisol in our system on a regular basis can lead to ill health effects, one of the dangers of chronic stress.[10] Cortisol is chronically higher in those with post-traumatic stress disorder (PTSD), predisposing those with PTSD—approximately 9 percent of the population—to greater reactivity and irritability. Emotional regulation, support, and connection tend to lower cortisol levels, which creates a physiological buffer to nervous system activation, arguments, and enables partners in relationship to more easily generate positive memories.[11]

Proficiency in regulating threat activation is known as having strong *vagal tone*. Similar to how good muscle tone enables our muscles to work better, faster, and recover with greater resilience, strong vagal tone modulates the body's threat responses via the parasympathetic (calming) aspect of the nervous system.[12] Once we are able to calm down again, the parasympathetic system can modulate our stress hormones, slow down breathing, and relax the gut, enabling us to be present, patient, and engaged. Strong vagal tone reduces inflammation, allows us to recover more quickly after threat activation, moderates our moods, helps us relax, and optimizes our social connecting behaviors. Reduced vagal tone is associated with anxiety, depression, and panic, while high vagal tone is associated with emotional resilience and advanced social skills such as attunement and empathy.[13]

When our threat response is mobilized, connection becomes more difficult, both physiologically and psychologically. Connecting behaviors that signal safety, security, and friendliness keep the nervous system on the right side of that equation. Furthermore, those safety signals also create a buffer to conflict by earning the nervous system's trust, making it harder to escalate interactions to arguments.[14] We can't prevent all triggers or conflict, but recognizing that we don't think or connect well when threat responses are activated allows us to take action in those moments to calm ourselves and one another, rather than persisting in an activating interaction. Soothing each other in moments like that can include taking a break from speaking, holding each other, offering a massage, or gently rubbing each other's belly or back to calm down the sympathetic response. This works with kids as well, who often respond quickly to physiological soothing.

Neurons in the gut, known as the *enteric nervous system* (ENS), also factor into our connection capabilities. This system is sometimes called the second brain because it is comprised of approximately 500 million neurons, more than twice the number found in the spinal cord.[15] The ENS can sense threats and mobilize our mood and body, in part by using the vagus nerve, and is one of the first responders of the body's security system.[16] Both the activating and calming elements of the autonomic nervous system connect to this gut network of neurons, allowing two-way communication between them and the brain. When you're under stress or anxious, your stomach may tense up. When your belly is relaxed, it's easier to connect. Sometimes rubbing the belly or hugging belly-to-belly can help communicate safety to the neurons in the gut. When the gut can relax, it has a calming effect on the brain, and vice versa.[17]

The ENS also holds 95 percent of the serotonin in the body and can make and release as much dopamine as the brain. Serotonin and dopamine are key neurotransmitters that help regulate mood, happiness, learning, pleasure, sleep, the seeking of connection, and motivation. Dopamine marks the feel-good reward attached to connection so that we seek it more often. It also controls the reward center in the brain, the same center involved in addictive tendencies. Our biology may use dopamine to create a kind of addiction to another person, or to love, in order to motivate us to seek out close bonds and maintain them. Studies involving prairie voles, one of the few species in the 3 to 5 percent of mammals that are monogamous, show high levels of dopamine involved in driving their pair-bonding tendencies.[18] Higher levels of dopamine are correlated with greater emotional interest in and attention to others, while lower levels are associated with less interest.[19]

Oxytocin, the "love hormone" produced by touch and cuddling, also facilitates bonding, by dampening the threat response, allowing for more stillness in the nervous system and more availability in the brain and body for connection.[20] Produced in the pituitary gland, oxytocin is a direct response to touch, sex, and breastfeeding and emotional bonding. It tends to heighten the senses relevant to connection, reduce anxiety, increase trust, and create a warm, fuzzy feeling and often works in concert with another peptide, vasopressin, in the biological attachment process.[21] Higher levels of oxytocin help us notice and amplify others' connecting behaviors, such as smiles and kind eyes, and increase our empathy and social attention.[22] It helps regulate our emotional responses in close connection with others and calms us so we can gaze at one another at close range and relax into physical intimacy.[23]

The role of the gut in producing neurotransmitters and mediating connection points to the importance of what is known as *visceral regulation*—managing diet, sleep, stress, sickness, and substance use so that internal organs can function optimally to engage in connection. Your relationships benefit when you take care of your body and engage in visceral regulation through self-care practices and handling physical and mental issues quickly and effectively.[24] When you're tired, sick, or stressed, it's easier to get into arguments. By keeping your body well regulated, you can bring your best self to partner interactions and maximize your emotional resilience and connecting abilities.

In relationships, we are always sending a signal to the other person's nervous system, which they then use to calculate connection, even if they are not aware of their nervous system's activity in measuring the exchange. To promote connection, we want to impress the nervous system with reliability and a sense of security, helping everyone's brains and bodies relax so we feel safe enough to be vulnerable and connect.

What Shapes How We Connect?

In Western culture, we often use verbal communication as a primary way to connect. While that makes sense in business settings, connecting more closely and bonding with loved ones requires more than words. However, our educational system focuses on conceptual and intellectual learning more than practicing connecting behaviors that improve emotional bonds between people, making it more difficult to develop the relationship skills we need. And due to cultural conditioning and other factors like the stress of social inequities, untreated mental health problems, addictions, and trauma, the relationship examples we witnessed growing up may not have modeled healthy and secure relationships with others. Some of the control over this is out of our hands, since much of our social engagement and attachment hardware in the brain is built by age two.[25] Most of us have no memory of our life prior to that, so it's very difficult to establish what experiences from those first years may have shaped our social wiring. Even without explicit memory, however, the ways we interact and respond to stress and the ways we either seek or push away care reveal much about our early experiences in childhood, acting as an implicit memory in brain and body. Yes, we can infer what we may have experienced in early childhood by assessing the family culture we do remember, but the way we are with others in the moment says even more about those early experiences. As a therapist, I often know more about someone's family history by watching them interact with another person for five minutes than if I ask them to tell me about their childhood. While our memory is selective, the results of those early experiences often show up in our behaviors. Our adult habits are a record of the automatic tendencies we developed, even if we don't understand or remember the experiences that may have influenced them.

How to Prioritize Connection

Prioritizing connection means that you tend to the nervous system and its desire to feel secure over imparting information to others. You connect instead of communicate, and your priority is caring for the base security needs of the relationship. If we meet the requirements of the attachment system well, others can more easily listen, understand, and care about how we feel and what we need. But if we don't take care of that primitive sense of trust with others, our verbal message often does not get the attention we wish it did.

To connect first and communicate second, begin your interactions by noticing physical and emotional cues about your partner. Take a "read" of them, and of yourself, with curiosity about what you need as a couple or as individuals to feel more secure. Begin by tending to those aspects of your interaction. Sometimes it's a smile, a friendly face, a hug, or sweet words such as, "Come here, I love you!" Or, "I appreciate you so much!" If we launch into a complex verbal exchange without connecting first, our conversations sometimes feel too transactional, platonic, or intellectual. We may even get into debates or annoying disconnects based on trying to mediate connection through ideas and words. Establishing connection first creates common ground of care and security, and allows our nervous systems to relax, opening our minds. Connection helps us *feel* loved and valued, making intellectual conversations more pleasant, even when you have differences of opinion.

In conversation, continue to tend to connection by holding hands, sitting close, making eye contact, and continuing to signal friendliness through body language and tone of voice. If the content gets frayed or annoying, try to come back to the common ground of connection. Make your interactions simpler, and move slowly enough to keep track of your emotions and needs. You can pause and hold each other without words for a while to communicate closeness, give each other an arm or shoulder rub, or take a walk together to reset a conversation. Words and ideas can be stressful to the brain, especially when we don't agree, so maintaining a focus on what does connect—touch, safety, trust, emotional support—gives you the edge to keep your bond feeling supportive.[26]

To relate more deeply with others' nervous systems, it is helpful to allow your face and tone to express the sentiment you feel so that others can readily experience it, not just hear it in words. If you can match your nonverbal cues and expressions to your words, your intent and meaning will be received with greater clarity. The more obvious you can make your kindness, friendliness, interest, and connection, the more easily those cues are perceived and support the relationship's sense of security. In love and romance, you often don't even need to use words a lot of the time to convey connection—a glance, touch, or a smile can say what you mean. Nonverbal communication is so important to the brain that words alone are not enough to convey meaning, especially if your nonverbals don't match your words. Some people complain that their partners misconstrue their message a lot. They may exasperate, "That's not what I'm saying!" Or, "I don't know why that doesn't get through or why it's not enough!" It can be frustrating and confusing for others to take away a different message than what we're saying with our words, but it happens frequently, especially under stress. Such discrepancies are sometimes due to our muddled nonverbal signals.

This disconnect happens often when those who are unfamiliar with emotional support attempt to comfort and soothe others. They may say the right things, but their nonverbals may not match, their facial expressions may be flat, and they may simply be awkward engaging in a new way of interacting. Sometimes people share their feelings verbally but there's little sign on their face and in their tone of voice that they really feel that way. This can happen with anyone who is a little guarded in their nonverbal expressions, and who is used to relying primarily on words and intellect to communicate. But it doesn't come without consequences, as the lack of matching our expressions and our words can confuse others and diminish the connecting value of an interaction. Allowing yourself to express and physically show tender emotions like love, care, and affection helps connect your words to your feelings, making it easier to read those sentiments.

Most of us can improve how we use nonverbals, shifting the heavy lifting of connection to the neurobiological system that's best designed to handle it, instead of placing the burden on our verbal communication. In short, if you want to increase love and connection in your relationships, allow your nonverbal expressions to communicate care and love directly to others' nervous systems. To help you begin doing this, below I offer six steps for how to prioritize connection over communication in your relationships.

STEP 1: Establish Mind-set

Focus your mind and intent on creating a sense of security with others when you interact with them, more than on getting things done or on communicating information.

To tend to connection over communication, the first helpful shift is one of mind-set. Remember: nothing impresses the nervous system more than directly communicating a sense of security in the moment. When you interact with others, especially your kids and partners, focus on creating an impression of safety in your contact. Over time, consistency in that effort will signal to their nervous systems that it's safe to relax and open up around you. Once this happens, evidenced by feeling relaxed and trusting of each other, then you can move on with everything else like exchanging ideas or playing together.

STEP 2: Be Aware of Your Presence

More than what you're saying or doing, be aware of how you're being. Try to communicate safety and friendliness through kind eyes, a smile, and a sweet tone of voice. When you're together, notice how you're being with each other over the activity you're engaged in.

To connect, we need to be aware of our presence in the moment. For example, are we relaxed? Are we focused or distracted? Are we able to receive our partner, or are we occupied with an activity? Being present enough to *receive* our partner is just as important to connection and intimacy as doing and saying things. Receiving includes noticing others, appreciating little things about them, and making room for them in our presence, physically and emotionally.

For example, if you're going to the grocery store together, don't just focus on driving there and getting the shopping done. Be available for emotional closeness, even in a mundane activity. Look at each other, connect, be interested in each other, play, laugh, and use the time to be with each other. Be present enough to appreciate your partner's sense of humor, quirks, unique personality and thoughts, and how they do things. Any time together is an opportunity to deepen your bond with each other in the moment as you prioritize how you are with each other over the activity.

STEP 3: Use Connecting Cues

Utilize nonverbals to communicate connection to the nervous system. Sustain eye contact a little longer so the eyes can meet and communicate connection (if culturally appropriate). Learn to soften your facial expressions so your partner and others can read them as friendly. And use touch and proximity to convey closeness directly to the nervous system (but know your person and be sensitive).

Security will first and most quickly be communicated through your eyes, face, expression, body language, and tone of voice. As we know, before you speak a word, the nervous system of the person you are interacting with has already received and analyzed the security information flowing from those nonverbal channels. So, before you try to express connection through dialogue, practice your nonverbal signals that communicate safety, security, kindness, and closeness.

A simple way to increase connection is to sit a little closer to each other when doing simple tasks like watching TV, watching the kids play, or eating. You might hold hands more often than you do, or put an arm around each other when you can. Physical proximity tends to communicate connection to the nervous system. The effect, however, can vary by culture and by individual depending on background, preferences, and experiences, so pay attention to the unique aspects of your specific relationship.

STEP 4: Share Feelings

Focus on sharing your feelings more than on transactional communication. If you've already engaged in much logistical talk about schedules, money, and chores, try to take your conversation into more emotional territory, like what someone is excited or anxious about.

Feelings are connecting. Emotional experience is why we love music, art, literature, plays, and memorable moments with others. Feelings are always new, because they have much subtlety in them—much more so than, "Hey, I'm going to the gas station to fill up," or, "Are you picking up the kids after school today?" Emotional experience is like traveling to a new, sometimes strange land, except the journey is built into your home life. Of course, we have to navigate the logistical chores of life as well, but don't let your relationship become too dominated by them. Some people report that their romantic partners feel like roommates after a while, because so much of their interactions revolves around chores and transactional conversation. Make time to ask about feelings, and to get to know each other deeply and as new people every day.

Feelings keep things exciting in relationships because they represent a deeper level of experience—one that taps into our subconscious and childhood impressions. They can be irrational—like dreams—yet point to important desires and frustrations you can learn more about by talking about them. They often capture our passion about life. Sometimes we don't completely understand why we feel a certain way, but exploring our experience with others helps us decode the feeling and get to know each other more deeply.

STEP 5: Prioritize the Process

Prioritize the process of your interaction over the content. Learn to pay attention in the moment to subtle changes of tone and expression that may indicate hurt or frustration, and use connecting tools to convey that your sense of security and care is more important than the content.

I cover process over content—the practice of prioritizing *how* you talk versus the topic—in-depth in chapter 6. But to touch on it briefly here: The nervous system evaluates connection in real time. It is always feeling the moment and scanning for security information that determines connection. A simple conversation can go south if someone misses an expression that signals frustration or feeling overwhelmed. Because some people miss these cues, they keep talking without pausing to care for the emerging feeling. Other times, we may notice these cues but not know how to shift the conversation to improve connection. When you're speaking, pay attention to your partner's eyes, face, and body language in the moment, and shift the conversation as needed. If we lose track of a person's state, our content can more easily derail a sense of connection, especially when there are differences of perspective, habit, and opinion. Tracking the process gives you the ability to stay ahead of upset and hurt feelings that get worse if not attended to.

STEP 6: Take Care of Each Other

Be ready to provide care and comfort in the moment if someone gets hurt or frustrated. What you have to say is not as important as caring for each other in real time. Practice offering empathy and physiological soothing. Offer hugs, hold someone's hand, and ask kind, curious questions. Practicing empathic behaviors makes them more natural with time.

If you notice emotional shifts in yourself and others when interacting, use that information to deepen the sense of care and security in the moment. Don't ignore emotions or dismiss them, but offer them care and support. Shifts in tone or facial expression or an averting of the eyes give you important cues about what your partner is experiencing. The same is true for your own feelings. Pivoting means you're willing to pause what you're doing and take care of each other, offering comfort and validation to each other so you feel important and acknowledged.

By implementing these six steps and the skills they represent, you can tend to your sense of connection instead of using conversation as the primary means to relate with others. By emphasizing closeness and security, you'll create deeper, more trustworthy bonds with others that then facilitate healthy, productive communication. Once you get good at tending to that sense of safety, you'll find that communication is easier, less contentious, and people become less defensive to the ways they need to grow, are more willing to examine and revise their habits, and have the support of the relationship and their partner to enact change.

Is Sex Connecting?

Sex has become a convenient and socially acceptable way to connect nonverbally, but if you're seeking a strong and close long-term bond, it is important to exercise other functions that communicate connection, such as emotional openness, friendship, kindness, interest in someone's mind and life, eye contact, holding hands, and reliably exhibiting security in your interactions with each other.

Sex is generally connecting for couples in that it involves physical touch and proximity, relaxation, and often emotional vulnerability and tenderness. But while sex can serve as a nonverbal connector, it is not necessarily the best approach to establishing or maintaining a secure bond. By itself, the act of sex does not establish security in relationships and cannot replace the full spectrum of behaviors that establish a sense of emotional safety. Sex does not always answer deeper security questions like, *Do you care about me?*, *Can I trust you?*, and *Can I rely on you?* It can also be disconnecting if partners are not attuned to each other's needs or pleasure. Some partners who are unfamiliar with how to share emotional intimacy rely on physical intimacy to create a connection, but sexual connection is not enough to endure the usual emotional challenges that arise in partnership life.

Nonverbal connection can include sex, but sex is not its main event. The connection the brain is seeking most in close relationships is one of safety and security. Once the nervous system feels a trusted bond, sex can enhance connection by being fun, offering shared pleasure, releasing endorphins and oxytocin, and cementing your connection at the subconscious level. Physical intimacy can relax anxiety and open a door for emotional connection, but it also heightens anxiety for some, and may fail at communicating other important features of connection. It's important to know your partner and assess if sex is connecting and from there discern how much your partner needs other ways of experiencing connection to feel close.

Examples

The following examples give you some real-world scenarios for how focusing on connection can keep you out of arguments and make your relationship more enjoyable.

Rita + Jen

Rita and Jen are smart, verbal women who have jobs in communication. Rita manages social media for a small corporation, while Jen is a legal assistant. When they come home from work at the end of the day, they often start talking right away, but sometimes the stress of the day causes them to get cross or start disagreeing about something in their life. It's gotten to the point where they almost expect to argue when they talk, and each has started spending more time away from the other with friends and going out to minimize time at home.

Rita and Jen needed to develop a security mind-set in order to focus on what their nervous systems really need to feel connected. When they come home, instead of talking right away about complex things, mostly while preparing something to eat and not really looking at each other, they needed to spend more time relaxing together, speaking less, looking at each other, and engaging in some kind of connecting touch or closeness before talking about the day.

They agreed to focus on connecting first before engaging in intellectual conversation when they come home, deciding it would be nice to de-stress a little before talking too much, and to connect nonverbally rather than recounting their day as a primary way of interacting. One way they did that was to give each other a long hug as soon as they were both home, then sit close on the couch and give each other a shoulder rub for a few minutes, only sharing details about the day once they felt connected. Even though this ritual only took five to ten minutes, it made a big difference in how they felt with each other after a long day. Through this shift of mind-set and behavior, Jen and Rita started to enjoy coming home to each other more, and they developed a habit of relaxing together when stressed, rather than just talking. Their evenings soon became more connected and less argumentative.

Doug + Jada

Doug and Jada want to connect more deeply but are struggling to figure out how. Doug tends to get mad a lot, especially when he's under stress at work, and Jada gets frustrated by the lack of meaningful time together and wants to have more fun with him. Sometimes they try going out and doing things, like going to a movie or dinner—they even tried paddleboarding once! But Doug often gets anxious and starts complaining about certain things, and Jada has a hard time opening up because she doesn't expect to have much fun with him anymore.

Doug and Jada needed to focus more on how they simply *are* around each other rather than on the activity they think might be connecting. Regardless of the activity, or if we're just sitting at home with one another, there are many opportunities to bond in how we share ourselves with others. Doug had to learn how to identify his stress and anxiety and ask for support and connection rather than just vent it out while on dates or at home. He needed to realize that under stress, his face and tone become tight and tense, alienating his partner. He learned how to share his feelings in the moment more proactively, which created a better bond with Jada.

Jada needed to open up a little more to emotional connection in the moment, and to revise her expectations, giving Doug a chance to prove they could move on from an old pattern. She practiced giving him reassuring signs that she was interested in him and wanting to connect, which helped him feel less anxious. And they both needed to realize that they could connect by being closer in the manner in which they interact, instead of thinking that they need an activity to bring them together. They started focusing on each other more in their activities by making eye contact, holding hands, being close, and prioritizing being together over the activity itself.

As Doug became more aware of his disconnecting nonverbal signals and asked for support when he was stressed, Jada could relax around him more and they could have more fun. Jada looked for ways to signal openness and friendliness to him without necessarily needing an activity, helping him feel more confident in their connection and thus able to better enjoy their interactions.

Jada started realizing she has her own blocks to intimacy, even though it seemed it was mostly Doug who would derail their dates. When Doug started learning how to better manage his stress by meditating and taking supplements, she started working to understand her own disconnecting tendencies so they could both improve and work toward each other. Jada began to see that as Doug relaxed, and as she opened to more connection, there was actually a lot more there in their relationship in the moment than she had given them credit for. They started to feel close again, have fun, and to build off that foundation.

Exercise to Build Connecting Skill

Sit down with a partner to talk, but before you talk, just face each other so your bodies are turned toward each other. Take a few deep breaths. Relax your spines and your jaws, then make eye contact, and gently gaze at each other. This is not a staring contest, but a gentle way to pay attention to what the eyes and face of your partner are expressing. Notice how you feel. Notice if you're tense, feel awkward, or are relaxed. Make a private mental note to yourself of a few things you feel in your body or emotionally, and a few things you notice in your partner.

When you're ready, move a bit closer and continue to face each other, now holding hands. Feel each other's touch, stay in each other's eyes, and notice what you see, and what you feel. At this point you can usually say something and your words have a stronger context of connection. When you're grounded together in the moment like this, your read of your partner is better and you can both see and feel the nonverbal aspect of communication.

Sometimes when people sit down to talk, they start using words right away to convey concepts, but they haven't really settled into each other yet, or connected nervous system to nervous system. Further, many people don't look at each other when they talk, which means they will miss important information as their minds are more likely to be distracted or in the realm of ideas. What we're practicing here is slowing down, being in the moment with each other, and connecting, nonverbally, before you speak. What you may notice is that you can feel connected more quickly this way, and that your words are misinterpreted less because all the nonverbal information is more obvious to each other.

The first few times you start by connecting this way, it may feel weird and awkward. But that's why it's helpful to practice and engage in the repetition of these types of exercises. The more you do it, the more normal sitting close, facing each other, making eye contact, and sharing feelings becomes. The best reason to connect this way more is that it works. If you notice benefits to connecting nervous system to nervous system rather than over-relying on words, you may choose to connect like this more often. Once you know you can interact this way, it gives you a resource for comfort and to de-stress, allowing your words to more accurately describe how you feel and what you want in your connection with each other. In this safe space, you can be more vulnerable, caring, and loving. Grounding into the moment opens up patience and increases our empathy with others. Give this exercise a few rounds to train your muscle memory around close connection. You'll find that these connecting moves start to become more your habit after a while.

Notes

1. Bonnie Badenoch, *The Heart of Trauma: Healing the Embodied Brain in the Context of Relationships*, Norton Series on Interpersonal Neurobiology (New York: W. W. Norton, 2017).

2. Stephen W. Porges, *The Polyvagal Theory: Neurophysiological Foundations of Emotions, Attachment, Communication, and Self-Regulation* (New York: W. W. Norton, 2011).

3. Joseph LeDoux, "The Amygdala," *Current Biology* 17, no. 20 (October 2007): R868–R874.

4. Robert M. Sapolsky, *Behave: The Biology of Humans at Our Best and Worst* (London: Penguin, 2017).

5. Stephen W. Porges and C. Sue Carter, "Polyvagal Theory and the Social Engagement System," in *Complementary and Integrative Treatments in Psychiatric Practice*, ed. Patricia L. Gerbarg, M.D., Philip R. Muskin, M.D., M.A., and Richard P. Brown, M.D. (Washington, DC: American Psychiatric Association, 2017), 221–241.

6. S. Breit, A. Kupferberg, G. Rogler, and G. Hasler, "Vagus Nerve as Modulator of the Brain-Gut Axis in Psychiatric and Inflammatory Disorders," *Frontiers in Psychiatry* 9, no. 44 (March 2018), https://doi.org/10.3389/fpsyt.2018.00044.

7. Porges, *The Polyvagal Theory*.

8. Stephen W. Porges, "The Polyvagal Perspective," *Biological Psychology* 74, no. 2 (February 2007): 116–143, https://doi.org/10.1016/j.biopsycho.2006.06.009.

9. D. S. Goldstein, "Adrenal Responses to Stress," *Cellular and Molecular Neurobiology* 30, no. 8 (November 2010): 1433–1440, https://doi.org/10.1007/s10571-010-9606-9.

10. Thomas G. Guilliams and Lena Edwards, "Chronic Stress and the HPA Axis," *The Standard* 9, no. 2 (2010): 1–12.

11. Rachel Yehuda, "Risk and Resilience in Posttraumatic Stress Disorder, *Journal of Clinical Psychiatry* 65 (2004): 29–36.

12. Stephen W. Porges, Jane A. Doussard-Roosevelt, and Ajit K. Maiti, "Vagal Tone and the Physiological Regulation of Emotion," *Monographs of the Society for Research in Child Development* 59, no. 2–3 (February 1994): 167–186.

13. Theodore Beauchaine, "Vagal Tone, Development, and Gray's Motivational Theory: Toward an Integrated Model of Autonomic Nervous System Functioning in Psychopathology," *Development and Psychopathology* 13, no. 2 (Spring 2001): 183–214.

14. Porges, *The Polyvagal Theory*.

15. J. Bahney and C. S. von Bartheld, "The Cellular Composition and Glia-Neuron Ratio in the Spinal Cord of a Human and a Nonhuman Primate: Comparison with Other Species and Brain Regions," *Anatomical Record* 301, no. 4 (2018): 697–710, https://doi.org/10.1002/ar.23728.

16. Emma Young, "Gut Instincts: The Secrets of Your Second Brain," *New Scientist* 216 (December 2012): 38–42, https://doi.org/10.1016/S0262-4079(12)63204-7.

17. Emeran A. Mayer, "Gut Feelings: The Emerging Biology of Gut–Brain Communication," *Nature Reviews Neuroscience* 12, no. 8 (2011): 453–466.

18. J. P. Burkett and L. J. Young, "The Behavioral, Anatomical and Pharmacological Parallels between Social Attachment, Love and Addiction," *Psychopharmacology* 224, no. 1 (August 2012): 1–26, https://doi.org/10.1007/s00213-012-2794-x.

19. Lane Strathearn, "Maternal Neglect: Oxytocin, Dopamine and the Neurobiology of Attachment," *Journal of Neuroendocrinology* 23, no. 11 (November 2011): 1054–1065.

20. Anna Buchheim, Markus Heinrichs, Carol George, Dan Pokorny, Eva Koops, Peter Henningsen, Mary-Frances O'Connor, and Harald Gündel, "Oxytocin Enhances the Experience of Attachment Security," *Psychoneuroendocrinology* 34, no. 9 (October 2009): 1417–1422.

21. C. Sue Carter, "The Oxytocin–Vasopressin Pathway in the Context of Love and Fear," *Frontiers in Endocrinology* 8 (December 2017): 356.

22. Dan-Mikael Ellingsen, Johan Wessberg, Olga Chelnokova, Håkan Olausson, Bruno Laeng, and Siri Leknes, "In Touch with Your Emotions: Oxytocin and Touch Change Social Impressions While Others' Facial Expressions Can Alter Touch," *Psychoneuroendocrinology* 39 (January 2014): 11–20.

23. Gerald Gimpl and Falk Fahrenholz, "The Oxytocin Receptor System: Structure, Function, and Regulation," *Physiological Reviews* 81, no. 2 (April 2001): 629–683.

24. Gary G. Berntson, Martin Sarter, and John T. Cacioppo, "Ascending Visceral Regulation of Cortical Affective Information Processing," *European Journal of Neuroscience* 18, no. 8 (October 2003): 2103–2109.

25. Allan N. Schore, "Attachment, Affect Regulation, and the Developing Right Brain: Linking Developmental Neuroscience to Pediatrics," *Pediatrics in Review* 26, no. 6 (June 2005): 204–217.

26. Phillip R. Shaver and Mario Mikulincer, "Adult Attachment Strategies and the Regulation of Emotion," in *Handbook of Emotion Regulation*, ed. James J. Groos (New York: Guilford, 2007), 465.

2.

The Language of the Nervous System

Emotional regulation flows naturally from being in the presence of someone we trust.

—Bonnie Badenoch

When measuring safety and security, what exactly does the nervous system pay attention to? It doesn't speak English, Spanish, Russian, or Wolof, but it does have its own language that it uses to measure connection. The Language of the Nervous System is made up of markers that convey security, safety, and connection to the brain, mind, and body. If you know how to speak security to others' nervous systems, you can deepen connection.

Neuroscience studies have determined what types of inputs the nervous system reads in making its calculations about closeness, a sense of safety, and bonding.[1] Both brain and body are complex, balancing a myriad of chemical and electrical signals and crunching the data together much like a supercomputer, measuring thousands of different data points simultaneously. As partners and as people, our nervous systems are in each other's care, and we can improve that care by becoming more fluent in this language. In the pages that follow, I focus on six components of this nervous system language that create a sense of trust and safety and deepen connection. These six elements make a big difference in how your nervous system experiences others, and in how easy or difficult it is to connect in any close relationship.

1. Proximity

"Proximity" refers to how physically close you are to another person when interacting. At a close distance, the brain can shift from measuring general anatomical features to capturing more subtle details about someone's state and emotions, potentially facilitating greater attunement. The brain also needs to determine if you're in danger, and if it decides you're not in harm's way, it sends a subconscious signal to the rest of the body that it's okay to relax.[2] That safety calculation helps prevent arguments and provides the brain with a positive feeling that it applies to the context of your communication. Close distance can also activate emotional intimacy and romance, offering more avenues for connection than the distance of normal conversation.

Proximity changes the meaning we take from verbal communication.[3] You can say the same words at a distance of three feet versus a distance of three inches and the brain will use the different contexts to take a different meaning from those words.[4] For example, talking about who's going to pick up groceries when you're on opposite sides of the kitchen might be experienced as a simple, logistical interaction, but move that conversation to a distance of three inches and the meaning might become flirty.

Usually, normal conversation distance is three to four feet apart. But in a relationship where you want to feel closer, or in which communication is difficult and you often get crossways with each other, try closing the distance to about three to six inches. Some of this happens subconsciously, but if you pay attention, you can notice if you feel comfortable or not at close range. If you don't, move back a little until you find the sweet spot. It's not worth trying to be physically close if it makes anyone nervous. When you move in close, just make sure you both feel safe and secure enough to interact at that distance; otherwise, use a distance that feels the best.

Moments of physical closeness can help create a sense of connection in your subconscious. The closer you are physically, the more clearly you send a signal to each other's nervous systems that says, *We are close and we are safe with each other*. Even if you don't notice a huge change in how you feel in that moment, physical closeness often conveys a sense of security deep into the nervous system and can help prevent a feeling of disconnection.[5]

2. Touch

Touch is a key marker of connection to the nervous system. Words are complex; they make the brain work to receive and understand language. Touch is simpler, more primitive, and allows the brain and body to relax into a connecting interaction that doesn't require much processing or interpretation. Most people respond well to touch, as it can generate a tender, soothing, and connecting signal to the nervous system.[6] Touch can often communicate better than words when you're trying to say *I love you* and *You matter to me.*

It's important to acknowledge that not everyone likes or responds well to touch. Reasons may include not being held, touched, or rocked much as an infant, growing up in a family that didn't engage in much physical soothing, one's personal preferences, or cultural habit. When touch does not feel attuned or safe as infants, it may feel unfamiliar or uncomfortable to the nervous system later in life.[7] In those cases, it's vital to establish consent before, go slow, and share how it feels. A secure relationship can create a safe place to retrain the nervous system and allow touch to become more comfortable in time.

There are different kinds of touch, and it's helpful to know which ones your partner likes the most. Research suggests that moderate-pressure touch is calming to the nervous system, whereas light touch can be activating, so if you are seeking to calm and soothe your partner, you might employ moderate pressure in your touch, like holding someone's feet with a nice, firm grip, holding someone in a tight (and loving!) hug, or using a little more force in a massage.[8] But everyone is different and a light, stroking touch feels relaxing to many. Some people like a static, holding touch; some like a moving, stroking touch. Practice different kinds of touch with your partner and find out what feels good. Some like it all!

Once you establish the kinds of touch that feel good in your relationships, you can use them more often to speak connection to the nervous system. If you're sitting next to your partner, you can hold hands. You might reach out and touch each others' arms or hands when talking. With kids, frequently cradle and rock them and engage in safe physical play that promotes bonding. With friends, you might try holding hands sometimes if that's comfortable, or plopping your feet on their lap when talking on a couch. All are ways of using touch to deepen connection.

Massage

Massage is a specific way to speak connection nonverbally to each other, which allows people to relax, open up, and feel connected without the stress or challenges of language. It's a wonderful act of giving, because your partner can literally feel your care, and it helps you receive your partner's energy and loving intent.

If words often land you in trouble as partners—if you tend to spar and feel disconnected in conversations—you might connect first via a brief massage of the hands, arms, or shoulders before engaging verbally. Generally, your nervous systems will feel more in sync after touch, and connection will be easier moving forward. It is important to learn your partner's preferences—how they like to be massaged—otherwise this activity can feel misaligned. Spend some time learning what feels good and trading tips as you begin to practice massage with each other.

Partner massage is one way to incorporate intentional touch that can also be romantic. It's helpful to establish ahead of time if it feels good to all parties to allow massage to progress romantically into sex. Friends can massage each other as well, and it can feel great—just have clear boundaries about what you want. Giving your kids a massage or letting them rub your feet or shoulders is also a good nonverbal way to connect. If you tend to run stressed, or if your kids have anxiety, creating opportunities for family massage time is a connecting way to de-stress and strengthen family bonds.

If you have the resources, finding a professional massage therapist who is attuned to your body can also help you learn to receive touch in a relaxing way, become more aware of what your body likes, and can help relieve stress and anxiety.

3. Tone

Your tone of voice often communicates more about what you're saying than your actual words.[9] The brain can read a wealth of information from tone, like intent, emotional state, mind-set, and the security of the interaction.[10] Our nervous systems listen much the way our dogs do, with tone of voice and inflection being an important part of determining meaning. Generally speaking, a friendly, soothing tone will relax others and put them at ease, while a louder, sharper, or more aggressive tone can cause stress and guardedness. Being mindful of this can change how others feel around us, allowing us to speak words that others can more easily hear and take in.

Many of us might think that our tone of voice is built in or just how we are, while it is in fact flexible and we can adjust it more than we may think. Our natural resting tone is generally a learned product of our early environment and conditioning, so those who grew up in a calm, quiet household may have a softer or flatter tone and those who grew up in a loud, boister-

> To use tone in the service of connection, it can be as simple as being more aware of the pitch and quality of your voice when you're speaking. Imagine your tone conveying a sense of security and soothing others just by the way you sound.

ous household may be louder or more dynamic.[11] Our vocal tone—known as prosody in research—develops in infancy to better connect with caregivers but evolves as we age based on environment and culture.[12] Just like it formed as an adaptation to connect better in childhood, it can continue to develop to enhance connection in our adult relationships.

One of the best examples of how we can modulate our tone in the service of connection is if we live in a foreign country, where intonations and the way feelings are vocalized are different. We may begin to adopt the intonations and manners of our new home culture in order to connect and communicate more effectively. Most of the time, however, being aware of our vocal tone to promote connection is less about our default, resting tone, and more about our tone when we're stressed, irritated, frustrated, or angry. The way we use our tone in such moments can disrupt our sense of connection with others by sending non-safe signals to others' nervous systems.[13] We can practice being more aware when upset, and intentionally use a softer, calmer, kinder timbre when speaking to others, even in those moments.

You might also practice more variation in your tone. As long as it does not become aggressive or threatening, variation is a sign of emotional range and complexity to others' nervous systems, which can help engender trust and connection. Tone variability can communicate empathy, care, and excitement more so than sounding flat. If you can vary your tone, getting soft for intimate and romantic conversation, higher pitched when you're excited, and louder when celebrating in a positive way, you may engage others more readily as you're conveying your emotional state. This sort of variation subconsciously conveys a sense of psychological flexibility to others by indicating subtlety and range in our processing abilities and sensitivity to nuances in the information we receive.[14]

Being aware of your tone when communicating with others will take practice at first, but eventually it can become second nature. Varying how you sound to others also becomes easier and more natural because you begin to realize that your body naturally expresses different tones based on state and emotion. As we remove mental barriers and social conditioning from our genuine expressions, we can better allow our voice to capture our feelings, which helps others read us more easily.

4. Eye Contact

The eyes convey rich information about fight-or-flight reactions in the body and feelings toward others. Most mammals use the eyes as an important way to measure nervous system activity, safety and security, and emotional states and intent.[15] For example, the eyes tend to widen in fear and narrow in disgust. And a soft gaze implies safety and friendliness, while a hard stare is indicative of anger. When we go into fight-or-flight and/or are sexually turned on, our pupils tend to dilate. And the direction of our eyes when we gaze toward someone indicates interest and connection.[16] We don't have to consciously know what these signals mean—thousands of years of evolution have wired our brains to interpret the data. But making our eyes available in interactions helps the nervous system know what's going on.

Because the eyes are so expressive and convey so much about the nervous system in real time, making eye contact is a useful way to follow internal experience, notice reactions and emotions, improve attunement, and deepen connection. While comfort level and duration of eye contact vary from culture to culture, in general, it accomplishes a few important functions that can assist in connection:

1. Eye contact communicates: *I'm here with you,* and *You have my full attention.*
2. The eyes communicate important information about safety and security, so by checking someone's eyes you can tell if it's

okay to relax or if you need to be wary, and others will do the same with you.

3. Eye contact allows you to notice what someone else is feeling and respond to it, and allows others to do the same for you.

4. Directing our gaze toward someone communicates interest to their nervous system.

5. The eyes quickly change to reflect emotional information in real time, so if you track the eyes closely, you can refine your ability to care for each other moment by moment.

Most people don't make enough eye contact, or hold eye contact long enough, to accomplish these tasks. Sometimes, when we speak, we glance at our partners briefly, then speak while looking away, or we may look away to think. While a glance at someone's face helps the brain gather some information about them, sustained eye contact allows you to gather information in real time and with greater nuance. For example, if you speak while looking away, you are likely to miss important information about how your listener is reacting to your words and to the interaction. Sinking into eye contact allows you to get past the initial anxiety and awkwardness of it and settle into tracking each other's states and feelings more deeply in real time. That allows you to be more attuned and catch stress, anxiety, or annoyance quickly before it escalates, as well as to convey love and affection through your eyes to others.

Learning to maintain more eye contact will give you connecting superpowers because you notice right away if someone is upset, bored, hurt, annoyed, or impatient in the interaction. You can then shift the interaction to respond to those cues, sometimes before your listener even registers their own feelings! You also get the benefit of noticing someone's loving gaze, or admiring eyes, allowing you to receive deeper love and connection in the moment.

The ways you attempt to increase the sense of security in your relationship need to be sensitive to cultural and individual differences. In some cultures, direct or sustained eye contact is less common and at times disrespectful, even between primary partners. If increased eye contact violates an important and established cultural norm in your or your partner's culture, then I recommend simply tuning your awareness to other signals in interactions, like tone or body language.

5. Body Language

The primitive systems in the body that measure connection closely additionally monitor body language.[17] Connecting body language can be as simple as facing each other in a conversation rather than standing side by side or opening your arms rather than having them crossed when you're having a discussion. It includes holding hugs so the nervous system can receive the full benefits of that touch (quick hugs are sometimes too fast to regulate the nervous system). And it includes having a relaxed body with others and noticing stress cues (in yourself and others) such as raised shoulders, flushed skin tone, or a stiff jaw.

Body language communicates our availability to pay attention, whether we are relaxed enough to take in information, and if we are physically prepared to connect. Stress is conveyed physically by the body and face and may signal to others that we are emotionally distracted or less available for an attuned interaction.[18] When your body language is open and relaxed, it indicates a readiness and willingness for interaction. When our body language is more closed, tense, or turned away, others may be more wary to engage. Softening our body language so it attracts others allows for co-regulation of stress and emotional states and creates bonding moments in relationship.

So what is connecting body language? Relaxing your body and taking a couple deep breaths so that your shoulders drop and your belly softens; facing your partner; signaling friendliness on your face and displaying soft eyes; smiling, if you feel content; and reaching out with your arms, sitting close, or holding hands signals a desire for closeness. All these expressions of body language will convey to others your sustained attention, prompting connection. This is especially true with kids, who may not open up right away when you engage them directly, but if they sense your relaxed presence around them, open up when they're ready.

Talking with small kids by getting on their physical level is a great example of this. Because adults are usually much bigger, kids often spend their time looking up at the world, but the size difference can create distance and be intimidating. Attachment research suggests that if you squat or kneel down before speaking with kids so that you're at the same eye level, it's easier for them to feel safe and bonded in the interaction.[19] We can use this physiological cue in all relationships. Instead of towering over others or sitting much lower than someone else, we can be mindful to create a greater sense of physical equality and generally attempt to interact at eye level to put the nervous system at ease.

Your face and body's position in part communicate your interest and willingness to interact. If your partner, friends, or kids often accuse you of being "hard to reach," it is likely that your mind gets engrossed in what you're doing to the point where you unintentionally or unwittingly tune others out. Since your mind may not easily switch off a task you're engaged in, turning your body toward others in an immediate physical response aids in sending a message that you care, as it helps your mind switch and avoids feelings of rejection in others. It also conveys to others that they are your priority.

The brain looks to body language to understand the meaning of communication and how to interpret words being spoken. When there is a discrepancy between words and body language, the latter wins in terms of the meaning the brain takes away from the interaction.[20] Nonverbal indications reign because the nervous system is always looking for safety cues from the primitive system when there is any doubt as to intent. Once security is verified, the brain is freed up to move into more abstract thought.

6. Speed of Response

Speed of response is an important but often overlooked measure of security and connection. Essentially, when we seek attention, the nervous system measures how long it takes for someone to acknowledge us and respond.[21] A quick response reassures our internal hardware that we can get support quickly, that others are paying attention to our needs, and that they care about us. This becomes a data point that communicates closeness and support to the mind.[22]

A delay in responding, even of two or three seconds, sounds an internal security warning: Can we rely on this person? Are they paying attention? Is what they're doing more important than I am? In such situations we may feel an emotional "drop," which is the movement from the anticipatory excitement of connection to the disappointment of realizing the other person isn't available or doesn't desire to meet us there. Speed of response is part of the mechanism that regulates neurochemicals like oxytocin that amplify the positive feeling of connection or, in their absence, leaves interactions feeling flat.[23] Even a two-second delay can cause the nervous system to question the connection and can cause that drop, transforming desire into rejection surprisingly fast. At times we may not notice the subconscious impression of the delay, but other times we will. Lags like this make it harder for others to trust moving forward.

Without knowing it, we calculate speed of response often throughout the day, and anytime we seek our partner's attention. In the modern era, we are often reading, watching something, or checking our phones or email when our partners seek our attention. The best way to use body language in these moments is to immediately turn our attention to others when they seek us out, moving our body, eyes, and mind. An immediate response sends the message: *You are the most important thing in my world*, and puts others' nervous systems at ease. Once you've responded, you can always let your partner know that you'd like to finish something important before engaging in discussion, and ask if that's okay. Being willing to stop what you're doing at a moment's notice and give your loved ones your full attention causes them to feel valued and loved, and is good practice in prioritizing connection and our relationships over mundane tasks.

When I talk about speed of response in workshops, people are surprised to learn that it matters to connection. "What's a couple seconds?" some ask. But the nervous system calculates attunement in microseconds, so a few seconds is a long time, and the delay causes questions about reliability that linger in the subconscious, contributing to a sense of disconnection and fueling arguments that may happen later. To some, pausing what you're doing to turn your attention to your partner or child right away sounds overly indulgent and co-dependent. I like to provide context: in a culture that values (sometimes to extreme levels) independence, productivity, and self-reliance, many healthy relationship behaviors can seem co-dependent. Turning your attention to others right away is not co-dependent but rather a healthy interdependent behavior that promotes close relationships.

If you're routinely too late in your responses to others, even if your eventual answer is caring, others begin seeking to avoid that mild feeling of rejection and may start seeking attention from other, more affirming sources. Such sources can include other people, hobbies, books, social media, family members, or new friends. Of course, a diversity of friendships and activities is healthy, but partners, family members, and friends should feel important when they seek one another's attention, not rejected or disappointed.

Here I offer some practical tips for how to speak the Language of the Nervous System and some exercises that will help you develop better connecting skill in these areas.

Practicing the Six Elements
of the Language of the Nervous System

1. Proximity

Tip: Take opportunities to be physically near, whether that's sitting closer on the couch, or standing next to each other when socializing with others. When talking, sit or stand closer than you normally would, and especially if there is some friction in the interaction.

Partner Exercise: Start a conversation at a distance of three to four feet. Maybe pick something mildly stressful to talk about. After a minute, move closer to each other so you're now at a distance of three or four inches. Notice how the distance changes the conversation. The proximity might make you laugh, or feel awkward or giddy. Your brain has a different context for the words at that distance. It may be harder to argue. The power of nearness can change your interactions and connection in real time.

2. Touch

Tip: Use touch often, as long as it's appropriate to the moment and feels good to your partner or others. For example, you might hold hands more often, or place a hand on their arm at dinner. You might give each other a shoulder rub at the end of the day to relax, or even trade ten-minute massages once a week.

Partner Exercise: Sit close to each other. In this exercise, you'll be caressing each other's arms to get a sense of the kind of touch your partner likes the most. Pick who will go first, and begin massaging your partner's forearm. Use a stroking touch for twenty seconds, then a static, holding touch, and ask your partner which they like better. Try it again, then trade. By discovering what different types of touch you each prefer, you learn the kind of touch that feels most connecting and relaxing to you and your partner.

3. Tone

Tip: Cultivate an awareness of your tone. Try to use a kind-sounding, warm, friendly pitch when speaking with others. Our tone often changes when speaking to babies and pets, an automatic feature of bonding that communicates attunement and connection, so you might think of those shifts in timbre as an example of how to signal care. If you tend toward a loud or aggressive-sounding tone, you might find that you elicit better listening and more empathy from others if you soften your manner of speech.

   Partner Exercise: Say something to your partner loudly and aggressively. Then say the same thing in a sweet, calm, friendly manner. Your partner gets to notice how different they feel despite the words being the same, and you can share your experience in each. Switch, so you both notice the difference.

4. Eye Contact

Tip: Try to make more eye contact throughout the day, and hold the eye contact longer than you normally might. Sustained eye contact may feel awkward at first, but it gets more comfortable with time. You may be used to looking away, distracting from the moment, or laughing it off, but sinking into the opportunity to see more information about your partner's state and emotions in their eyes and on their face can enhance connection. If you take a few deep breaths to help your body relax into moments of eye contact, they will become a more natural and automatic part of your interactions in daily life.

   Partner Exercise: Sit across from each other, get comfortable, relax your bodies, and make eye contact with each other. Instead of hard-staring into each other's eyes, use a soft gaze, and explore your partner's face. Check and see the exact color and shade of your partner's eyes. Is the color around their pupils uniform or does it vary? Guess at the number of eyelashes they have, and notice the fine lines on their face. Notice the quality of your partner's gaze—is it soft or tense? Do their eyes look happy or sad? Practice for about twenty seconds, then pause and share with each other what you noticed. Do it again for twenty seconds and share any specific emotions you think you saw in your partner's eyes. Your partner can let you know if your reads are true or not. As you learn to read others' eyes more closely, you can respond to what you see in real time by offering care or asking deeper questions, creating a stronger connection than if you simply listen to the words in conversation.

5. Body Language

Tip: Try to be more aware of your body language when you're around others. You might turn your body to face others more often rather than interact side by side. Soften your body, and if your body runs tense look for ways to physically relax around others. Especially notice if your belly, shoulders, or jaw are tight. Beware of multitasking too much when interacting with others. Focused, direct body language is a powerful way of saying, *I'm here, and I'm paying attention.*

   Partner Exercise: Sit next to each other on a couch and have a conversation while both looking forward, similar to how you might speak in the car. Notice what that feels like. Then face each other, start the conversation again, and notice how it feels different to be able to see someone's face and eyes and have their body facing you. Another scenario you can use is to have your partner pretend to do something that faces away from you, like washing the dishes or multitasking. Ask them a question and have them answer without turning to look at you. Then ask the same question and have them turn and face you to answer. Notice how those interactions feel different.

6. Speed of Response

Tip: When your partner seeks your attention, respond immediately. Look up from what you're doing and give them your full attention right away. Your quick response signals attentiveness and communicates security to their nervous system. If you have to continue with what you're doing, turn your attention to others first, then negotiate continuing with your activity. In this way you can avoid feelings of rejection and strengthen your connection.

   Partner Exercise: Have one person take out a phone and stare at it, pretending to check social media or email. The other will seek that person's attention. Ask the person on their cell a question, like, "Do you want to go out tonight?" or, "Can I tell you something?" The first part of the exercise is for the person on their phone to not respond or look up for a full three seconds, and for the person asking to notice how that feels. Then, to notice the contrast, play out the same scenario again, but this time respond immediately, looking up from the phone right away.

Notice what a difference it makes to have to wait versus getting someone's attention right away. When waiting, we often feel unimportant compared to the phone. When responded to right away, we feel special and like we're a priority to our partner. That little shift can make a big difference to how secure people feel in relationship, because so much of connection is a determination of *Are you there for me?* Switch roles, so you both get to experience the exercise as the asker. Being more aware of that "dropped" feeling where desire turns to disappointment helps you remember why responding quickly to each other matters.

The Language of the Nervous System offers ways of relating to others that deepen connection and that communicate security directly to the primitive parts that measure it. You can use these cues to build stronger, more reliable and stable relationships with others. The more you practice this language of connection, the more it becomes second nature—wired into your automatic behavior like any habit—and it's there for you even when you're not thinking about how to act or when stressed. Looking for opportunities throughout the day for physical closeness goes a long way to improving a sense of connection in your partner relationship. As partners and as people, our nervous systems are in each other's care, and we can improve that by becoming more fluent in the Language of the Nervous System. Despite having so much technology to communicate through, the bottom line is that we still need direct human-to-human contact to establish a trust.

While these cues will help you communicate love and warmth to others, the Language of the Nervous System is also about reading others' emotional signals so you can respond more quickly and in a more attuned way. Hurts and disconnects that linger will eventually make their way into long-term memory, making them more difficult to revise and repair, so noticing emotional information as close to real time as possible is helpful to maintaining connection.

This language also helps you be more aware of how you might *receive* loving care from others, such as a kind glance, smile, or empathic look and tone. You can better notice those moments to soak in others' love from their touch, proximity, and eye contact and so go beyond words to send clear, full-body signals that communicate connection.

Notes

1. Stephen W. Porges, "Making the World Safe for Our Children: Down-Regulating Defence and Up-Regulating Social Engagement to 'Optimise' the Human Experience," *Children Australia* 40, no. 2 (June 2015): 114.

2. Stephen W. Porges, "Love: An Emergent Property of the Mammalian Autonomic Nervous System," *Psychoneuroendocrinology* 23, no. 8 (November 1998): 837–861.

3. Andrew S. Imada and Milton D. Hakel, "Influence of Nonverbal Communication and Rater Proximity on Impressions and Decisions in Simulated Employment Interviews," *Journal of Applied Psychology* 62, no. 3 (1977): 295.

4. Judee K. Burgoon, David B. Buller, Jerold L. Hale, and Mark A. de Turck, "Relational Messages Associated with Nonverbal Behaviors," *Human Communication Research* 10, no. 3 (March 1984): 351–378.

5. Stephen W. Porges, "The Role of Social Engagement in Attachment and Bonding," *Attachment and Bonding* 3 (2005): 33–54.

6. Tiffany Field, "Touch for Socioemotional and Physical Well-Being: A Review," *Developmental Review* 30, no. 4 (December 2010): 367–383.

7. Bessel A. van der Kolk, "The Body Keeps the Score: Memory and the Evolving Psychobiology of Posttraumatic Stress," *Harvard Review of Psychiatry* 1, no. 5 (January–February 1994): 253–265.

8. Miguel A. Diego and Tiffany Field, "Moderate Pressure Massage Elicits a Parasympathetic Nervous System Response," *International Journal of Neuroscience* 119, no. 5 (2009): 630–638.

9. Lynne C. Nygaard, Debora S. Herold, and Laura L. Namy, "The Semantics of Prosody: Acoustic and Perceptual Evidence of Prosodic Correlates to Word Meaning," *Cognitive Science* 33, no. 1 (2009): 127–146.

10. Jurriaan Witteman, Vincent J. P. Van Heuven, and Niels O. Schiller, "Hearing Feelings: A Quantitative Meta-analysis on the Neuroimaging Literature of Emotional Prosody Perception," *Neuropsychologia* 50, no. 12 (October 2012): 2752–2763.

11. Pilar Prieto and Núria Esteve-Gibert, eds., *The Development of Prosody in First Language Acquisition*, vol. 23 (Amsterdam: John Benjamins, 2018).

12. Shari R. Speer and Kiwako Ito, "Prosody in First Language Acquisition—Acquiring Intonation as a Tool to Organize Information in Conversation," *Language and Linguistics Compass* 3, no. 1 (February 2009): 90–110.

13. Jonathan Culpeper, "'It's Not What You Said, It's How You Said It!': Prosody and Impoliteness," *Discursive Approaches to Politeness* 8 (2011): 57–83.

14. Witteman, Van Heuven, and Schiller, "Hearing Feelings."

15. Michael Brecht and Winrich A. Freiwald, "The Many Facets of Facial Interactions in Mammals," *Current Opinion in Neurobiology* 22, no. 2 (April 2012): 259–266, https://doi.org/10.1016/j.conb.2011.12.003.

16. Nathan J. Emery, "The Eyes Have It: The Neuroethology, Function and Evolution of Social Gaze," *Neuroscience & Biobehavioral Reviews* 24, no. 6 (September 2000): 581–604.

17. Fatik Baran Mandal, "Nonverbal Communication in Humans," *Journal of Human Behavior in the Social Environment* 24, no. 4 (2014): 417–421.

18. Beatrice de Gelder, "Towards the Neurobiology of Emotional Body Language," *Nature Reviews Neuroscience* 7, no. 3 (March 2006): 242–249.

19. Porges, "Role of Social Engagement."

20. Deepika Phutela, "The Importance of Non-verbal Communication," *IUP Journal of Soft Skills* 9, no. 4 (December 2015): 43.

21. Leslie Atkinson, Eman Leung, Susan Goldberg, Diane Benoit, Lori Poulton, Natalie Myhal, Kirsten Blokland, and Sheila Kerr, "Attachment and Selective Attention: Disorganization and Emotional Stroop Reaction Time," *Development and Psychopathology* 21, no. 1 (2009): 99–126.

22. James E. Swain, Pilyoung Kim, Julie Spicer, Shao-Hsuan Ho, Carolyn J. Dayton, Alya Elmadih, and Kathryn M. Abel, "Approaching the Biology of Human Parental Attachment: Brain Imaging, Oxytocin and Coordinated Assessments of Mothers and Fathers," *Brain Research* 1580 (September 2014): 78–101.

23. Ibid.

3.

Being Present Enough to Connect

Time isn't precious at all, because it is an illusion. What you perceive as precious is not time but the one point that is out of time: the Now. That is precious indeed. The more you are focused on time—past and future—the more you miss the Now.

—Eckhart Tolle

Being present in the moment with each other is one of the things I generally watch for in the couples I work with. Most of us miss the *pause*, that moment when we can sink into the present with someone else and intimacy can happen. I don't mean romantic intimacy, necessarily, but the emotional closeness of love, connection, and seeing and receiving another person in a focused way. We miss the pause and get distracted from it, start an intellectual conversation, look away, fidget, or get busy. What gets lost here is the opportunity for love to flow between you in a way you can really perceive. While many of the couples I see in my practice complain of a lack of connection, few come into the present moment with each other where that connection can happen. Granted, they may be hurt by a previous interaction or have learned not to trust their partner due to challenging emotional patterns, but even then, the opportunity for repair of hurts exists in the moment. Most of the time, what I notice is that people are uncomfortable connecting directly and intimately, making it difficult to correct errors and repair hurts in real time. It's also important to spend some time connecting directly in order to be able to practice bonding skills that can then become more natural.

Part of my interest in seeing couples engage in the present moment comes from many years of studying spiritual traditions beginning in late adolescence and into the current day. Growing up in the fast-paced and productivity-oriented culture of New York City, I went seeking wisdom about what it really means to be alive and how to best use the opportunity of having consciousness. I traveled to many countries, learning indigenous and ancient spiritual traditions, and sought out many teachers in the United States as well. From those experiences, I have witnessed the power and value of training the mind to have more focused presence. Our attention naturally moves in many different directions at once, but we can train it to focus on the things that matter most.[1]

Spirituality is sometimes described as a person's deepest existential thoughts and feelings, and I think many of us would place our relationships in that realm of experience. We may wonder, *Am I with the right person? Can I really have love in this relationship? Can I get what I need?* Or, *Is this how I should be spending my time and my life?* Being in the moment allows you to bring those existential thoughts and feelings into the joint space where they can be explored, and you get to see how the relationship can show up with its love, attention, and care when you give it a chance. Clinical psychologist Dr. Steven C. Hayes, the founder of Acceptance and Commitment Therapy (ACT), associates being fully present in the moment with psychological flexibility and adds a spiritual and mindfulness take on that ability. He defines psychological flexibility as the ability to "make contact with experience in the present moment fully and without defense."[2] According to Hayes, psychological flexibility allows you to navigate life's ups and downs and remain grounded in your values and long-term perspective on life.

That relational space we share with others reminds us that love and meaning can exist in connection and don't have to be sourced individually or through financial and professional success. In other words, connection can be deeply satisfying as it relates to our purpose in life. As we deepen our relationships, our world can take on new meaning—one that revolves more around the love we share with others. While many aspects of our lives may fluctuate, creating enduring love with others offers long-term fulfillment and feeds that relational sense of purpose.

One of the biggest complaints people have in relationships is that their partner is not present—not engaged or emotionally attuned, often distracted, and doesn't spend enough time with them. It's understandable: near-constant distractions fill our modern world, like TV, the internet, our phones, work, parenting, exercise, friends, hobbies, and responsibilities such as cleaning, cooking, fixing things, grocery shopping, appointments, caring for pets, and more. But the real problem is not that we don't have the time or are powerless against modern distractions—it's more often that we're uncomfortable being fully present in the moment.

Connection asks us to be present and attuned *together*. Being present *at the same time* means that you recognize the opportunity to slow down, drop what you're doing, make eye contact, and give the relationship a chance to share love in an obvious way. A real moment of connection can last all day. When you bond like that, you're not just giving lip service to love; you're showing up with your mind and body ready to offer and receive it.

Most relationships are able to experience and share more love, support, and empathy than it may seem. We can most easily access this by opening to receive what's available in the moment and slowing down, looking at each other, and opening our hearts. Intimacy asks that we be available for real emotional contact, in touch with our feelings, grounded in our bodies, and connected to the truth of what we want. We need to be aware of when we are talking about the past or the future and have the courage to be in the now with each other, ready to co-create a depth of love.

Being present reminds us why we're together—not just to manage life, parent, make money, and do chores, but to revel in the awesome opportunity we have to share and experience life on the planet together. When I feel buried by life's chores, I sometimes imagine myself in a void of total darkness, prior to being born. I try to imagine that if I knew, in that state, that I had a chance to come to this planet, be alive, and share love with others, how excited would I feel? And what would I do once I got here? Would I focus on paying taxes, handling bills, and managing logistics, or would I take time to look into people's eyes, open my heart, and make use of this awesome journey we're on to seek out and celebrate the love and connection available between us and others?

What Is the Present?

We all have fleeting moments of presence in our lives, moments when we land in real time without distractions, our hearts and minds open, and we can share love deeply with others or just feel it in ourselves. Every now and then, the whole universe seems to rush into the moment and we realize the amazing beauty of life. We may be watching our kids play from a distance, tenderly caring for an older family member, or experiencing something special in nature. That sense of connection, vibrancy, and excitement can last longer than the moment. But rather than wait for these times to land in our laps, we can create them through the practice of being more present. The energy of our connection can help pull us out of our limited perspectives and inspire us with love and good feeling.

While Western culture offers many technological advances and opportunities to feel content through material comforts and things, there is no substitute for the feeling of deep connection and a sense of harmony within yourself and with others. I saw this in the years I spent traveling and learning from indigenous cultures, which showed me that happiness can come from more than material things. My work with wealthy and A-list celebrity clients has further reinforced that understanding. Regardless of our income, status, power, or influence, what we seek most is love, peace, connection, fulfillment, and a sense of home and meaning.

Many Native peoples I have spent time with seem able to find contentment in the moment as a state of mind and in their relationships. Being fully present with other people is a source of comfort and support to all of our spirits and bodies. Some poor families I lived with exhibited an uncommon happiness that clearly came from their hearts and how they are with others. I would notice them being fully present in their interactions, showing much love to one another, expressing and sharing emotion, and possessing a generous quality of mind. While we will always lack some material comforts compared to others, we all have the opportunity to find richness and fulfillment in our closest relationships. In fact, people at the end of life often say that what mattered most to them was the love and closeness they were able to develop with others.[3] We need to be wary to not be so busy that we lose the opportunity to connect deeply and form quality relationships.

The observation that people can be happier when they focus on their close relationships rather than on increasing material success is not new.[4] We need certain things to be comfortable and to meet our survival needs, but beyond that, what really matters—and drives happiness—is the quality of our connections with others.[5,6] In order to derive meaning and joy from close relationships, we need to be emotionally present and in the moment to share love with people.

In Senegalese culture, for example, it is unusual, and considered impolite, not to stop and chat with someone you come across throughout your day. You might even spontaneously decide to go grab a soda and let your conversation go longer. In that culture and in others around the world, people are more willing to stop what they're doing to connect because relationships are a top priority above chores and productivity. In the modern Western world, prioritizing being present and connecting is less common, so we have to be intentional about making it a focus.

Connection as Part of Evolution

Evolution has honed the nervous system over hundreds of thousands of years to measure safety and security, using primitive cues to know who to get closer to and who not to. These evolutionary mechanisms often run in the background, calculating information about health, genetics, fertility, interest, and emotional states out of conscious awareness.[7] For example, the brain can detect subtle chemical signatures that provide information about stress levels and nervous system activity.[8] Connecting via technology can be helpful in many ways but may not use the same evolutionary channels to establish connection as touch, close eye contact, and physical closeness. Evolution happens slowly over many, many years, and our nervous systems have not yet adapted to these new digital ways of mediating our connection.

In addition to chemical and visual signals that measure emotional states and fitness, our evolutionary wiring also wants to know that the people in our lives are paying attention and available to collaborate with us as needs and threats arise. When your partner feels distant or distracted, it can affect your existential sense of well-being, consciously or unconsciously. Your nervous system starts to feel alone and untethered. In the absence of connection, we often develop adaptations to help our nervous systems maintain a sense of security, organization, and confidence, yet those work-arounds can lead to overly independent strategies.

For example, someone who was emotionally neglected in childhood may develop a superiority complex to help them feel important, or a tendency to keep emotions in and not seek support due to not trusting others' care. Someone who had an argumentative parent may develop a loud, aggressive tone of voice so they feel capable of standing up for themselves. When home life is not emotionally connected or attuned, we develop adaptations to our environment to feel secure, and while they play a valuable role when we need them in childhood, they can interfere with forming relationships in adulthood.

We can become aware of these adaptations and improve them. Sometimes they live outside our conscious awareness and we're confused as to why our relationship life may not be working well. Because feeling secure is so critical to the brain and nervous system, we often maintain these tendencies even when we know they cause problems. It takes courage, much exploration, the feedback of others, curiosity, humility, and sometimes therapy to understand and unlock defenses that may be interfering with our relationships.

Relationship is a litmus test for these adaptations, because our loved ones will give us feedback on what's working and what isn't in our lives together. If you're willing to examine your defenses, you can use others' feedback to assess your behavior and connect the dots to experiences in your past. This kind of awareness can point to how you can relate more effectively by undoing defenses you built in childhood and create deeper, trustworthy bonds.

Connecting Is Not a Function of Time

Sometimes people attribute their lack of connection to not having enough time to tend to the relationship. If both partners are working and parenting, it can be hard to find downtime when they're not exhausted. While it is true that in some cases people start to feel disconnected because they don't have enough time together, most of the time the real issue is what people do with the time they have. Connection can be created in just a few minutes but can last throughout the day.

Some couples I see worry that tending to their relationship will take too much time out of their busy lives. They don't want to sacrifice important things they're working on, or hobbies, and don't want to foster co-dependent tendencies. These individuals may believe that each partner should handle their own emotional needs and show up in a pleasant mood when they do have time together. The problem with this approach is that partners may be living parallel lives too much to receive the benefits of the relationship and so may not feel emotionally supported. Connection does not require much time, but it does require a mind-set that values bonding and being present in each other's emotional experience so that partners feel seen, known, and cared for.

Our brains and nervous systems don't need a lot of time to connect, but they do need some—enough to feel and receive another person. Texting and email don't quite cut it, and neither do quick pat hugs or just saying, "Hi!" And while having extended time together is not the primary determinant of connection, it can help to not feel rushed in your time together. Sometimes people worry that if they slow down, stop what they're doing, and sink into the moment they won't be able to get things done and the day will be wasted. But connection can happen in a few minutes and can actually clear space in your day by putting your mind at ease, avoiding time-consuming disagreements, and giving you the good feeling that you're prioritizing deepening love. If you allow yourself to be in the present moment with your significant others, openhearted and available for connection, you can connect quickly and deeply in shorter windows of time. You can sink into the moment and not feel rushed, confident that there's enough time for connecting and the chores of life.

Learning to connect quickly and efficiently is important to the security of your relationship. The window for bonding is narrow sometimes: you may only have an hour between all your obligations, such as work, kids, chores, and extended family. The dishes have to be washed, the toilets cleaned, friends are calling, and a stack of overdue mail and bills needs your attention. *Is now a good time to connect?* What I tell my clients is that if you have time to brush your teeth, you have time to connect. All it takes is a few minutes of deep, focused presence with each other, undistracted, face-to-face, showing interest, care, and friendliness, to remind you what the relationship is all about.

You can relate in small windows of time throughout the day. Sometimes partners make the mistake of waiting until right before bed to try to connect, but that's a long time for the nervous system to wait and puts the emphasis of your relationship life on engaging in logistical chores. Consider the balance of your time and focus that goes to transactional activities versus connecting moments and try to increase the ratio toward connection. You can look for brief moments in between activities to show love and care, offer a hug, hold each other, or say something sweet. Think of our need for connection like our need for food. Our nervous systems appreciate several "meals" a day to feel bonded.

In the modern world, many people work a lot of the time and are never "off." They take phone calls at night and check emails first thing in the morning. It's important to have clear and effective boundaries on work activities so that your time, body, and mind can shift to a connecting mood and space where there is opportunity to experience deeper bonds with the people around you. It helps to "close the shop" at regular times to prioritize family and relationship time; not just to create time for connection, but to free up your mind so you're mentally and emotionally available to connect. Don't just schedule dates—it's equally important to decompress from work so that you are more available to the people around you in your presence.

Connection tends to stay more stable when maintained regularly, rather than when long stretches of busyness go by and then you have to "reconnect." If you're around each other, a hug can suffice, or a check-in with eye contact: "How are you?" If you're in separate locations, a cute text or a loving message helps to maintain a connected feeling until you can be together. If you travel or are out at work all day, bringing your partner into your daily life and trying to keep them in the loop can help maintain connection. For example, you might text them a photo of the hotel you're staying at: "Look where I'm staying!" Or what you ordered for lunch: "I thought this would be yummy—I haven't tried it before!" In that way, you feel more present in each other's lives when there are long stretches of time apart. Notice the times of day that you and your loved ones tend to be tired, and try not to have those be the only times set aside for connection.

Being present does not mean that you have to connect all the time. Introverts and independent people, especially, need time to themselves or to do their own thing. The key is to create enough connection that you can have independent activities without either partner feeling neglected. Often, being present and connecting for a few minutes followed by, "Would you mind if I took some time to myself to do [x, y, or z]? I think it would help me relax and I have so much fun doing it," is enough to set up separate activities while still tending to the connecting needs of a relationship. I'm not suggesting you sit around for hours every day staring into each other's eyes talking about feelings. There's a natural ebb and flow to each day where you can focus on work, chores, relationship, alone time, relaxation, and more. The problem is when partners engage in more independent activities without giving their emotional connection its due. So even in busy life, with many things to get done, it's helpful to be present enough to connect emotionally so that our relationships feel vibrant enough to impart that acknowledgment and inspiration. Remember, connection is more a function of your mental, physical, and emotional presence than your time, so don't just shift your schedule to make more time if you need more connection; you also need to shift your mental and emotional state to open up and share more intimately.

Landing on the Same Little Patch of Grass

This is a metaphor I use to help people practice landing in real time with each other. It came from noticing that with many of the couples I work with, when one partner was ready and available for connection the other would not be, would get distracted, or would otherwise take away from the opportunity to connect in that moment. Then the partners would trade, and when the other seemed ready to connect, the first would get distracted or think of a problem. It seemed that being available to connect at the same time created an uncomfortable possibility of connection in the moment that was unfamiliar, so they would avoid that anxiety by trading readiness. The trading was just enough to claim they wanted more, and to show a reaching out for it, but not consistent or coordinated enough between them to actually feel it.

Landing on the Same Little Patch of Grass is being fully present in the moment and ready to connect *at the same time*. The idea is: If you just had a little patch of grass between you to stand on, could you meet each other there, fully present in mind and body? This is easier said than done, because landing there together creates an intimacy that can be awkward. If one of you is ready to connect and the other is thinking about the stock market or the laundry, it's hard to land on that little patch of grass together, but if you're willing to practice being in the same moment with each other and work through the anxiety and unfamiliarity, you give the relationship a chance to show its magic.

Four important elements of being fully present are:
1. Being Physically Present
2. Being Mentally Present
3. Being Emotionally Present
4. Being Present in Time

1. Being Physically Present

Being physically present begins with being grounded in your body when you're with others and aware of your body language. If you don't feel relaxed, that's an important diagnostic point to explore. For example, you might be curious about why you feel tense with someone and what force in your life or in the relationship may be causing the stress, then develop a plan to address it. When you're together, being physically present means turning your body to face your partner. Try to release distractions and give your partner your full physical attention instead of multitasking. Try to settle into the moment. Sometimes I tell partners to imagine they're in a warm, relaxing hot tub with each other so that they relax into the moment. That level of calm gives your bodies a chance to slow down together without feeling rushed or like the moment is simply a quick step on the way to the next activity.

Being physically present also includes taking care of your body and having healthy habits that support your mood, energy, and relationship life. It includes resolving any sleep issues, as those wreak havoc on your ability to regulate mood, emotions, and interactions with others. Engaging in regular exercise, eating well, and abstaining from overuse of drugs or alcohol are also ways to be more physically prepared for connection. And managing any physical or health problems as best you can is part of the responsibility of joint life. Mind and body are so intertwined the results are likely to show up in your interactions with others.

2. Being Mentally Present

Once your body is available for connection, how about your mind? Is your mind distracted, or focused on your partner? Are you thinking of a hundred things you need to do, or can you develop a singular point of attention on someone else in the moment? Our minds naturally think of many things at once and draw us in different directions. But that tendency of the mind often causes our loved ones to feel they are not a priority. Learning to focus our mind when interacting allows us to be present enough to notice our feelings and those of others, and details like facial expressions and emotions, so that we can interact in an attuned way. It allows us to drown out the background noise of our daily lives and make our loved ones feel special.

This focus is similar to meditation but with the presence of another person. The quality of mind one develops in meditation is the same one you're looking to bring to your relational interactions—calm, focused, and with your full attention in the present moment. Of course, time with our loved ones asks for more than just focus—we also seek play, emotional openness, and connection, for example—but being able to bring your mind fully into the moment with your partner sets the foundation for those dimensions as well.[9]

When interacting, try to bring your mind fully into the present, and resist the tendency to think too much about the past or future. Don't rattle off a list of things you need to accomplish together or just discuss logistics. Try to be less transactional and be more in touch with your feelings, ready to share love and emotional connection with each other. Receive each other's presence, which means noticing your partner, taking in their mood, emotions, and facial expressions. Notice and be interested in the details of their expression and what they say.

Connection happens *now*, not later. It's not worth waiting for that impossible moment when all your tasks are done, because too often the relationship waits too long to connect. Relationships deserve love and care as a priority above the tasks of the day, not as an afterthought when we're done handling our business.

The irony is that if you tend to your connection well, you are often freed up to focus on other things. The relationship can serve as a foundation for projects and meaningful endeavors in other spaces. But when you don't feel connected, that sense of isolation consumes mental space, generates emotional stress, and makes it harder to enjoyably focus on other things in life.

Relationships often have more juice than we give them credit for, because we may limit the love in our relationships through our own habits and behaviors. Think of how when you squeeze a lemon or an orange, if you just squeeze it halfway there's still a lot of juice left in it. If you trust there's more there, you'll squeeze it more, getting all the good stuff you can out of it. Deepening connection is like getting everything out of the orange. You trust the relationship to offer more and deepen in its love by creating opportunities to get more juice out of it. Sometimes, when we're willing to be present, we notice that more love was there, waiting for us to be ready to grasp it. We only thought it was missing because we weren't in the moment to receive it.

3. Being Emotionally Present

Emotional presence is where relationships and bonding can really take off. We can be present in our bodies with people and focused in our minds, but it is not until we open up emotionally that our connections become powerful and strong. Emotional bonds elicit love, care, and interest. Being present physically and mentally is the appetizer for the main course of emotional connection. Deep relationships typically occur through sharing meaningful experiences, relating around impactful moments, allowing ourselves to be seen and known for who we really are, and sharing how we feel with others in real time.

I realize how daunting this may seem to some. Emotional connection is where I have struggled the most in my relationships because it wasn't part of my family life, which was intellectual and formal. Emotions were not commonly discussed. Someone might ask you what score you got on a test, but not how you're feeling about life. I also lacked support to talk about the difficult things I experienced and therefore didn't develop a habit of trusting or opening up to others. I retreated internally and still struggle to share my feelings as much as I would like. What I've learned is that the more I challenge myself to speak about how I feel, listen to others, and validate my and others' emotional experience, the more fulfilling my relationships become. Opening up emotionally is still a work in progress for me and I need to continually challenge myself to be vulnerable, transparent, and open. But when I overcome my tendency to be inward, the results are well worth the effort.

Emotional connection keeps relationships new and exciting. Emotions are full of rich associations and variation and offer opportunities to explore experience beyond "I'm fine." Connecting around feelings is a way to keep your relationships fresh and meaningful because of the powerful way we experience feelings in our minds and bodies. Emotional connection helps us blaze new ground, get to know each other better, and keep the flame of our interest alive. If you don't really *know* each other at a deep level, it's hard to love each other in those secret and tender places that common small talk doesn't get to.

Of course, some people are more analytical in nature—their minds are strong in logical thought, and emotional connection can seem like a foreign, confusing space. If this describes you, I'd like to offer you a cheat sheet with a straightforward description of the behaviors you can practice that elicit emotional connection:

1. Listen for emotional key words in someone's speech, such as them saying they feel sad, happy, or frustrated.

2. Follow up on those emotions by asking directly about them. If it's a negative emotion, you might say, "I'm so sorry you feel that way. Tell me more about it." If it's a positive emotion, you might say, "Wow, that's so great! Tell me more about it!" Show you care and ask them to share more about that emotional experience with you.

3. Be willing to feel your own emotions too. If you have trouble identifying emotions, you can use an emotions chart[10] and pick the one you feel closest to.

4. When others are sharing feelings with you, try not to be intellectual or factual about the details, and don't solve their problem. Just listen, empathize by saying you care, show interest, and let others rely on you for comfort and as a trusted listener. When you provide this type of presence, you become valuable as a source of support. When you listen well and share your own emotions, allowing others to also care for you, an emotional bond is being established.

Being emotionally present is as much about sharing difficult emotions as it is about sharing positive ones. We all feel more stressed when sharing or hearing difficult material, but it is normal in relationships to have both positive and negative feelings, and our relationships can suffer when we hide the negative ones. If you can develop a safe emotional space with your loved ones, it makes sharing those tough, inconvenient emotions easier. And when you feel positive emotions, don't keep them to yourself; share them! Let people know how you feel about them, as these emotions can amplify the good feeling in relationships and can supercharge your bond.[11]

People want to be understood, and our perspectives, habits, and preferences can change as we age and learn. If you are partnered, you are probably not going to be the same people you first met as you move through life. To continue to get to know each other, it helps to openly share relevant feelings, positive and negative, and open your mind to new perspectives. Sometimes negative feelings point the way toward the valuable growth the relationship needs, and you can embrace that work by being curious together. Feelings help you adapt the relationship as needed in different phases of life.

Discomfort with Emotional Intimacy

Most of us did not grow up in families where people sat down with each other, faced each other, made eye contact, held hands, and talked about feelings. Unless you're an outlier who grew up in an emotionally intelligent household, people probably didn't ask you about yourself in a sincere way of really wanting to get to know you. You may not have felt safe to open up emotionally with those in your home, or it just wasn't the culture. Even when we know that connecting emotionally is helpful to bonding, we may not engage in it because it's not our habit.

Just like going to the gym, the exercises you need to do to make certain muscles stronger don't always feel natural or easy at first. But with practice and repetition, those muscles get stronger and the activity gets easier. The same principle is true in developing your emotional muscles. If you have some discomfort in emotional intimacy, I recommend you run through some of the techniques in this book even if they feel uncomfortable or awkward at first. As you challenge yourself to move toward your partner, remove distractions, be fully present, and open up to share and listen in the moment, it will become second nature—it just takes practice.

When I started trying out these skills, it felt really awkward at first. I just had very little experience with emotional intimacy. Luckily, I had a forgiving partner who was willing to be patient and work with me as we went. One thing that helped was making my growth project explicit: I made it a goal I could point to and talk about, so that when it did not go well I had some cover to say, "Whoops! I guess

I'm still working on that!" Instead of secretly trying to be better at connection, it helps if you and your partner can talk about the practice. In my case, I would share how I felt I was doing and the struggle I felt practicing new behaviors and the transparency would buy me some goodwill to keep fumbling through for a while. I've since come to think of this approach as a valuable loophole we can use while building the skill we need to actually connect emotionally. If we don't have those skills yet, we can at least open up about how it feels to be developing them, which is connecting in and of itself, and maybe our partner can relate to the effort.

The good news is that the body and mind learn fairly quickly through repetition. I needed to put myself in position to practice connecting behaviors—like opening up about feelings, showing interest, and validating others' experience—before they became more natural. Because connection feels good, these behaviors are self-reinforcing: As they deepen your skill at relating, you want to use them more and develop a taste for loving, supportive interactions. The more you practice, the more confident you are likely to feel about your ability to create strong, supportive connections with others, giving you the power to shape your relationships and have healthy interactions.

Developing the ability to be emotionally present with our partners is a key to closeness. If your family was like mine growing up, the training ground for those skills was nonexistent. But we know when we are being challenged to develop that skill because our partners or friends ask for more closeness from us. You may want more of that from your partner. When you first begin practicing being fully present, mentally, physically, and emotionally, you may experience some anxiety, pressure, or discomfort. Your nervous system may not be accustomed to being in such a direct, intimate space. That's okay. Rather than relieving your anxiety or awkwardness by distracting from that intimate presence, sink into the moment, breathe, and work those emotional muscles. Your partner will notice the effort, and it will get easier with time to be fully present, listen, and engage directly with emotions.

4. Being Present in Time

Love Is Now.

Relationship is always in the now. To be there, we have to be willing to open up to what the moment is offering. Maybe we were pissed at our partner yesterday, but maybe today, if we're paying attention and open to it, our anger may soften when we see that they're looking at us with loving eyes. Maybe when we were in our own thoughts this morning getting ready for work, the relationship did not feel very satisfying, but now, in the present moment, if our partner takes our hands, looks at us, and shares how much we mean to them, it feels different.

Connection in the now takes us out of our random thoughts and into a relational space where love can be co-created in the moment. Maybe you've heard of how love writer Mandy Len Catron reenacted an older research study designed to make people feel closer and she and her partner in the reenactment actually fell in love.[12] Love is seen as a mysterious feeling, but it can be created with interest and care. Catron later published more of her experiences in her memoir, *How to Fall in Love with Anyone*, emphasizing how love is an action and how we can all be more intentional about developing it with others.[13] Catron's reenactment was based on the work of psychologist Arthur Aron, a well-known relationship expert who has studied intimacy for decades. His original study suggested that greater closeness could be generated by asking thirty-six questions that show emotional interest and then looking deeply into each other's eyes for four minutes.[14] The relational space has its own power beyond our own thoughts as individuals, and when we plug into it love can happen in ways we may not have imagined.

Being in the present is also about accepting the reality of the moment rather than wishing it was different. The moment may not be what we thought it would be or what we want it to be, but it is exactly the test of intimacy that moment has created. Sometimes we get disappointed that moments don't fit our expectations. We get frustrated that our partner is in a certain mood, or on a different page. Connection offers a way to accept and embrace the moment, yet also shape it by moving in tandem with someone else to create what we want. If we're passive, we're often left with just complaining. We can be active and use connection with others to create the relationships we want. Rather than resist the realities of each moment, we recognize that if we can connect well, we can co-create a different experience together. If we resist the reality of the moment and deflect, reject, ignore, or withdraw, we miss a chance to be present with the fullness of life, the whole nature of our partner, and to move our relationships toward what we need.

When you get disappointed in interactions because they're not going the way you want, try to use your connection to bend them toward something mutually fulfilling instead of allowing disconnection, passive-aggressive behaviors, or criticism to take over. If you trust in your connection, you can recruit your partner in a sweet way to something that would feel better. For example, you might say, "I'm starting to get a little frustrated in this conversation, but I really care about what you're saying. Can we try to talk in a way that helps me relax and enjoy it more?" Trust that your partner also wants an interaction that feels good and in which both people are heard and feel cared for. You need to remain present enough in the moment with others to coordinate that shift, because if you disconnect out of the relational space you lose a lot of important levers to shift the moment toward what you need. When negative habits take over, the relationship misses a chance to prove it can handle any moment with resilience, love, and trust, and to be connected enough to meet both people's needs. But by sharing what you need, how you feel, and asking sweetly for what would make you feel better, you can shift interactions in real time to the kind of connection you're seeking.

Being present with feelings in real time is especially important if you've gone through something difficult, dealt with a relationship trauma like an affair, or if one or both of you had past hurts. When relationships experience traumas like infidelity, abandonment, or loss, the emotional pain of those events can make it harder to be present with our partners in the moment, look them in the eye, and open our hearts. Vulnerability feels like it might just generate more pain, so we stay closed. It's tempting to be in the past, feeling the pain of what occurred but not present enough with others in the moment to repair what happened. Or we cut to the future: *I'm looking forward to getting past this phase so we can connect better.* But for healing to occur around painful events, you need to connect now more than ever, and that happens when you have the courage to be emotionally present with each other in the moment.

When people have had difficult childhoods and relational and attachment wounds, those traumas can create patterns that make real-time connection difficult, because the nervous system doesn't trust connection with others.[15] But connecting in the moment with others is exactly what the nervous system needs to heal. The eyes need to see and test the reliability of a connection over time to heal and trust others again. We need to feel someone else being completely present enough with us in a safe and reliable manner to get the message that we matter and can be cared for. Such care and repair can't be done with words alone—it is the caring presence of another that helps heal the nervous system. Trying to heal such traumas by ourselves is also inefficient—relational wounds often need a trusted bond to offer up a new experience and for a new, secure impression to stick.

Being in the present moment with others is a shared meditation that creates the opportunity for connection. With practice, your mind becomes more free of clutter when you're with others and more available in the moment for the richness of love that wants to unfold between you.

Stress and Anxiety in Relationship

Many people live with both stress and anxiety. Generally, stress is considered a normal response to change in one's environment. It is typically episodic and can be dealt with by adjusting to the new condition or dealing with the stressor. Stress also often decreases while sharing a supportive presence with others, which means that overall, healthy relationships can manage stress just fine, especially when you know how to help each other relax in a way that's bonding.

Chronic stress, however, can be a problem. Sometimes it results from an intense job, a difficult family situation, a physical health condition such as pain, or friction in the relationship itself. It is not only physically unhealthy, but it also makes it harder to connect. It's important to identify the stressor and take steps to reduce it, as well as to develop ways of de-stressing with others such as allowing others to comfort you or make you laugh, and by playing and having fun with friends, kids, and partners. Learn tools for individual stress management, such as meditation, exercise, a healthy diet, getting good sleep, supplements, and learning how to share and address feelings and emotions. Discuss the chronic stressor with others and explore ways of eliminating the source of it.

Anxiety, which is different from stress, can wreak havoc on relationships despite your best intentions. Anxiety is an unhealthy mental condition that often includes persistent nervous system activation and excessive worrying, even in the absence of specific stressors, and keeps one in a hyperactivated nervous system state where interactions with others may not bring it down. Further, it can cause your body or nervous system to be too tense or frenetic to share a warm, friendly, reliable connection and often causes individuals to act domineering as they attempt to relieve their anxiety by controlling others and their environment.

There are different types of anxiety and they can result for a variety of reasons, so if you notice anxiety in yourself or in your partner (or kids) it may be helpful to have professional support in understanding the type you have and to learn how best to reduce it. Treating anxiety doesn't necessarily mean taking medicine. It can sometimes be treated through counseling and lifestyle modifications alone, but a mental health professional can help you make that determination and sort through the options so that anxiety is not negatively impacting your ability to connect with others.

Some therapists say that managing anxiety is half the battle in relationships. Anxiety often moves us to control our environment to find relief but can leave those around us feeling belittled, bossed around, or condescended to. Anxiety can make us speak more harshly or be irritable, struggle to take in other perspectives, and also make it difficult to connect intimately and emotionally with others due to a lack of calm and the frenetic quality of mind it imparts. And anxiety makes it harder to downregulate our nervous system, handle emotions, and move through life in a relaxed manner. The negative impact of anxiety often outweighs the concerns our anxiety causes us to worry about.

The good news is that while anxiety is a common mental health issue, it can typically be resolved. It may take working with a professional who specializes in anxiety and coming up with a plan to address it, but in almost all cases there is a way to lower anxiety so it is not such a problem in your life and relationships.

Being Present in Busy Modern Life

There are endless activities in modern life that limit the amount of time and mental space we have to connect with our partner or others. Luckily, there are key connecting moments throughout the day that offer opportunities to be present in meaningful ways if we take advantage of them. Let's explore ways to be more present and connect more with others even in the midst of a busy schedule.

1. **Transitions.** There are times throughout the day when the nervous system engages in extra measuring of connecting cues. These include times when you are about to be away from each other, coming back together after being away, when you switch activities, and the times around sleep. If you manage these transitions well, you get extra points for the connecting value of those moments. Dr. Stan Tatkin has written extensively on the value of connecting more during transitions.[16] He recommends partners be fully present in saying good morning and good night, and connect during transitions such as before and after work to settle the nervous system.

   Transitions are key moments when the nervous system reevaluates connection and seeks to answer security questions. Because the brain runs so much off memory, it seeks to confirm that its perception of our partner is still accurate. It seeks to measure mood and state because those may affect the security of being together or away. And since sleep is a transition into and out of consciousness, it's a vulnerable time when the brain seeks security both before and after. A simple hug, meaningful eye contact, or some sweet words can be enough to connect in a transition.

2. **Coming home.** Dr. Tatkin designed a powerful exercise called The Welcome Home for partners to use when they reunite at the end of the workday.[17] When you come home at the end of the day, you hug first instead of talking, and hold the hug until both partners' bodies relax. This physical touch, and especially belly-to-belly contact, gives your nervous systems a chance to relax into each other and sync up, so that you're physiologically more connected. After the extended hug, you can then engage with words. The Welcome Home creates a nonverbal connecting ritual to a major transition in your day, and is effective at supporting your sense of security with each other. This works for romantic partners as well as with children and other loved ones.

3. **The two-minute connect.** If you have time to brush your teeth, you have time to connect at least once a day. I recommend setting aside a couple minutes and being intentional about focusing that time on connection. You might sit down with your partner or loved one face-to-face, make eye contact, and ask them about their day or share how you've been feeling. You can do this any time of the day—it doesn't need to be in the morning or evening. Connection requires attuned presence but doesn't need to take a long time. Even just a couple minutes of connecting like that can make a big difference. Start practicing today and see how it feels!

4. **Opportunities for touch.** If you're making food, doing chores, or helping the kids with homework, look for little opportunities to sit close and engage in some touch. Even thirty seconds of holding hands at dinner reassures the nervous system that you're connected. You can sit in each other's laps to take phone

calls, cuddle on the couch while watching TV, and give each other hugs when you move from room to room. Touch is an easy, nonverbal way to connect, even in the midst of a busy day.

5. **Brief, meaningful words.** Use the time you have together wisely in the service of connection. If you only have twenty seconds, take a moment to feel what your partner means to you, and express something sweet about how much you appreciate them. How would it feel if they were suddenly gone from your life? Sometimes imagining their absence puts you in touch with the value of their presence. Speak what's in your heart—don't worry about being cheesy. You might say, "I really appreciate having you in my life," or, "I love you; you mean so much to me." By expressing your appreciation directly, you're boosting your connection, and others don't have to guess as to how you feel about them.

6. **Relaxing together.** Independent relaxation is important, but look for ways to relax together, because when you do the brain is able to connect your relaxed state with being together, which establishes a sense of security in your neural circuitry and supports your bond. Some ways to relax together include joint meditation, sitting outside looking at nature, or drawing a bath for your partner and reading to them. You can make yourselves some tea and sit down to enjoy it, or give each other a shoulder rub. Most of us need calming activities together to balance out how active we are throughout the day. Engaging in calming activities as a couple reinforces your ability to be in a calm state with each other. For something a little more lighthearted, you might pick a funny book and lie in bed reading it to each other. Since relaxing is time well spent, doing it together gives you a way to improve self-care and feed your relationship at the same time.

Quiet Love

Couples who stay together long-term have often learned to use real and deep connection to create excitement, not just relying on the novelty of a new relationship.[18] Essentially, depth of connection takes over from the stimulating feelings that are prevalent at the outset of a relationship. Getting to know each other better, especially in your deep thoughts and feelings, lights up the brain and stimulates bonding and closeness, which results in positive chemical releases similar to the physiology of new relationships. *Quiet love* encompasses the ability to connect in calm, emotionally intimate moments, as well as to engage in side-by-side activities sometimes known as *parallel play*.

These moments of quiet love are distinguished from the thrill that a new relationship may begin with.[19] This type of love refers to those slow, calm moments of emotional intimacy, where you can sink into the moment, really get to know each other, show care, and bond. Such moments prove that you can be fully present with each other, and allow love and tenderness to be felt and to grow. Quiet love also includes parallel play, such as relaxing in the same room with each other, engaged in separate activities.[20] While together, you may not necessarily be interacting. Relaxing in parallel with each other is a sign you have a trusted connection and don't always need to stimulate it. When you trust your bond, parallel play exhibits one of the key goals of a mature relationship: achieving a balance between being independent people, yet connected and together.

Being present enough to connect is vital to facilitating real and meaningful connection in relationship. Interacting face-to-face, eye-to-eye, with touch and proximity, and offering your full, engaged, undistracted presence is an effective way to deepen connection. Relationship is always now, not later, and your physical, mental, and emotional presence allows you to show up together in the moment, ready for connection. When you can meet in that intimate space with others at the same time, sparks can fly. Are you ready for love and connection? It's ready for you.

Notes

1. Brent J. Atkinson, "Mindfulness Training and the Cultivation of Secure, Satisfying Couple Relationships," *Couple and Family Psychology: Research and Practice* 2, no. 2 (2013): 73.

2. Frank W. Bond, Steven C. Hayes, and Dermot Barnes-Holmes, "Psychological Flexibility, ACT, and Organizational Behavior," *Journal of Organizational Behavior Management* 26, no. 1–2 (2006): 25–54, https://doi.org/10.1300/J075v26n01_02.

3. I. Byock, *The Four Things That Matter Most: A Book about Living*, 2nd ed. (New York: Atria Books, 2014).

4. Laura Camfield, Kaneta Choudhury, and Joe Devine, "Well-Being, Happiness and Why Relationships Matter: Evidence from Bangladesh," *Journal of Happiness Studies* 10, no. 1 (February 2009): 71–91.

5. George E. Vaillant, Charles C. McArthur, and Arlie Bock, "Grant Study of Adult Development, 1938–2000," Harvard Dataverse V4 (2010), https://hdl.handle.net/1902.1/00290.

6. Mark Anielski, *The Economics of Happiness: Building Genuine Wealth* (Gabriola, BC: New Society, 2007).

7. James V. Kohl, Michaela Atzmueller, Bernhard Fink, and Karl Grammer, "Human Pheromones: Integrating Neuroendocrinology and Ethology," *Neuroendocrinology Letters* 22, no. 5 (2001): 309–321.

8. Lilianne R. Mujica-Parodi, Helmut H. Strey, Blaise Frederick, Robert Savoy, David Cox, Yevgeny Botanov, Denis Tolkunov, Denis Rubin, and Jochen Weber, "Chemosensory Cues to Conspecific Emotional Stress Activate Amygdala in Humans," *PloS ONE* 4, no. 7 (July 2009): e6415.

9. Daniel J. Siegel, "Mindful Awareness, Mindsight, and Neural Integration," *The Humanistic Psychologist* 37, no. 2 (2009): 137.

10. You're welcome to use the emotions chart on the PRESENCE wellness center website at presencewellness.co/emotions-chart.

11. Bethany E. Kok, Kimberly A. Coffey, Michael A. Cohn, Lahnna I. Catalino, Tanya Vacharkulksemsuk, Sara B. Algoe, Mary Brantley, and Barbara L. Fredrickson, "How Positive Emotions Build Physical Health: Perceived Positive Social Connections Account for the Upward Spiral between Positive Emotions and Vagal Tone," *Psychological Science* 24, no. 7 (July 2013): 1123–1132.

12. Mandy Len Catron, "To Fall in Love with Anyone, Do This," *New York Times*, January 9, 2015, https://www.nytimes.com/2015/01/11/style/modern-love-to-fall-in-love-with-anyone-do-this.html.

13. Mandy Len Catron, *How to Fall in Love with Anyone: A Memoir in Essays* (New York: Simon & Schuster, 2017).

14. Arthur Aron, Edward Melinat, Elaine N. Aron, Robert Darrin Vallone, and Renee J. Bator, "The Experimental Generation of Interpersonal Closeness: A Procedure and Some Preliminary Findings," *Personality and Social Psychology Bulletin* 23, no. 4 (April 1997): 363–377.

15. Mary D. Salter Ainsworth, Mary C. Blehar, Everett Waters, and Sally N. Wall, *Patterns of Attachment: A Psychological Study of the Strange Situation* (London: Psychology Press, 2015).

16. Stan Tatkin, *Wired for Love: How Understanding Your Partner's Brain and Attachment Style Can Help You Defuse Conflict and Build a Secure Relationship* (Oakland: New Harbinger, 2012).

17. Ibid.

18. Bianca P. Acevedo, Arthur Aron, Helen E. Fisher, and Lucy L. Brown, "Neural Correlates of Long-Term Intense Romantic Love," *Social Cognitive and Affective Neuroscience* 7, no. 2 (February 2012): 145–159.

19. Sue Johnson, *Love Sense: The Revolutionary New Science of Romantic Relationships* (New York: Little, Brown Spark, 2013).

20. Mario Mikulincer, "Attachment, Caregiving, and Sex within Romantic Relationships," in *Dynamics of Romantic Love: Attachment, Caregiving, and Sex*, ed. Mario Mikulincer and Gail S. Goodman (New York: Guilford, 2006), 23–44.

4.

Working Together as a Team

Talent wins games, but teamwork and intelligence win championships.

—Michael Jordan

Couples can learn a lot from teams that have to operate under stress in a coordinated manner to accomplish difficult missions.[1] A couple is essentially on a challenging mission: to stay connected, while managing differences, often under stress, and learning how to move as one to accomplish a common goal of achieving an enduring and durable love and support for each other and those around them.

Some of the training used by professional sports teams and elite military units offers lessons that primary partners can use to better navigate life together. Special forces soldiers, for example, are taught to stay connected under stress, to have one another's backs, and to place the team objective above their own personal preferences. Sports teams practice moving in a coordinated manner, utilizing the synergy effect to amplify individual talents, and focusing their minds on that coordination even when they're tired.

Such team principles work to help humans maintain connection and a joint focus on mission in challenging circumstances.[2] One of my dreams is to build physical obstacle courses for couples that help partners practice connecting in tough situations, helping each other when tired, and strengthening their focus of mind on a common goal. Such obstacle courses would be fun and help train partners' procedural habits to move together in a more coordinated manner. Soldiers and athletes engage in much training in order to be able to execute on team principles when tired and under stress. They practice to not get split off from one another, go after one another, or lose focus on the greater objective due to a set-back. If you're in a primary relationship, you might imagine that you're engaged in training to be a stronger team as you read this book, with the goal of learning how to move together, use your individual talents in a coordinated manner, and have each other's back at all times.

Important components of functioning as a team in relationship are as follows:

- You set an intention to move through life together as a unit, rather than living parallel lives as individuals.
- You set the team's mission and purpose—what success will look like.
- You take joint responsibility for issues.
- You coordinate well—life tasks, responsibilities, et cetera.
- Instead of blaming each other and pointing the finger in failure, you work together to improve.
- You track and prioritize what's good for the team, not just for each individual.
- You turn differences into assets rather than dividing forces.
- You offer each other positive encouragement and support in personal growth while defining goals for improvement.
- You have each other's back, protect and defend each other.
- You turn toward each other for support during stress, not away from each other or attacking each other.

By reflecting on these principles and how they show up in your relationship, you can strengthen your teamwork enough that few life stressors can knock you off-balance.

Collective Life

The concept of moving through life as a team runs counter to many Western ideas about independence, individualism, and relationships. Some cultures around the world are more collective and seem to better understand that the success of each of us is tied to that of others. The team concept also runs counter to some new age ideas about relationships, such as the idea that you are responsible for your own feelings and no one can make you feel a certain way. That notion is not based in science and promotes an individualistic approach to relationship that undermines the collective reality of sharing life together. Healthy people are impacted by others and react accordingly if treated well or poorly. Being in touch with one's feelings is a good thing and part of why having healthy relationships matters. People who don't feel emotions in response to others' behaviors often have emotional blocks that can negatively impact connection. The team concept in relationships is that the actions of one affect the other and choices either makes can affect everyone on the team. That's the reality and why we need to learn to move together in a coordinated fashion to benefit the team and the individuals in it.

Healthy relationships exhibit what is known as *mutuality*, a key concept in relationship health that simply means making sure things feel good to you *and to others*. Some people defer too much to others, giving up what they need in the process. These people give themselves away in relationship, but it's not healthy and doesn't benefit the team as much as they may think. Others are more self-centered and tend to their own needs over those of others. Taking this too far, these individuals can act selfishly and too independently and don't care well for joint needs, which can cause those relationships to become distressed or fail. Collectivism helps you aim for that balanced middle, where you and your partner feel good in the relationship, where you take care of individual needs but not at the expense of the team. It also extends to family members, such as kids living in your home. Giving them a say, encouraging them to share how they feel, and having family meetings to establish what everyone needs are great ways to function collectively.

Pulling other people in to help you when you're having trouble as a couple or family unit can be a good idea. Partnerships live within a structure of community, friends, and family, and most good teams have a coach. In fact, a common part of some wedding ceremonies is asking those in attendance, "Who will help this couple when they need it?" When you're not able to come up with ways to manage differences on your own or you find yourselves arguing a lot, you might reach out to trusted friends, family, or a therapist and enlist their support to develop better skills. High-level sports and military teams don't succeed by accident—their teamwork is the result of countless days spent in practice, often working with a mentor who stimulates their growth. By engaging in drills, taking situations they don't do well and working them together to improve, and often with quality instruction, such teams learn to function at an elite level. Our partnerships can benefit from the same principle: sometimes we need support or a good coach to help us take the next steps.

A "We" versus "I" Mind-set

We are often taught to share our feelings in "I" form, such as phrasing our emotions in the form of "I feel [x]" rather than "You make me feel [x]." "I feel" statements allow us to share our feelings in a way that is less accusatory and tend to elicit less defensiveness in others. But too many "I feel" statements can also create polarization in relationships and reinforce separate camps, especially when it is difficult to empathize with others' feelings or challenging to find a common perspective.

While being heard in our individual truth can be fulfilling—especially if our partner is empathic—there is a powerful, relational mind-set shift when we take joint responsibility for issues and address them as a team. Greater relief can come when the relationship gathers its collective energy to take responsibility for issues as a unit. For example, rather than trading "I feel" statements, which may not line up, it can be nice for the relationship as a team to say, "We have an issue here. How can we get better at this? How can we work together and support each other to improve?" That collective mind-set takes the burden off each individual, minimizes blame in both directions, and shares resources to address problems. The "we" mind-set is especially helpful when it comes to practice: once you agree on how the relationship needs to improve to handle an issue or situation, it becomes easier to identify how to train together to arrive at the needed skill.

Taking Joint Responsibility

Taking joint responsibility for issues in relationship is a sign of maturity and is more effective than assigning responsibility to one person. As mentioned, relationship is a team sport and taking joint responsibility for your strengths and weaknesses exemplifies good teamwork. Instead of being critical of each other on an issue, you might recognize that most relationship dynamics are created and maintained by both partners, so you might as well work together. Relationship patterns are very circular—one's behavior affects the other, which affects the partner again. It's very hard to parse out where dynamics begin and end, especially after years of being together. Working together as a team allows you to avoid impossible analyses of who is responsible for an issue and simply collaborate to improve your habits. Solving issues in this manner also creates skill that is mutually reinforcing, meaning that when one of you has a bad day the other still knows how to carry the team skill or objective.

An important caveat: shared responsibility is not a replacement for individual responsibility; it's an add-on. Each person in relationship still needs to be humble and willing to own their part in order for growth to occur. There are also exceptions where joint responsibility is not a positive force in relationship: issues of alcohol/drug abuse, anger problems, emotional manipulation, or physical abuse all require individual responsibility and commitment to change to clean up before a partner should take responsibility with the individual displaying such behaviors. Chronic issues of deception—including affairs, lying, and hiding things—also may fall into the realm of individual responsibility and may require professional support to navigate successfully as a team.

Even when one partner needs to take individual responsibility for an issue, they often deserve the support and encouragement of their partner in that effort. Individuals who are willing to offer their partner love, support, and encouragement in their personal healing process may find that support enables greater change and can help keep the relationship healthy in the process.

Relationship as a Path of Growth

This book presents a radical premise—that we become our best selves in close, connected relationships with others and that we discover our full selves in a relational context. It's not just that we want healthy, fulfilling relationships; it's also that we need such bonds to help us become the fullest expression of our selves.

Neuroscience has shown that deepening your relationship is one of the most effective ways to engage in self-actualization: personal growth that matures us as individuals.[3] The human brain learns most efficiently in a relational context, beginning at birth and all the way through the life-span.[4] Relationships challenge us, stretch our perspective, expose our blind spots, and invite us to become more whole versions of ourselves. Relationships continually ask for new and different behaviors, habits, and improvements. The complexity keeps the brain stimulated and seeking growth, and the nonverbal and verbal feedback of others acts as a thermometer that measures if we're on the right track.

While some independent activities can be helpful to personal growth, few match the challenge and complexity of relationships to expose our weak areas and broaden our minds. We all get frustrated in relationships, but much of that is the friction needed to help us grow. If we can embrace the challenge and face it together with the support of others, all of life becomes a journey to know ourselves better and break through limitations as we mature as individuals and build a more comprehensive mind-set for life.[5]

One of the key skills of emotional resilience is the ability to lean on others in long-term, committed relationships. Emotional resilience encompasses our ability to withstand, navigate, and recover from emotional events but also our ability to see positive meaning in emotional challenges. If we can see the growth available for us in stressful events, that aspiration forms part of our resilience. Emotional resilience is enhanced by acknowledging stress and developing empathy and self-compassion.[6] And by remaining present and embodied in emotional experience, and then sharing our experience with others, we make use of the brain and body's natural abilities to be resilient under stress.[7] As relationships deepen their own resilience, they can impart it to the individuals in the relationships, helping protect from destabilization in emotional events.

Some researchers have pointed out that emotional resilience is not only a desirable individual trait that can be developed through practice but also a social goal that places responsibility on relationships, systems, and organizations to support individuals emotionally.[8] Individuals can seek to develop their emotional resilience in order to better weather emotional events and support themselves and others, but systems also have a responsibility to offer support, which then becomes part of each individual's system for accessing resilience.

Through relationship life and good teamwork, you can become a more loving, patient, wise, open-minded person, and those traits and skills can then transfer to every area of your life: with your kids, at work, and with friends, and even with yourself. Because our sense of self and our self-esteem are derived in large part from an internalization of how others see us,[9] improving connection helps you develop greater confidence in yourself.

Thermometers

Rule of thumb—we often overrate ourselves and our relationship prowess. I came up with the concept of "thermometers" in my practice a few years back in order to help partners understand that it is not them but rather their partner who needs to sign off on satisfaction and improvement on key issues. I work with a lot of influential people, and they are sometimes accustomed to making determinations about issues and when things are good enough. But in relationship, assessing satisfaction and improvement is always a team project. We may not know how our partner experiences something unless we ask sincerely, and we often assign a rosier picture to our own behaviors than we really deserve.

Asking the right thermometer for their assessment of whether you're improving or not in key areas is a more accurate way to hold yourselves accountable as partners. You are the key thermometer on issues that bother you and your partner is the key thermometer on issues that bother them, but you get to weigh in on how any issue feels. It's good practice to check in with each other from time to time and see how you're doing in specific areas of improvement you're working on. Getting those cross-evaluations is critical to assessing your actual (rather than perceived) skill and places the evaluation where it belongs—with the partner it bothers and on how the improvement feels to the relationship, not just to an individual. Using the concept of thermometers also helps to fill in blind spots in our awareness as individuals, since we often can't see problem areas in the same way our partner might. And it keeps you working together to solve problems rather than isolating around individual perspectives.

Managing Differences

Managing differences well is one of the most difficult, yet rewarding, aspects of relationship life. After all, none of us partners with someone who is identical to us, and differences we have with the people we live with can create friction. Your differences are not going to go away, nor can you smooth them over by trying to get your partner to be more like you, although there is an averaging that tends to happen as partners remain together over many years. Transforming your differences into assets is part of the journey.

To manage your differences with others well, you first have to see differences you have with others as valuable. Rather than judge them, or blame them for friction and discomfort you feel, ask yourself how a difference may be useful as a counter-weight to your own tendencies. We often judge the qualities we have talent in, expecting others to measure up to our strengths, but people are distinct and have various aptitudes. Managing this involves showing respect to differences of person-ality, perspective, habit, culture, and talents and recognizing that different strengths and weaknesses can be complementary and advantageous in relationship.

For example, many of my high-performing clients judge their partners for not being as driven, detail oriented, and organized as they are. They say things like, "Why can't they get their act together and do [xyz]!" But sometimes their partner is more talented at relaxing, not piling on too many things to do, better at manag-ing stress (or not creating it in the first place), having fun, connecting emotionally, engaging in self-care, offering empathy, and many other important aspects of rela-tionship and family life. When we share life with others, different qualities can bal-ance our strengths and make our team more well rounded. When I point out to an individual that their partner's emotional intelligence and ability to have fun might help them lead a more balanced life, many people can recognize that may be true. Even though our default tendency may be to judge our partner's qualities that are different from our own, seeing their qualities in that positive, complementary light helps us be less judgmental and appreciate those differences.

I was at a conference a few years ago and a couple who had been married for decades came onto the stage. One of the partners said, "Our relationship is simple. She makes me responsible and I help her have fun." I could tell they had great maturity as a couple and one might imagine that their statement represented years of working to understand how to manage their different personalities. They were a good example of a pair who could have simply gotten frustrated by their differences but instead found a way to appreciate them as assets to the team.

Embracing Diversity

Relationship asks us to find unity in diversity: to have a sense of togetherness in a sea of different opinions, perspectives, habits, goals, and cultures. The concept of unity we are using is one that embraces diversity, complexity, multiplicity, dif-ferent approaches and mind-sets, and which experiences an integration of those as part of a whole.[10] This type of unity does not define oneness as similarity or cultural homogeneity but rather sees the diversity of life as an expression of that unity. This kind of unity is not exclusionary and does not seek agreement-by-similitude or single-mindedness; it represents the balance between secure attachment (a peaceful home base) and individual expression (support for individual qualities and freedom).

Resisting diversity and clinging to a rigid mind-set leads to arguments, disconnection, defensiveness, resentment, and sometimes the end of relationships. This type of friction can occur in any relationship, not just with primary partners, and occurs quite frequently with our children, who push us to embrace new points of view and habits reflective of a new generation. Much has been said about how embracing diversity can make us smarter—we're able to see the world from multiple perspectives, develop greater emotional intelligence, and improve our empathy and theory of mind.[11] The rubber meets the road for the development of those qualities in our relationships, where differences are front and center in our lives and we need to learn how to live with them. You can't try to dismiss or avoid dealing with differences in relationship; you have to meet those differences and tangle with them head on.

Diversity is sometimes present at the outset of your relationship. Other times, it may develop as you go. A partner can have a shift in their identity or orientation, go back to school and discover a new perspective, or take on a new hobby. Physical health issues can also introduce diversity, as do shifting dynamics with extended family members. People may develop different interests and preferences, seek to expand their romantic and sexual life, experience financial highs and lows, or dedicate themselves to a new religion or cause. Relationships that are able to embrace shifting identity aspects and openly discuss the impact of those shifts in a collaborative and respectful manner can adapt well to changes over time.

Part of being a good team is being aware of power differentials and aspects of privilege in your relationships. There may be a power differential based on gender, wealth, education, social class, race, culture, language, immigration status, age, social connections, proximity to family, or any number of other factors that can imbalance equality in relationships. To foster a strong connection, it is important to root out these inequities and systemic privileges, be aware of them, and seek to correct and balance them so that you feel like equal partners.

Systemic inequities can affect connection in relationships as well as impart an individual experience of marginalization to either partner. Embracing diversity in your relationship is being aware that social forces are not just "out there" in the culture but are at play in your relationship. They influence you, your partner, and how you act with each other. Such systemic forces are hard to eradicate because they are woven into our beings and society, often the product of our socialization in childhood. For example, depending on your background, you may be comfortable asserting yourself and your opinions, interrupting or talking over others, raising your voice, and feel deserving of respect, or you may have been socialized to defer to others and be polite, to please others and place them before yourself, and be demure about what feels good in sex. You may feel worthy of affection, attention, and generosity, or you may not, just accepting what others choose to give. You may have learned to feel good about your body, confident relative to others in society, and safe when you go out, or you may have learned to be ashamed of your body, suspicious of authority and others, to hide your true self in public, and to feel unsafe when out in the community. You may have developed judgments of others based on race, religion, or sexual orientation from the family or culture you grew up in.

Intersectionality is the idea that overlapping aspects of diversity all contribute to a person's experience of themselves and their place in society, and that identities and the cultural experiences that flow from them are complex, not just rooted in one identity structure such as race or sexual orientation.[12] Kimberlé Williams Crenshaw originated the term as part of an exploration of how diverse and marginalized identity structures impact our experience in life, with ourselves, and with others. As you get to know others intimately, you are also learning about and navigating their unique cultural experiences, beginning in childhood. As you get to know them, you can appreciate how their background impacts the way they show up in relationship. You can also be mindful of how your partner dynamics mirror larger social forces that create power imbalances and assign privilege based on particular identities, helping you uncover ways connection and trust may be getting stifled or can be enhanced in your relationships.

An immigrant in relationship with a native-born national may be reluctant to question cultural frameworks or push too hard against perceived privilege. A person of lower socioeconomic status (SES) may feel inadequate with a higher-SES partner. You may have been taught as a child that girls should be polite and defer to boys or act a certain way, or that boys should be tough and not cry or show their tender emotions. These are all examples of how socialization impacts us and our adult relationships in real ways. Discussing oppression and larger cultural forces such as sexism, patriarchy, and racism within your relationship can be helpful for rooting out hidden privileges and increasing the sense of safety, security, equality, and connection.

To maintain a strong bond, it helps to validate and show respect to others even when you disagree with their opinions. Supporting your partner even in an activity you don't appreciate or understand is a way to show respect to their preferences and ability to think for themselves. Being aware of identities and personal factors in yourself that are marginalized or oppressed in the culture at large may help you understand some of the feelings you have in your relationship. You can use that awareness to work together to disable power dynamics learned from culture that do not promote a sense of equality or connection. Your relationship is a stable and influential platform from which to take care of each other, and a strong relationship can help heal divisions in society. Developing healthier relationships reminds us to work toward fairness and equity for all: to promote healthy relationships in our homes and in the culture at large.

Polyamory and Open Relationships

While people have always pursued and practiced open and polyamorous (poly) relationships, Western culture has only recently become more accepting of non-monogamous relationship lifestyles, a change driven in part by Millennials and Gen Zers,[13] and by the growing integration and positive influence of same-sex relationships.[14] Gay men, for example, do not usually assume by default that their partnership will be monogamous and often engage in frank communication around their romantic and sexual preferences.[15] While there is still considerable judgment of non-conventional relationship lifestyles and of LGBTQ+ individuals in some sectors of society, younger people as a population bloc are more accepting and willing to celebrate each person's unique attributes rather than believing individuals should conform to traditional standards.[16]

Poly and open relationships can be just as secure and healthy as more traditional partner relationships.[17] In some cases, they may be more so, due to the added maturity, resilience, awareness, and communication needed to navigate such arrangements successfully.[18] Open and poly couples may be able to teach monogamous couples important elements of teamwork because those relationship structures often require an extra measure of skilled communication, awareness, and negotiation to be secure.[19] For example, swinging couples are sometimes assumed to look outside their relationship for stimulation because they are having trouble connecting with each other, but research suggests otherwise.[20] Such partners often have stronger bonds than couples with more traditional romantic lives because they have a shared activity they enjoy and because their lifestyle often deepens their friendship and communication.[21] It is also important to define what success means, because for some poly, open, or even monogamous couples, staying together for a long time may not be part of the definition. A vibrant relationship that is healthy and enjoyable for a period of time may be considered a success by some partners.

Some research suggests that there may be a biological basis for a person's preference for monogamy or non-monogamy, much like there is with sexual orientation.[22,23] For that reason, and so as to not prejudice non-monogamous preferences, I will use the term "relationship orientation" here. In my work with nontraditional couples who practice an open or poly lifestyle, I have isolated three primary factors that seem to allow such partnerships to function securely and that allow partners to feel successful in a non-monogamous relationship. These are valuable principles for monogamous couples as well, as they tend to facilitate stronger security in any relationship.

1. **Self-Awareness.** Advanced self-awareness helps non-monogamous partners successfully navigate the emotional ups and downs of their lifestyle. They need to know where to set boundaries, what feels okay and what would feel too threatening, and if such a lifestyle is really right for them and matches their true preferences.
2. **Enhanced Communication.** Poly and open partners need to have above-average transparent communication in order to understand each other's preferences and boundaries, accurately and vulnerably describe their true thoughts and feelings, and broker shared agreements that feel good to all partners.
3. **Tracking.** Once a non-monogamous lifestyle is set in motion, it is not enough to let it run on autopilot. It is important to continually gather data on how the arrangement is feeling and reassess rules and boundaries as needed.

The Phases of Relationship

While no consensus exists among researchers about the phases of primary relationships, there is some agreement as to how long-term partnerships evolve on their way to deeper love and security. Developing a strong team is in some ways about navigating these phases successfully and strengthening the bond in each one. Each phase presents challenges in a unique way, and, as you pass, your team can emerge stronger into its next phase of relationship.

My summary of the general phases of relationship is inspired by M. Scott Peck's classic book about community building, *The Different Drum: Community Making and Peace*, in which he outlines four stages of community.[24] While it is not about partner relationships, it is an excellent guide to understanding the dynamics that come up in all relationships and the opportunities and challenges they present. These stages map a path from individualism to collective existence, and to the teamwork that helps us have meaningful, respectful, and fulfilling relationships.

1. The Honeymoon Phase

In this initial phase, we are inspired by our dream and vision of what the relationship can be, and we feel hope at the start of the journey. Neuroscience shows that the body produces certain chemicals in higher doses during this phase, including oxytocin, which helps us bond; dopamine, which gives us a kind of joyful high; and nerve growth factor (NGF), which also produces a sense of euphoria.[25] Our mental belief in, and physiological response to, the new relationship allows us to overlook flaws in our new partner and in our relationship with them and be excited about the path ahead.

This physical and mental high, sometimes called limerence or new relationship energy (NRE), is intoxicating but is bound to mature as we get to know people more closely, and especially as we begin living with them and sharing daily life. As relationships deepen, our expectations sometimes lead to disappointment, because people aren't perfect, and we have to reckon with reality. It is often recommended that people date for a few years before choosing long-term partnership in order to experience more aspects of each other than what is revealed in the honeymoon phase. In the first six months of a relationship, your partnership is not very battle-tested in difficult circumstances and your knowledge of each other is limited. Teamwork in this phase is about knowing that the reality phase is coming and to prepare for it, and to start being honest about your weak areas and how the relationship will handle and support those. Ideally, you try to develop maturity and awareness while enjoying the awesome high of a new, exciting bond.

2. The Reality Phase

The reality phase sets in as you get to know each other better, go deeper in relationship, maybe begin to live together, and have to deal with the completely normal and necessary friction that differing habits and perspectives elicit. You can't hide your flaws very well in this phase, and your partner can't hide theirs either. How you reconcile your differences becomes vital to the relationship's survival and to a sense of fulfillment.

Teamwork in this phase is about learning to navigate conflict, manage your differences elegantly, and develop a process for improvement as a couple. You won't be smooth here because that comes from experience, but you don't want to be toxic either. It's important to learn how to de-escalate conflict, be vulnerable, and offer empathy and care for each other in the emotions you experience.

Much of the conflict of this phase is positive conflict, meaning it's friction that is trying to make you better. But sometimes toxic conflict can set in—the kind that is intentionally mean and hurtful as a retaliation for feeling hurt ourselves. You have to guard against this toxic conflict as it is destructive. Positive conflict champions the relationship and wants to see it grow but still requires that you work through it and not neglect the issues that come up. The reality phase is difficult to navigate, but if you hang in there and keep developing healthy habits you can find your way to the next phase. It can help to get professional support from an experienced therapist if you need it.

3. The Humble Phase

In the best case, the reality phase takes us to the realization that we don't have all the answers; it humbles and reminds us that we need to collaborate with our partners to develop a more fulfilling relationship. In the humble phase, you drop unnecessary defensiveness and grow more curious about the parts of you that may cause issues in relationship. You are willing to learn and grow, and that mind-set allows you to build the skill you need more quickly. It can be a fun phase, especially if you collaborate on joint growth, but also a vulnerable one that can come with some shame at times. The more support you can give each other, the better.

Teamwork in this phase is about working together to achieve deeper connection. It's about holding each other gently with compassion as each person becomes more aware of the limitations of their skill set. Sometimes honest conversations need to be had about personality qualities or problem dynamics, and you do your best to have them with love, care, and support of each other. This is a great phase in which to work with a counselor, because each partner is open to learning and change and you can challenge yourselves to grow and deepen connection more quickly. You can also hold that growth mind-set at home, practicing the skills that carry you into the next phase of relationship security.

4. The Secure Phase

The secure phase is what most people seek in a long-term relationship: a reliable base that is strong enough to be there for you in thick and thin and that offers consistent fun, care, and empathy. Marriage is designed to help make a relationship feel more secure, but neither a marriage certificate nor a wedding ceremony magically imparts the skills you need to build such a relationship. Security is earned through commitment, dedication, humility, and perseverance, dealing with conflict, and bringing love, warmth, kindness, respect, and genuine care to that process. With continual attention, such a relationship can pay incredible dividends, physically and emotionally, in terms of a shared lifestyle, a friendship, and support for the tasks of life.

Living as an individual can be hard, but relationship life can be as well when it's not secure. When you move through life alone, you're responsible for every aspect of caring for yourself, and friends can be fleeting or busy with their own loved ones when you need support. In a secure relationship, the partnership can support you to pursue your individual goals and cares about what makes you happy, but it will take work and continual tending to make it secure. Some people find more peace in individual life, and some seek the team approach. If you choose to partner up, a team mind-set makes your individual and relationship dreams easier to achieve.

Examples of the "We" Mind-set

We've explored the difference between an "I" and a "we" mind-set and how the latter can help you take joint responsibility for issues and exhibit teamwork in improving your skills. In the following examples, I will illustrate ways in which a "we" mind-set can help support your growth.

Example 1: Conflict

Michael and Aleysha often get into arguments. They get frustrated with each other, and when they talk about issues they often blame and criticize each other, leaving them both feeling unheard, isolated, and dismissed. Aleysha expects Michael to be better at things he's not very good at, like remembering plans and offering emotional support, and feels disappointed by his level of listening and care. Michael is tired of being criticized, her negative perspective, and sometimes feels that his partner will never be happy with him.

On good days, they can share how they each feel by owning those feelings and saying, "I feel sad," or, "I feel frustrated," rather than criticizing each other's behavior, which makes it easier for them to listen to each other and care. But those conversations sometimes turn into a battle for whose feelings matter the most and whose version of reality is true, with each of them feeling like the other only cares about their own feelings in the relationship.

To work as a team, rather than stopping with their respective "I feel" statements that don't always unite them, they can sit close, hold hands, and set an intention to address issues together. They can use "we" language to agree on what the issue is and what they can get better at as a couple, so they can support that growth and assign less individual blame to each other. They can discuss what would make their interactions more pleasant and team up to practice those moves as a team.

Aleysha might say, "Maybe we can sit closer when we start to argue."

Michael could respond with, "That's a good idea. And I think if we touched and expressed something positive and reassuring about the relationship, we wouldn't be so on edge."

Aleysha: "Good point. The problem is we each start to feel alone and then we both want the other to really get how we feel, but we're not really coordinating well."

Michael: "Yup. I think we often feel blamed or criticized by the other. Maybe if we each make sure to validate each other's feelings before we make our point or move on, we'd feel more heard and respected."

Aleysha: "I agree. And I'm appreciating right now how we're talking about getting better at communication together; it feels less attacking and I'm way less defensive."

You can see how Michael and Aleysha have found a way to share responsibility for their poor communication and to work together as teammates to improve it. Instead of just "I" statements, they're talking as a couple, not just as individuals, and it's helping them feel less polarized in the dynamic. Teamwork is about moving toward each other to connect when there's an issue, not blaming or criticizing each other on issues or under stress. A team mind-set establishes the opportunity to practice new skills together until they feel familiar, an aspect of relationship improvement I explore in the next chapter.

Example 2: "I Need Support"

Tarek and John are a sweet couple. They met when they were both living in Boston but moved to Arizona so John could pursue a new job. When John started working, Tarek was still unemployed and started to feel lonely while John was out all day. To make things worse, Tarek started to feel like he wasn't contributing as much and started to feel inadequate compared to John, who was really enjoying his new job.

Sometimes, when John would come home, Tarek would sulk and withdraw. Other times, Tarek would talk about how he felt all day—lonely, like he wasn't as important or successful as John. Tarek would do a good job conveying his feelings at times, explaining from an "I" perspective that he felt de-prioritized and bad about himself. John would listen attentively but not really know what to do to make things better. Sometimes these conversations would make them feel more disconnected, with Tarek not really feeling valuable and John getting frustrated that there was nothing he could do to help Tarek.

By using a "we" mind-set, Tarek and John can move out of that stuck place where John doesn't know how to help and Tarek feels low about himself. A team approach will likely help Tarek feel less like a screw-up and John like he has to find something he can do to support his partner.

One of them might say, "Man, this is a tough problem. We really love each other. I wonder what we need to do to improve the situation?"

The other might respond, "You're right; it's been kicking our ass since the move. I wonder what our relationship is needing more of right now."

Tarek might say, "I think when I feel lonely and down I'm comparing myself to you and how excited and successful you seem right now."

"I know," John could reply, "and I don't know what to do to help you feel better."

John: "I wonder if we didn't handle the move that great and we took care of me but not enough of you."

Tarek: "I don't know; I just didn't predict we would feel like this. I guess I had a lot more friends in Boston."

John: "Well, let's really think about what we need to feel like we're thriving again. What if we went out together a few nights after work and made some new friends as a couple?"

Tarek: "That could feel fun."

John: "And maybe if we tried mountain biking together and learned some of the trails on Saturday? That's pretty popular around here."

Tarek: "I suck at biking, but sure, it'd be fun to explore the areas around our house. I'm glad you're not just looking at me and asking me why I'm so low lately. When you do that, it makes me feel worse, even though I know you care."

John: "Good. I'm glad we're not having that conversation either. I just get confused about how to support you and then we start feeling really distant. This approach of doing it together feels way more fun and productive."

By talking about their issue as a team, they were able to avoid highlighting the disconnecting individual experiences they were having and defined common ground for improvement. Discussing the issue as a team got John and Tarek out of their rut where they could mobilize the relationship to act as a unit. They took joint responsibility for the issue of Tarek feeling low, and committed to action together that joined them in connection, which eased John's frustration and didn't make Tarek feel like a problem partner.

Example 3: Noticing Differences

Sasha is a clean freak and her partner, Natalie, is not. Sasha always appreciated Natalie's free spirit, spontaneity, and nonconformist attitude, but now living with her is tough. Natalie leaves her underwear on the floor, doesn't make the bed, doesn't rinse the bathtub after she uses it, and leaves takeout on the kitchen counter, where it stays until Sasha cleans it up the next morning. Natalie always appreciated Sasha's sense of order, and responsible nature, and felt secure with someone who is good at adulting and taking care of details. But living with Sasha, Natalie feels that she is too uptight, anxious, and over-concerned with unimportant things. Sasha feels that Natalie doesn't respect her and her need for a clean home to feel organized and relaxed.

When Sasha and Natalie talk about the issue, the conversation usually doesn't go well or resolve anything. Sasha feels that Natalie isn't willing to exert the effort to respect her more, and Natalie feels that Sasha wants her to be a different person. Sasha expresses feeling frustrated and annoyed, and Natalie expresses feeling condescended to and stifled. Both are usually left feeling like the other just doesn't get it, and alone in their experience.

Huddling up as a team, Sasha and Natalie can move from being on opposite sides of the issue to being on the same side—them against the problem. They can talk as a "we" about how they don't feel as connected as they used to and how living with someone who is different is hard. They can take joint responsibility for the issue and remind themselves that the relationship needs to step up to this challenge and the change that's needed is not just in one of them or the other, or in changing their personalities, but in coordinating better as a team.

They might start by asking themselves, "How can we handle this problem better?"

"We have natural differences that we appreciate, but how can we minimize what's annoying about those differences?"

Sasha might say, "You know, we are who we are, and that's probably not going to change that much. We need some systems in place to protect us from the annoying part of our differences."

Natalie could agree, "Instead of changing our personalities, let's figure out some way of supporting ourselves that doesn't elicit the things we both don't like."

Sasha: "Might be easier said than done, but maybe we can think creatively. The problem is, I like things neat and you're just not built that way. I hate reminding you to pick up, and it's hurting our relationship, but I just don't feel relaxed when the place is messy."

Natalie: "And I hate making you feel that way, but I'm just not the person who is detail oriented, and you're, like, the queen of that, so it feels unfair for you to think I could match that."

Sasha: "I like that you're a free spirit—*most* of the time. But in living together, it's hard."

Now that they're tackling the issue as a team, it may be easier for them to come up with something that works—a better way to manage their natural differences, rather than constant conversations about how their tendencies are a problem. Acknowledging that they have different personalities and probably aren't going to change that much gives them a better opportunity to find the right approach. Finding a way to manage differences without asking people to change the way they are also works well with money differences, which often elicit chronic arguments. With a "we" mentality, the myriad possibilities for improvement open up in a creative space of thinking together about the issue.

"You know what?" Natalie says. "I just thought of something. You know that guy down the hall from us who is a little shy and has been out of work for a while? Maybe he'd be willing to come by once a day and help us pick up. He's been wanting to hang out with us some anyways, and we'd be helping him until he finds something else."

"Not a bad idea," responds Sasha. "If he agrees that he would really like that. It would be weird if we were paying him and he wasn't that into it. But he often says he needs more to do and more interaction."

Natalie: "Okay, let's check with him."

They spoke to their neighbor down the hall, and he was excited to come help once a day. He not only appreciated making a little money but also enjoyed a chance to interact with Sasha and Natalie, since he often felt isolated and wasn't getting out much. He also loves keeping things neat and feels a satisfaction from that and from helping others, so supporting the two partners to bridge their differences and get along better felt meaningful to him. It turned out to be a win-win-win with Sasha and Natalie getting some support to keep the apartment neater and their neighbor feeling helpful and more connected.

While Sasha and Natalie still argue sometimes, it is a win for them to stop pointing the finger at each other and hold responsibility for the issue together in a way that is respectful toward both of them. They found a way to minimize the annoying side of their differences by thinking creatively and getting outside help, preserving their sense of connection and admiration for their differences.

Exercises to Improve Teamwork

Exercise 1: Championing Each Other's Cause

This exercise is designed to help you get better at supporting each other's important causes and needs, reduce defensiveness, and improve teamwork. I sometimes call it Picking Up Each Other's Flag because of the imagery of carrying your partner's mission and flag and bearing it as your own. Both names convey the intent of the practice, which is to take up your partner's cause on an issue you differ or disagree on and advocate for their side and needs as if they were your own.

Pick an issue you have a difference of opinion on. Not a major issue—keep it easy for now. Spend a couple minutes discussing the issue from your usual perspectives, each of you sticking up for your own side. Then defend your partner's side for them. You need to be able to make the arguments they would make and to know what is important to them about the issue. Go one at a time so the other can listen to the effort. This exercise helps develop empathy and *theory of mind,*[26] which allows you to put yourself in others' shoes and understand their needs, even if they are different from your own. It helps you to develop a two-person psychology that can account for the needs of two people at once, rather than a one-person psychology where you mostly track your own preferences.

Higher empathy gives you the ability to stretch your mind into a different perspective from the one that comes most naturally to you and so validate others' needs. By switching roles, you learn to be less defensive of one viewpoint, more appreciative of diverse approaches, and able to show your partner a willingness to stick up for them on things that they care about. If you ever find yourselves in an argument or debate that's disconnecting, you can use this exercise to disable the argument, show each other you care, and find common ground as a team.

Exercise 2: Improving Joint Responsibility

Usually, the best solutions and ways of addressing issues come from working together on things. After all, you move through life together, so you'll typically need to collaborate on improvement to make sure your approach works well for both of you. Here is a simple exercise to practice taking joint responsibility.

Take an issue that you feel disappointed about in the relationship or that you and your partner sometimes see differently on. Write it down on a piece of paper. Decide together what you want it to say so that you both understand the issue and feel committed to addressing it. Distill it down to just a few words or one sentence. Next, tape the piece of paper to a wall so you can view it from a few feet away. Then stand together, side by side, holding hands, and look at the paper together. By "externalizing" the issue and being united as a team, it's easier to remember that you're on the same side addressing a problem together.

The practice is to look at the issue together and brainstorm on it. What can you do together to improve this issue? Feel your connection, your bodies touching, and focus on the problem itself taped to the wall. The problem is *out there*, and you two stand together as a team. Don't let the issue split you off from each other. Stay connected as you discuss the possibilities. While you might look at each other more in an ordinary conversation, this exercise helps you learn how to externalize problems and face them as a team.

Whether it's an issue that one of you primarily cares about or one that you both want to address, it's important to approach any dispute as a team. Practicing with concerns that your partner cares about more than you do helps to develop your empathy for their experience. Whether it's an agreed-upon problem or an individual cause, the relationship should be able to marshal its energy to champion change on the issue. This sense of addressing problems while being on the same team reduces defensiveness, helps you think creatively together about solutions, and supports you in practicing teamwork on any challenges you may face.

Notes

1. Tessa Melkonian and Thierry Picq, "Opening the 'Black Box' of Collective Competence in Extreme Projects: Lessons from the French Special Forces," *Project Management Journal* 41, no. 3 (June 2010): 79–90.

2. Eduardo Salas, Nancy J. Cooke, and Michael A. Rosen, "On Teams, Teamwork, and Team Performance: Discoveries and Developments," *Human Factors* 50, no. 3 (June 2008): 540–547.

3. Marion F. Solomon and Daniel J. Siegel, eds., *How People Change: Relationships and Neuroplasticity in Psychotherapy*, Norton Series on Interpersonal Neurobiology (New York: W. W. Norton, 2017).

4. David Osher, Pamela Cantor, Juliette Berg, Lily Steyer, and Todd Rose, "Drivers of Human Development: How Relationships and Context Shape Learning and Development," *Applied Developmental Science* 24, no. 1 (2020): 6–36.

5. Joseph LeDoux, *Synaptic Self: How Our Brains Become Who We Are* (New York: Viking, 2002).

6. Dr. Harry Barry, *Emotional Resilience: How to Safeguard Your Mental Health* (London: Orion, 2018).

7. Sweta Rajan-Rankin, "Self-Identity, Embodiment and the Development of Emotional Resilience," *British Journal of Social Work* 44, no. 8 (December 2014): 2426–2442, https://doi.org/10.1093/bjsw/bct083.

8. George A. Bonnano, "Loss, Trauma and Human Resilience: Have We Under-estimated the Human Capacity to Thrive after Extremely Adverse Events?," *American Psychologist* 59, no. 1 (January 2004): 20–28.

9. Marcus Mund, Christine Finn, Birk Hagemeyer, Julia Zimmermann, and Franz J. Neyer, "The Dynamics of Self–Esteem in Partner Relationships," *European Journal of Personality* 29, no. 2 (March/April 2015): 235–249.

10. Daniel J. Siegel, "Mindful Awareness, Mindsight, and Neural Integration," *The Humanistic Psychologist* 37, no. 2 (2009): 137.

11. Lee Gardenswartz, Jorge Cherbosque, and Anita Rowe, "Emotional Intelligence and Diversity: A Model for Differences in the Workplace," *Journal of Psychological Issues in Organizational Culture* 1, no. 1 (April 2010): 74–84.

12. Sumi Cho, Kimberlé Williams Crenshaw, and Leslie McCall, "Toward a Field of Intersectionality Studies: Theory, Applications, and Praxis," *Signs: Journal of Women in Culture and Society* 38, no. 4 (Summer 2013): 785–810.

13. Tristan Taormino, *Opening Up: A Guide to Creating and Sustaining Open Relationships* (Jersey City: Cleis Press, 2008).

14. Geri Weitzman, Joy Davidson, R. A. Phillips, James R. Fleckenstein, and C. Morotti-Meeker, "What Psychology Professionals Should Know about Polyamory," *National Coalition on Sexual Freedom* 7 (2009): 1–28.

15. Douglas C. Wilson, *Gay Male Couples and the Issue of Monogamy versus Non-monogamy* (Santa Barbara: Pacifica Graduate Institute, 2012).

16. Alison Keleher and Eric R. A. N. Smith, "Growing Support for Gay and Lesbian Equality since 1990," *Journal of Homosexuality* 59, no. 9 (2012): 1307–1326.

17. Jessica Fern, *Polysecure: Attachment, Trauma and Consensual Nonmonogamy* (Portland, OR: Thorntree Press, 2020).

18. Franklin Veaux and Eve Rickert, *More than Two* (Portland, OR: Thorntree Press, 2014).

19. Taormino, *Opening Up.*

20. Justin Wilt, Marissa A. Harrison, and Cobi S. Michael, "Attitudes and Experiences of Swinging Couples," *Psychology & Sexuality* 9, no. 1 (January 2018): 38–53.

21. Carolyn Rose Nash, *Monogamists and Consensual Nonmonogamists: Comparing Attachment Styles, Use of Relationship Therapy, Satisfaction with Therapeutic*

Services, and Overall Relationship Satisfaction (Fullerton: California State University, Fullerton, 2018).

22. Marianne Brandon, "Monogamy and Nonmonogamy: Evolutionary Considerations and Treatment Challenges," *Sexual Medicine Reviews* 4, no. 4 (October 2016): 343–352.

23. Angela Willey, *Undoing Monogamy: The Politics of Science and the Possibilities of Biology* (Durham: Duke University Press, 2016).

24. M. Scott Peck, *The Different Drum: Community Making and Peace* (New York: Simon & Schuster, 2010).

25. Gary W. Lewandowski, Jr., "AsktheBrains: What Physiological Changes Can Explain the Honeymoon Phase of a Relationship?," *Scientific American Mind* 24, no. 4 (September/October 2013): 72, doi:10.1038/scientificamericanmind0913-72a.

26. Theory of mind is a psychological concept that refers to the ability to understand others' perspectives as valid and equal to your own, to put yourself in someone else's shoes, have empathy for others' emotional experience, and see the world through their eyes.

5.

Developing a Practice Culture

Meaning and understanding emerge from new experiences rather than the other way around.

—Pat Ogden

Few of us start out equipped with the skills we need for healthy, long-term relationships, much less the skills we need for the particular people we're with. Every person is unique, as is our bond with them. So even if we consider ourselves capable of healthy relationships, we still need to grow into how to best relate to the specific people in our lives. Building these skills takes time, but it also takes training. Sadly, for most of us, our families were not very good examples of how to have healthy, supportive relationships, and our schools did not offer substantive training in this area, so it's up to us to put ourselves in position to gain that learning and engage in the practice of key skills. Developing insight about our behaviors is important and discussing our goals with our partner is also helpful, but when it comes to really re-patterning behavioral tendencies, practice is key.

I started noticing the power of practice in my own life as I tried to improve my relationship skills. Even though I was learning about relationship health, attachment, and the science of connection, the concepts alone weren't enough to change my habits—I had to place myself in awkward situations and try new relationship behaviors until they became smooth. For example, I couldn't say "I love you" when I first started trying these things, because it wasn't a phrase my family used growing up, and I always felt embarrassed saying it. I felt love, but the words were not easy to get out, so I had to force myself to say it until I could connect the words to how I felt. Further, I wasn't good at offering hugs, or asking for them. I was terrible at saying I needed alone time (I would usually just disconnect) and I didn't know how to talk about my feelings.

I didn't know how to offer emotional support and would usually just look like a deer in the headlights if someone came to me with an emotion. I lacked empathy and had to work hard to keep another person's experience in mind and show interest, care, and compassion. I learned the concept of practice from some of the neuroscience research I was reading and began to see why it's important and how it works. When I started using it, I made the big gains and changed fast. To make it less awkward, I would tell my partner I was practicing, and then I would try saying things and doing things that were unfamiliar. It was sort of fun but also sort of terrifying, because trying new behaviors like that is exposing. The results, however, were amazing.

The key to practice is the "fake it till you make it" concept of learning. While that method is not useful without authentic vulnerability and connection (often people who try to fake confidence or skills they don't have feel even more isolated since no one knows their real struggle), combined with transparency and support it works very well. Fake it till you make it helps boost relationship skills because it involves actual action and procedural memory rather than simply mental learning. Relationship skills really benefit from engaging in the physical movements, words, and nonverbal expressions that are connecting until they become more natural. If the learning just lives in our head, we never bring it out in an awkward way that helps us get better. The interesting thing about this method is that at first sometimes people complain that it feels fake. They worry that it's not authentic to who they are. But after time, once they are more comfortable saying "I love you," offering hugs, communicating care and support, and offering kind eyes and facial expressions to others, it does feel genuine.

In other words, fake it till you make it returns us to natural relationship skills that represent how we really feel and the types of relationships we want to have, but since many of us are not socialized around those connecting moves, they can feel inauthentic and awkward at first. The key to this method is to make yourself uncomfortable, take emotional risks, and say and do things before they feel like you. Over time, you'll notice the difference in your relationships, and the connecting skills will feel authentic to who you are. Trust me, I didn't have any of these skills at first. And I couldn't have fulfilling relationships as a result. But once I practiced these moves for a while, I felt more in charge of how connecting an interaction I could have with others, and capable to communicate love and care and make others feel safe and supported.

Developing a practice culture is part of ensuring growth in your relationship.

One of the biggest differences between relationships that succeed and those that remain challenging or dissolve is whether partners bring a growth mind-set to life together.[1,2] Some people remain stubborn, set in their individual ways and resistant to revising their habits. When partners are able to bring a humble and curious mind-set to their relationship and are willing to explore their behaviors and blind spots in an effort to improve, that team approach allows the relationship to evolve and get healthier, and also imparts ever-growing individual skills to each partner.

The neuroscience of connection shows that most of our relationship behaviors are automatic—driven by immediate, instinctive patterns wired deep in our bodies and psyches.[3] Relationship behavior that seems choice driven is often spurred by these automatic tendencies and the subconscious, with habits shaped by developmental experience in childhood, when many of the brain's social systems are built. Emotions, reactions, and facial expressions often precede thought. Some of these automatic habits are learned behaviors that form part of the "procedural memory" system, the same automatic system that is trained by hours of practice playing an instrument or practicing a sport.[4] The good news about understanding how automatic we are in relationships is that we can bring compassion and a sense of humor to the silly things we do, or to habits that do not serve connection, knowing that they're often not intentional.

Human interactions light up the brain like nothing else—brain to brain, we take in a profound amount of information, much more than we can be conscious of. Because relationship interactions involve a tremendous amount of complexity and information moving at a high rate of speed, we need to engage procedural memory to improve our automatic habits—much like training our fingers to play the right keys on the piano faster than the speed of thought. That's partially why approaches to couples therapy have been shifting from talking about issues and reflecting on better habits to practicing skills live in the moment.[5] The automatic system doesn't listen to thoughts and measured plans—it needs to practice.

While deliberate repetition is an established way to develop skills in many endeavors, it is seldom utilized by couples to improve relationship skills. Yet intentional practice is one of the most effective growth activities in relationship, imparting practical skills you can use right away.[6] I don't think I've ever had a couple walk into my office who were already employing practice to improve their relationship patterns, but once they start, their skills improve. Leading marital therapists use practice often because of how effective it is at retraining conscious and nonconscious physical and mental systems that affect how we interact with others, and because the learning achieved through such repetition is more stable in the face of stress, tiredness, and upsetness, as compared with insight-based learning.[7,8,9]

Developing a practice culture means you're willing to act out difficult scenarios until you can do them better, not just talk about them. Instead of talking about how to communicate better under stress, for example, you would try different approaches, rate them, select one that works well, and repeat that one over and over until it is embedded in memory, the same way a soccer team might drill taking shots on the goal.

Practice has gotten more attention lately for developing connecting skills because neuroscience has helped us understand that many of our relationship behaviors are automatic, driven by procedural memory, and the main way to improve such default tendencies is through repetition and practice.[10] Couples therapy models based on this neuroscience include methods designed to help partners shift from bad habits to behaviors that are friendly and connecting. This means spending time practicing friendlier, more supportive behaviors toward ourselves and others, getting feedback, and repeating new connecting behaviors that at first may seem awkward or unfamiliar. Even therapists make use of deliberate practice for their personal craft. While they engage in empathy and connecting behaviors daily, research has shown that the deliberate practice of therapy skills leads to elite ability and improved outcomes.[11]

Practice helps partners re-train automatic tendencies by identifying and repeating key skills, same as how we pursue improvement in any endeavor that relies on procedural memory.[12] Practice gives you hope that your relationship can step up and improve, because you see your partner exerting effort in real, practical ways, not just saying they'll try to do better later. And it brings you together, sharing responsibility for issues and improvement. In addition, practice can be fun, bonding, and playful and give you a focused way to spend quality time together. It helps to shift chronic problems, including patterns that have become embedded habits of behavior, and creates a compassionate culture where mistakes are well tolerated.

Chronic conflicts are typically rooted in a pattern of interaction and are not just issue specific. Practice helps disarm these chronic habits by addressing them at their root, improving your mind and body's default habits. Solving a single issue is usually not enough, as our communication patterns tend to carry over into discussions on many fronts. Practice helps you revamp a problematic pattern of communication itself, which allows you to bring better skill to all your interactions. In other words, practice helps improve the way you interact, and that positive skill carries over into your interactions in general.

A practice culture imparts a sense of compassion and tolerance for missteps. We're all going to make mistakes constantly in our relationships. In fact, they're not really mistakes—humans are too complex to not step on one another's toes at times. The brain is error prone in relationships because human interactions send the brain a lot of complex information at a high rate of speed and many of our evaluative systems are primitive. It's important that your connections have the trust, goodwill, and resilience to accept mistakes and support one another to improve as a team. Practice implies that these skills are a work in progress, which they are. It reminds us that we don't have it all figured out, and that we need to be compassionate and supportive regarding the things we're not good at.

Just like any team that practices their craft week-to-week, a growth culture reminds us that improvement requires continual effort. We can't take our growth for granted—we have to put in the time and energy. The structure of practice as a way to address issues can be fun, playful, connecting, hilarious, and unifying, much like an improv acting class. Rather than get split off from each other for weeks with resentment, you can remember to bring the issues you're experiencing into a session and work them in different ways to see what works, improving a problem dynamic together.

A Culture of Growth

From the minute a relationship begins, the merging of two or more minds, hearts, habits, cultures, and perspectives asks us to grow, learn, and adapt. A growth-minded approach to relationship takes **humility, vulnerability, and curiosity** and can pay tremendous dividends to the individuals and relationships that embrace it. Having empathy for others and learning to appreciate differences between viewpoints are critical relationship skills that can bridge connection between people and communities. If we do that well, we can create a shared culture and reality that sustains our relationships.[13] If we don't, we may be signing up for years of stress, friction, and arguments.

Part of having successful relationship is recognizing that our own reality is not so precious. Sure, we have our own thoughts and ideas, but a shared reality is way more fulfilling and interesting. Our individual perception is limited by our own experiences, memories, and thoughts. There's a whole new world out there ready to be experienced if we allow ourselves to open and share someone else's

worldview, habits, and perspectives. Shared reality makes us smarter, helps elimi-
nate some of our blind spots, and develops new qualities in us that make us more
mature and capable in a variety of situations, both personal and professional.[14] It
prepares us well to raise children, appreciate co-workers, and helps us be wiser,
more patient, and self-reflective individuals.[15] Opening to a shared reality helps
us embrace diversity in our communities and imparts psychological flexibility that
allows our minds to keep up with changing times, both in society and in the evolution of our personal relationships.

If you're able to stay humble and curious about yourself in relationship and
willing to put forth the effort to learn and grow, your bond can improve over time
and you can solve issues that arise. A culture of growth makes the difference
between a relationship that is struggling but worth working on and one that may
need to end. When people are not willing to learn and grow, or self-reflect, it's
difficult to change problems. But when partners are motivated to learn and grow
together with the humility and dedication that takes, then the future is typically
brighter than the status quo and it's worth seeing what the relationship can do.

I often tell people that they will collect the best data about their partnership
when they work together to improve it. If you sit on the sidelines or just gripe
about the relationship, you don't know what it can do. Sometimes relationships
will surprise you when you put some effort in. Your partner may show up in ways
you did not expect. Developing a culture of growth helps you and your partner
continue to improve, and there are many ways to pursue it. While some individual
growth activities can be helpful to developing relationship skills, you will need to
practice improving together to get the most benefit.

Relationship is one of the planet's most advanced schools of personal
growth and an active spiritual practice. Many of us seek a sense of peace that
can withstand the ups and downs of life. Relationship life as a practice can help
strengthen you for those waves and help you to develop a resilient state of being.
Rather than seeking a unity in relationship that aims to minimize differences in
order to achieve peace through sameness, partners who seek a unity that is embracing of differences will find a greater and stronger secure base for their love
and greater resilience in themselves for the experience of life.

The age-old tension between connection and individuality is settled in secure relationships. The dichotomy between independence and strong partner
bonds is a false one—secure relationships offer individuals freedom to pursue life
goals and dreams while also offering support and shared resources. That question I had long ago about whether it's worth getting into a serious, committed
relationship has been answered for me: not only can relationship life offer valu-

able support when functioning securely, but the learning and growth available in relationship also acts as a graduate school for individual growth.

Blind Spots

Psychological and neuroscience research shows that we all have blind spots—ways we impact relationships that we have a hard time seeing and being aware of.[16] Blind spots are the result of the brain optimizing for what it needs most and not being able to develop talent in all aspects. Partnership tends to reveal our blind spots, helping us to understand ourselves if we embrace another's perspective on us and their feedback.

Sometimes our pride gets in the way of being able to see these weaknesses, which then makes it difficult to improve them. We may get defensive when our partner gives us feedback because it doesn't fit our self-image. Even if our partner can't describe what they notice about us with complete accuracy—after all, they have their own issues—their feelings often point to important areas where we can learn about ourselves and improve. Much of the time, however, even when we're willing to accept responsibility, it's just hard to bend our minds to see what others may experience about us because we're so used to seeing the world through our own eyes.

If we are curious and humble and use relationships to illuminate our weak areas and blind spots, we can more clearly understand how we negatively impact connection, and have a chance to make tremendous gains in our maturity and self-awareness. Admitting our faults also helps our partners be patient with us because they know we're working to grow and improve. There's almost no relationship where one partner is creating all the issues—generally, problem dynamics are co-sponsored by both partners. Practice culture gives you concrete ways to support the relationship's growth and each other's progress.

The Healthy Relationship Lifestyle

Developing a practice culture is easier to implement if you are partnered, but as an individual, you can use it with friends and family members as well. If you desire focused practice in a more organized setting, you might consider joining an interpersonal process therapy group that provides a dedicated training ground for relationship skill building and the opportunity to practice with others. While this book highlights how partners can benefit from working together to improve their connecting skills, I also recommend that individuals, partnered or not, commit themselves to a *healthy relationship lifestyle*. That means setting your intention to have only relationships that feel good, that exhibit mutuality, that respect you, care for you, and serve your needs.

Whether you are in a relationship or not, committing to a healthy relationship lifestyle helps you develop better habits by attracting people who are prepared to have strong, secure bonds. And it helps prevent the development of bad habits by reducing your exposure to friends with unhealthy patterns. Healthy friendships give you opportunities to practice beneficial skills such as receiving care, asking for what you need, setting boundaries, offering empathy, and being more emotionally open. Some toxic relationships may need to end to make room for healthier new ones. As you move unhealthy relationships to the sidelines of your life, you'll see your time and energy going more toward links with people who can match your desire to have secure, trustworthy connections.

If you are not in a committed relationship, you can start practicing in your friendships, with co-workers, and with family members, trying to improve connection and communication and building skills for any future relationships. Begin to move toxic people out of your life and bring in healthier people who care about you and your felt experience when you interact with them. Relationships typically only work well if the individuals in them are prepared to genuinely care for each other and are not just focused on individual objectives. Notice any selfish tendencies in your friendships and with family members or dating partners and commit to improving those relationships or focusing on people who can respect and support you.

If you're single and eventually want a great partner relationship in your life, start practicing healthier, deeper connections with friends, in your social group, with co-workers, and with family members. That way, you're preparing yourself to be ready for a connected relationship and are more likely to attract someone who has healthy connecting skills.

If you are partnered, you can commit as an individual to the principles of a healthy relationship lifestyle and expect those qualities in your current partnership. That commitment is a way of depersonalizing feedback and expressing what you need to a partner by discussing your values rather than their character or weaknesses. By having standards, you can compare your relationship and partner's behavior to those personal values helping provide you with clarity on what needs to change and what goals or boundaries you may need to set to ensure a healthy bond. The goal is to have a definition of what relationship health looks like in your given partnership and to challenge yourselves to work toward and achieve that goal.

Of course, healthy relationships don't feel good *all* the time, meaning that friction isn't always a bad sign and it can be helpful to stay dedicated through tough times. But unhealthy relationships that cause heavy, chronic stress or that treat you disrespectfully as a default habit need to be improved quickly or possibly brought to an end. An individual commitment to heathy relationships can help with that, because instead of being critical or judgmental as a way to set boundaries, you can compare the relationship to the healthy standards you have committed to and highlight any discrepancies.

Practice Culture

There is nothing difficult in life that we do easily without training or practice. Relationships are no different. In fact, the complexity and challenge of relationship life outpaces the difficulty of most other endeavors, yet we often have a better-developed practice culture in hobbies and sports. Developing a practice mindset in your relationship means that you're willing to put in effort to train better skills, revise your assumptions, listen to your partner, and grow together. It means you remain curious and humble in looking at yourself and at the relationship itself. And it means you're willing to practice—not just talk about—the relationship skills you're trying to build as a couple to be more successful.

To practice effectively, you first have to assess what's getting in the way of your connection and identify the areas you need to improve.[17] Some of the skills you can develop in practice are not just choice-driven behaviors but also automatic tendencies, like the nature of your gaze, tone of voice, expressiveness, and your nonverbal communication of empathy. These automatic cues can be shaped by training in the same way that actors learn to be aware of them and harness them to communicate effectively.

Practice reshapes both choice-driven and automatic behaviors toward more connecting actions and reactions based on partner feedback. In partner bonds, another's experience of us acts as a mirror we can use to polish our tendencies, try different things, and learn what feels secure in that given relationship. People and partnerships have unique qualities, so it's important to test what creates connection in your given relationship. While practice can seem awkward when beginning, especially when retraining automatic tendencies, it feels good to learn how to connect better with your partner and realize you have the power to increase love between you.

Relationships can seem complex, confusing, and almost impossible to improve at times. That's where practice comes in, as it can offer you a simple and familiar structure for how to get better. The nice thing about practice is you take joint responsibility to support each other in getting better. Just like actors rehearsing a scene, you figure out how you want those scenes to go, then run lines and practice your movements over and over until you're confident in those new skills you can use in challenging moments.

The key difference between talking about issues and practicing them is that the former mostly involves words and concepts, whereas the latter involves the parts of the body, brain, and nervous system that engage in those patterns. Practice means you enact scenarios that tend to cause problems, you try out different things to see what works, you play with it until you find something that feels good, and you engage in repetition of the new way of doing it. You learn how to negotiate your individual needs, not just in concept, but in terms of how an interaction feels in real time. Instead of committing to do things better in the future—often the result of a "talk"—you've actually practiced doing it better already, so your confidence that you can rise to that challenge as a couple goes up and your native skill to do it better is more available the next time you need it.

Why Practice Works

Like many activities that rely on the automatic procedural system for the needed skill to succeed, relationships utilize natural habits and involve complex cues traveling at a fast rate of speed. The pace of human interactions is too fast to think through every action, so to connect consistently, we need to train those reflexive parts that will send our partner information before we even have a thought. Ideally, we want those subconscious cues to communicate security and friendliness to others' nervous systems so that our connections can be strong.

The brain tends to build new capacity based on need and demand. If a need for new capability is sent to the brain, it begins building the capacity to meet that claim. But developing new neural hardware is expensive from a biochemical standpoint, so the brain doesn't pay attention to just any demand signal. It pays attention to those that carry intensity and have frequency. That is why some types of friction in relationships can be helpful—the conflict can stimulate the brain to develop new neural capacity.

It's like when a town grows in importance yet the only road leading into it is old and bumpy. For a while, people may put up with it, but eventually the demands to replace it become impossible to ignore. This is like a demand signal being sent to the brain for new relational skill. Eventually, the local authorities (or the brain) realize that they need to upgrade the road or risk losing the people who live in the town and the new people they want to attract. Upgrading the road may be difficult and take time and resources, but it's what will allow the town to evolve into its new phase. Relationship friction is like the people of the town asking for a new road. We may not listen the first time, or the second or third, but eventually the relationship puts pressure on our system to develop new skill, and the brain goes to work to build new capacity to meet that demand.

Practice elicits those demand signals because when you're working together you can noticeably *feel* the lack of skill you're needing and there is demand pressure in that moment from our partner to find it. Simply talking about issues doesn't require us to actively display the skill we are working on and therefore puts less pressure on the brain in that moment.

Once the brain decides to build new capacity based on demand, it then has to engage in those new behaviors often enough to develop automatic skill.[18] Repetition is how the procedural system learns new tricks, so thinking about doing something better is not enough. We have to practice that new behavior with enough frequency until it becomes easy and natural and we can do it without thinking.

In groundbreaking research, Dr. Stephen Porges found that social engagement parts of the brain go offline under stress, leaving us with primitive strategies for attack and defense.[19] We can learn important insights about healthy relationships in a talk setting, but what happens when our fight-or-flight system engages? In those times when we feel threatened and our stress hormones start pumping, we can't recall or rely on the fancy strategies we have learned—instead, we resort to primitive defenses to protect ourselves. Practice helps impart relationship skill into your muscle memory so it is more present in those primitive reactions when stressed. While your frontal lobes may not be as accessible in such moments, your body can have more relational moves wired into your nervous system and available as options for action.[20]

How to Practice Relationship Skills

At a basic level, practicing relationship skills is like practicing anything else: we take a problem, or something we want to improve, we test or design a better way to do it, and we rehearse that better way over and over until it feels familiar and natural. Doing this with your partner allows you to make the best use of both your perspectives and it can be fun and playful.

Here are the important steps of practice:

1. Set an intention to practice something together that you don't do well.

2. Remember that the growth is for the team. Take joint responsibility—don't assign a lack of skill to just one of you as an individual.

3. Pick an issue that causes some problems. If you're new to this, pick something easier first, not your most difficult issue or topic.

4. Generally, focus practice on your process of interaction, not on a topic. Instead of trying to answer a question or solve a debate or disagreement, focus on your communication skills and how the interaction feels.

5. Practice the scenario in different ways to see what feels good. At first, it might feel like you are acting, but you're not—this is an issue you actually care about! Role playing elicits *state-dependent memory*, meaning it reminds us of how we feel when a specific thing happens. Once you feel the issue in your body and emotions rather than just thinking about it, the practice becomes more real and effective in those moments.

6. Try different things and watch how your partner reacts. You can also ask them what works best. This gets you working together to decide how to best support each other in challenging moments.

7. Once you find something that works well, repeat it over and over again—at least several times. Establishing new muscle memory requires doing something that works well more than once. You want this new and better habit to be there for you automatically and under stress.

8. Once you're done, pat yourselves on the back and go relax. You deserve credit for working on your relationship. Practicing like this builds your native skill. You can trust that over time practice will improve your natural habits. Instead of getting critical or giving up in tough moments, you'll have some moves you've tried that are more available for you to use.

Examples of Practice

Example 1: Differences of Opinion

Joshua and Kayla are having a hard time talking about money. Joshua is more spontaneous and comfortable spending money on things he enjoys, whereas Kayla is a long-term planner and saver. In psychological terms, Joshua would be known as more of a short-term gratification type of person, meaning he derives satisfaction from living in the moment and doing things that bring him immediate pleasure. Joshua's spending habits make Kayla nervous. She's more of a long-term gratification person, meaning she derives satisfaction from planning well, budgeting, and feeling like they have a solid financial foundation.

Ideally, Joshua and Kayla's personality differences would be complementary, each helping the other with their talents. Joshua might help Kayla to let go, relax, and have fun in the moment, without always thinking about what things cost. Kayla could help Joshua be more prudent, think about the future, and be kind to his future self, not just his current self, by saving more.

In their current situation, Joshua feels stifled by Kayla and Kayla gets stressed out by Joshua's habits. His way of making decisions makes her anxious, and she sometimes feels resentful that she has to be the responsible one in the relationship who helps cover his financial habits. Let's look at how practice might help Joshua and Kayla resolve their differences and get on the same page.

When Joshua and Kayla sit down to talk about money, they often get into arguments. Since the type of practice I advocate is oriented around the *process* of interaction more than the *content*, the way they speak to each other is a good place to begin. They would first identify, as a team, what happens when they talk about money. Kayla might notice that Joshua gets impatient, starts to raise his voice, and seems unable to appreciate the stress she feels about his habits.

Joshua might notice that Kayla seems intent on doing things more her way than his, and that she doesn't "get" who he is and how important his way of being is to his enjoyment of life.

After identifying the obstacles to feeling connected and what causes the conversation to go south, they have some points of practice. The next step is to pick one to start working on. In this case, Kayla and Joshua decide to practice what they do when Joshua gets impatient. "I don't want to get impatient," Joshua says, "but the conversation just makes me so frustrated after a while, and I can't get through to you!"

"Okay, so let's practice what we do when that happens. Maybe you can try some different things and I will too," Kayla says. They then pretend to have one of those conversations and Joshua begins to feel what it's like when he gets aggravated. From here, he can practice a few things and see what works best and feels more connecting in the interaction.

Joshua practices letting Kayla know that the conversation is getting irritating for him and he may need some sort of reset to stay engaged without getting impatient. "I don't want you to feel that way," Kayla says, "I want you to feel relaxed, and open, so we can try to understand each other. What do we need to do to help you chill out?"

"I don't know; maybe if we hold hands, or do foot rubs while we talk, that might be a way to stay connected and do something relaxing," says Joshua.

"Okay, let's try it," Kayla responds. They take off their socks and give each other foot rubs while they talk. It makes them laugh and they notice they're already feeling more connected.

"Okay, but what if I start to feel like you're trying to put me in some weird box that feels too strict?" Joshua says.

"I don't know," says Kayla, "but let's practice some ways to deal with that."

"Well, if I tell you I'm feeling that way, can you practice changing your tone, or approach, or something?" Joshua asks.

"Sure, let's try some ways of doing that," responds Kayla. When Joshua gives her that feedback, Kayla practices trying to open her mind to a different perspective, and also reassures Joshua that she wants him to feel happy in life and supports his need for that.

"That last part felt awesome!" Joshua says. "I don't think I've ever heard you say that you support me feeling happy in life. It meant a lot."

"Good," says Kayla. "I guess I can do that more often, and you can tell me when you need to hear that. What I need is for you to respect how nerve-wracking it is for me to not have a solid plan for our financial future."

"I hear you," says Joshua. "I really want you to not feel anxious about things."

"If I start to feel anxious," Kayla says, "like the conversation is not going to solve anything for me, can we practice you caring for me in that place and helping me?"

"Sure," says Joshua. "You know that I care, but we just have big differences here that feel important to both of us."

"Okay, let's practice it, then," says Kayla. "I'll connect to that anxiety that comes up for me, and let's try to do better in terms of conveying care for that and supporting me." They start talking about their spending habits, Joshua acts defensive (on purpose, they're starting to get into the play element of practice here), and Kayla shares, in a nice way, that the conversation is now making her really anxious. Joshua tries a few different approaches to caring for her in the moment. First, he tries an old technique: "Well, I have feelings too," which lands like a dud. Then he tries, "I'm really sorry you're anxious. I love you and I want the best for us, but I can't be a different person."

Kayla rated that last one as having a good start but then closing the door to positive change. Trying again, Joshua gave it another shot: "What if I said, 'I care about you and I don't want you to have to worry. Let's work together to have a financial plan you feel good about, but I also need to be appreciated for being different than you. I need you to recognize that that is a good thing, not a bad thing'?" says Joshua.

"Deal," says Kayla. "You support us in creating a plan, and I'll let you know I appreciate how you're different from me."

"That would feel really nice," says Joshua.

Kayla and Joshua have already started improving their money conversation. Not only do they have some good strategies for better conversations, but they also were able to share some of the underlying feelings they have on the issue and they bonded in the practice and have more hope that they can bridge their differences. Their willingness to practice helped them try out different improvements to how they normally talk, as well as receive feedback about what works and what doesn't. By having open minds and staying humble, they learned from each other and came up with a team approach to a touchy topic.

Example 2: Differences of Habit

Steve and Jacob met two years ago and are now engaged to be married. They've only been living together for a few months, but they're already running into some issues that were less of a problem when they had separate places. Jacob is a morning person who feels a lot of energy early and likes to consider all the possibilities the day may offer. Steve is the opposite: He feels energized at night and is slow to get going in the morning. He likes to sleep in and is often moody until he's had some time to settle in.

Steve is happy to discuss the day with Jacob once he's had his coffee, but Jacob wants to talk the moment Steve wakes up. Jacob gets frustrated with Steve's slower morning energy, and Steve gets annoyed with Jacob wanting to chat and plan right when he gets up. Their two most recent arguments have happened in the mornings because their habits are so different. Steve feels frustrated and Jacob is starting to feel he can't be himself and enjoy days the way he likes to. Let's see how practice might help them bridge these differences.

They identify that the way they interact in the mornings is hurting their relationship. With a good "we" mind-set, they acknowledge that they need to learn to manage these differences better and not let them hurt their connection. "Let's practice how a morning could go that feels good to both of us," says Steve.

"Okay," says Jacob. "I'll stand in the kitchen and imagine I've been up for two hours. I've already done an hour of exercise, showered, and am making breakfast for us, ready to talk and make plans for the day."

"Sounds good. I'll do my usual slow-to-wake-up, kind-of moody thing, and let's see if there's a way to connect in that situation."

Steve and Jacob literally act out the scenario: they don't just sit on the couch and imagine it, but rather they go to the kitchen to make it as realistic as possible. Acting things out physically as close to the way they actually happen helps to activate state-dependent memory, the memories and emotions we feel in those scenarios. Being in the kitchen pretending to make breakfast, Jacob remembers what it feels like to be annoyed in the morning. Steve stumbles in, but he doesn't want to talk or look at Jacob; he just goes for the coffee. Jacob can feel Steve's morning moodiness and tries to think of ways to connect with Steve that won't bother him. Steve tries his best to reach out and connect with Jacob without just pretending to be chipper. They try different things, noticing what works, what doesn't, and what feels good. This kind of practice can be creative and playful—you don't have to get it right immediately; it helps to try different approaches and get feedback so you can develop what works together.

Through the practice, Jacob notices that Steve is open to some contact, as long as he keeps it light and casual and doesn't ask Steve to shift completely from the state he's in. Steve does need time to wake up but can connect lightly if he doesn't feel a ton of pressure to plan the day. Steve starts to feel more respected; he sees the effort Jacob is making to figure out how to bridge their difference. He feels some room to connect more to Jacob by kissing him on the cheek, saying good morning, giving him a sweet look, and then going for the coffee. "Just give me thirty minutes and we can talk about the day," Steve says. The fact that he's connecting a little and giving his partner a time frame feels like an improvement for Jacob. To Jacob, thirty minutes feels okay and much better than worrying he might have to wait an hour or more to plan their day, and he's glad they're not arguing before the day has begun.

Jacob practices saying good morning and kissing Steve without interrupting his wake-up routine or putting pressure on him to interact much or plan. Steve practices being a little more engaging and also aware that Jacob probably doesn't want to wait too long to plan the day.

After trying a few things, they land on a sequence that feels good to both of them. Steve connects more with Jacob right when he wakes up, and Jacob respects Steve's need for a slower morning. Beyond having the concept in theory, they now know the moves that feel good to bridge their difference. Steve gives Jacob a clear timeline to when they can plan the day, which allows Jacob to look forward to that moment rather than wondering when it will feel okay. They practice it a few more times just to make sure it's familiar to them, and then set their intention to use it the next morning and see how it goes.

It would have been easy for Steve and Jacob to keep arguing about the mornings, their different ways of waking up, and continue getting frustrated with each other. Sitting and talking about it wasn't resolving much, but practicing the motions with their bodies helped them feel confident as a couple that they could conquer that situation and know how to better care for each other in those moments.

Exercise

Think of an issue you have with a loved one or partner. Consider how those interactions begin and how they go south: What is the sequence of events in terms of mood, words, or behavior? If you can invite that person to practice with you, that is best, but if not, you can do this exercise on your own. If you're practicing solo, simply imagine being with the person you have the difficult issue with and consider what a smoother interaction might look like. What do you each need to do differently? Visualize a practice session with them and think about how you would each practice different behaviors until the new pattern feels more connecting. How would you take joint responsibility for the issue? What different behaviors might you try? How would you set an intention as a team to get better, then try things in a playful manner to figure out what works? And would you feel comfortable repeating the successful interaction until it's more ingrained in procedural memory?

If you do have a partner for this exercise, here are steps you can follow:

1. Pick an issue (not your worst issue).

2. Describe what doesn't go well together and get on the same page with the problem.

3. Sit facing each other at close range and make eye contact, just so you can connect and set the intention for practice. If the scenario involves standing or moving, you can then get up to act it out.

4. First, do the interaction in the usual and problematic way, so your bodies and emotions remember how disconnecting that feels.

5. Then practice a better way of having the interaction, with both of you coming up with new approaches. Get feedback from your partner on what you're doing and watch their reaction to see what works.

6. Once you find a better way of interacting on the issue, practice the new pattern and skills over and over—at least three times— until they feel familiar. That moves the new behavior and skills more into procedural memory, where they are available to you under stress, such as when you get triggered or argue.

Keep the practice fun and lighthearted if you can. Don't use your most sensitive issue first, but train with something more manageable until you have experience with the process. Do your best to avoid judgments or criticism. Support each other in trying new things.

You can also practice with your kid(s). They might think it's fun to act out problem patterns and think of ways to improve those interactions and will likely appreciate your effort to include their sensitivities and feedback into finding better solutions. It gives them a voice in your dynamic, allowing their thoughts, feelings, and ideas to shape how you do things. And practice is physical, which can be more fun and engaging than talking about an issue. For example, if you have a problematic morning routine with your kiddo getting ready for school, you might set up the scenario and practice it for ten minutes, looking for ways of moving through that time that are more connecting and better serve both your needs.

Dedicating ourselves to growth, bringing humility and curiosity to conversations, and allowing our relationship to help shape us into better people are all key parts of practice culture. Identifying the specific areas that we need to adjust, devising a strategy for growth, and engaging in repetitive training and practice that improve our default skills in those areas give the brain and body the support they need to develop new skills and retain them.

Even couples with longtime negative patterns can benefit from practice. I've worked with partners who have been married twenty or thirty years, and they have still been able to improve their relationship significantly and achieve much greater satisfaction with each other. No matter how long you have persisted in an unhealthy pattern, the future can be brighter, your friendship can improve, you can learn how to relax more around each other, and you can enjoy your time together.

Yes, the longer you have persisted in a rut, the longer it may take to change it. Instead of seeing this as a reason for despair, this can motivate you to dedicate even more time and effort to improvement in order to accelerate change. If your relationship is newer, you can be inspired to handle issues before they become chronic and establish good connecting habits at the outset of your relationship. Whatever your circumstance, don't lose hope. I've seen couples in a bad cycle for a decade or more who then turn it around and have an incredible, rich, and fulfilling future. Everything you do to improve relationship skills is a good investment in yourself, your sense of well-being, and your family's health.

The power and beauty of practice is that it can be fun, it normalizes the process of giving each other feedback and filling in blind spots, and it is effective at improving relationship skills. The title *More Than Words* refers to the fact that humans measure connection in important nonverbal and subconscious ways, but it also refers to the fact that conversations are often not enough to improve the skills we need in relationship. We have to retrain our procedural systems through practice and repetition, involving our bodies, nonverbal behaviors, and communication. Once you understand what you're up against—years of conditioning around negative habits from our developmental years in childhood and years of using those default behaviors in relationships—then you have a sense of what it takes to improve those habits: effort, dedication, and repetition. But even just a little practice can improve a problem scenario and give you hope that you have a system for addressing issues that shares blame rather than offers criticism. I've seen even just a ten-minute practice session be helpful. Give it a try!

Notes

1. Sudha Shashwati and Preksha Kansal, "Is There a Right Way to Love?: Mindset in Romantic Relationships," *International Journal of Innovative Studies in Sociology and Humanities (IJISSH)* (February 2019).

2. John Gottman and Nan Silver, *The Seven Principles for Making Marriage Work: A Practical Guide from the Country's Foremost Relationship Expert* (New York: Harmony, 2015).

3. Daniel Goleman, "New View of Mind Gives Unconscious an Expanded Role," *New York Times*, February 7,1984, 1.

4. Daniel Siegel, *The Developing Mind: Toward a Neurobiology of Interpersonal Experience* (New York: Guilford, 1999).

5. Stan Tatkin, "How Couples Change. A Psychobiological Approach to Couple Therapy (PACT)," in *How People Change: Relationships and Neuroplasticity in Psychotherapy*, ed. Marion F. Solomon and Daniel J. Siegel, Norton Series on Interpersonal Neurobiology (New York: W. W. Norton, 2017), 320.

6. Allan Rosenblatt, "Insight, Working Through, and Practice: The Role of Procedural Knowledge," *Journal of the American Psychoanalytic Association* 52, no. 1 (March 2004): 189–207.

7. Francine Lapides, "The Implicit Realm in Couples Therapy: Improving Right Hemisphere Affect-Regulating Capabilities," *Clinical Social Work Journal* 39, no. 2 (June 2011): 161–169.

8. Stan Tatkin, "Applying a Psychobiological Approach to the Identification and Treatment of Socialemotional Deficits in Couple Therapy," *Psychotherapy in Australia* 19, no. 4 (August 2013): 14.

9. Rosenblatt, "Insight, Working Through, and Practice."

10. Solomon and Siegel, eds., *How People Change.*

11. Daryl L. Chow, Scott D. Miller, Jason A. Seidel, Robert T. Kane, Jennifer A. Thornton, and William P. Andrews, "The Role of Deliberate Practice in the Development of Highly Effective Psychotherapists," *Psychotherapy* 52, no. 3 (2015): 337.

12. Addie Johnson, "Procedural Memory and Skill Acquisition," in *Handbook of Psychology*, 2nd ed., vol. 4, *Experimental Psychology*, ed. Alice F. Healey and Robert W. Proctor (Hoboken: Wiley, 2012).

13. Susan M. Andersen and Elizabeth Przybylinski, "Shared Reality in Interpersonal Relationships," *Current Opinion in Psychology* 23 (October 2018): 42–46.

14. Maya Rossignac-Milon and E. Tory Higgins, "Epistemic Companions: Shared Reality Development in Close Relationships," *Current Opinion in Psychology* 23 (October 2018): 66–71.

15. Maya Rossignac-Milon, Niall Bolger, Katherine S. Zee, Erica J. Boothby, and E. Tory Higgins, "Merged Minds: Generalized Shared Reality in Dyadic Relationships," *Journal of Personality and Social Psychology* 120, no. 4 (July 2020).

16. Richard F. West, Russell J. Meserve, and Keith E. Stanovich, "Cognitive Sophistication Does Not Attenuate the Bias Blind Spot," *Journal of Personality and Social Psychology* 103, no. 3 (September 2012): 506.

17. K. Anders Ericsson, "The Differential Influence of Experience, Practice, and Deliberate Practice on the Development of Superior Individual Performance of Experts," in *The Cambridge Handbook of Expertise and Expert Performance*, ed. K. A. Ericsson, R. R. Hoffman, A. Kozbelt, and A. M. Williams, Cambridge Handbooks in Psychology (Cambridge: Cambridge University Press, 2018), 745–769.

18. K. Anders Ericsson, Ralf T. Krampe, and Clemens Tesch-Römer, "The Role of Deliberate Practice in the Acquisition of Expert Performance," *Psychological Review* 100, no. 3 (1993): 363.

19. Stephen W. Porges, "The Polyvagal Theory: New Insights into Adaptive Reactions of the Autonomic Nervous System," *Cleveland Clinic Journal of Medicine* 76, Suppl. 2 (April 2009): S86.

20. Pat Ogden, Kekuni Minton, and Clare Pain, *Trauma and the Body: A Sensorimotor Approach to Psychotherapy*, Norton Series on Interpersonal Neurobiology (New York: W. W. Norton, 2006).

6.

Process over Content

Redirecting attention from conversation to present-moment experience and from the past to the present engages exploration and curiosity.

—Ron Kurtz

Process over content is an approach to interactions that prioritizes connection over communication, helping you to stay close and improving your communication, verbal and nonverbal. The concept can be a little hard to get at first, and when I work with my clients on it, it takes a few times to get the hang of it. We're so used to focusing on what we want to say and not used to keeping track of how it feels, how we sound, or how we might score the overall interaction based on its connecting value. Remaining aware of the *process* of talking over the content of the dialogue takes some practice. One little trick to use is to measure your connection at the start of an interaction using a 1 to 10 scale and then measure it again in your head every five minutes. Is this interaction increasing connection? If not, why not? Often, it's because we're persisting in disconnecting behaviors or focusing too much on the content and not making enough room for connecting moves that communicate care and security. With a little more attention on our *process* of communication, we can connect much more effectively.

Legendary relationship researcher Dr. John Gottman noticed the power of prioritizing process over content in observing hundreds of couples and noticing which ones stayed together and had satisfying relationships.[1] He noticed that on the one hand, healthy partners were not exempt from arguing, but what distinguished them from unhealthy couples was *how* they argued and how quickly they made up. Healthy couples took care of each other more in conversations, noticed changes in mood, and balanced the conversation to keep arguments in a more tolerable range. They managed stress and relaxation well when communicating, sensing when one person was getting worked up and taking steps toward alleviating stress in the moment. And healthy couples even tended to build some compliments into their disagreements, easing the process of conversation. On the other hand, unhealthy couples did not care for each other well in arguments and argued in more self-centered ways that prioritized one individual at the expense of the other.[2]

Often, disputes escalate because we don't pause in the moment to care for how we're feeling. One person gets frustrated and starts elevating their voice and getting more defensive, or both people do, and the argument is then off to the races. If you're watching your process carefully, you might pause in those moments to check in on such feelings: "Why is the conversation frustrating? Is there anything we can do to bring down the stress of it?" Checking in when conversations start to go south helps you connect in the moment and collaborate on making the conversation feel better. If you keep focusing on content once difficult feelings show up, it's likely to lead to a worse argument. But if you can trust the relationship enough to be vulnerable around how the process feels, it keeps you in a healthy range of communication.

Neuroscience describes why attention to the process of relationships is so important. Our minds have trouble staying open and curious when our nervous systems feel threatened or under stress. When a process of interaction feels unpleasant or precarious, we get insecure and anxious and lose the ability to see someone else's point of view and hold differences flexibly.[3] Our ability to empathize, care, and share feelings in a constructive manner goes down.[4]

Under the stress of an unhealthy process, we resort to more primitive strategies of engagement. We get loud, fight for attention, close our minds, and get defensive. We get so caught up in what we want to say and our individual experience that we lose track of how the interaction feels to others. We miss facial expressions that tell us in real time how someone is feeling. Even when we do register that information, we sometimes blow past it and keep talking to make our point. We sometimes want others to listen to us regardless of how we're sharing, but speaking in an alienating and self-centered way doesn't serve our purpose, and alters the sense of goodwill and the context in which your words are understood.

When we notice difficult patterns in our interactions with others, we need to focus on *how* we're talking instead of *what* we're talking about and practice a process that feels safe, pleasant, and secure before we get back to the content. Ultimately, when you take care of your process of conversation, you develop more trust in having healthy communication, allowing you to relax. You anticipate enjoying your conversations and feeling cared for. You might need to slow down at first to practice this, but it gets more automatic with time and then you find you can dialogue at normal speed while still monitoring how it feels. Practicing this creates safety and trust in the nervous system and opens your minds to new learning so you can grow and explore new possibilities together.

Process over content involves:

- Placing a greater priority on how the conversation feels over what you're talking about
- Pausing the conversation if it starts to feel off or stressful, and collaborating to interact differently
- Pivoting to care for each other, take a break from the conversation, change your state, or simply reset and pay attention to how each of you is feeling before returning to the content

When conversing with your partner, if it feels good, carry on! If it doesn't, commit to noticing the disconnect in the moment and pivot, whether it's in yourself, helping the person you're talking to shift or feel soothed, or doing something together to improve the interaction. When you're process focused, you trust that the content of your communication will get handled even more effectively and enjoyably if you pause to regroup.

The Pause and Pivot

Having a process focus requires that you track little—and not so little—cues that reveal how the communication is going. You'll know from your partner's facial expression or their eyes, tone, or body language if the conversation feels safe and connected or not. Some of the early signs of stress are more subtle, so you have to pay close attention to catch them before they become frustration or hopelessness.

Next, learn to "pause and pivot" when you notice disconnection. Noticing signs of distress but not changing your approach is a surefire way to create escalating arguments. The *pause and pivot* gives you an opportunity to return the interaction to a more pleasant and comfortable way of speaking before continuing with the content. For example, if one of you is getting defensive or feeling hurt or insulted, you can pause the topic of the conversation to ask about those feelings and care about them. If a person is tired of talking, you might take a break. If someone is having trouble maintaining attention, you may need to walk and talk, massage hands, or continue over a meal. If the conversation feels toxic, you might need to discuss how to change your approach so it feels less hurtful before you go on. In all cases, you address how the process is feeling for both partners in the moment so that negative emotions don't escalate and so neither of you gets flooded by stress or overwhelmed.

Prioritizing process over content is a joint responsibility. If one of you pauses to check in on how the conversation is feeling, the other understands the method and can also get curious about how it could feel more pleasant. If one person is committed to content and can't pivot, or doesn't want to focus on process, it's difficult to turn the ship and the conversation may continue to escalate in a negative direction. And like most relationship skills, the more you practice this technique, the easier it becomes to pull it off. And because it's so effective at creating more enjoyable interactions, it becomes self-rewarding: each time you use it tends to reinforce how much easier it can make your communication and can help resolve difficult patterns, causing you to want to use it more.

Process over content also makes use of an important principle in relationships: that partnership bonds can help heal wounds from the past that surface in our interactions. Sensitive conversations often elicit core wounds and triggers—things that make us anxious or hurt and that connect to past wounds in childhood or in previous relationships. Those triggers can make us less rational, or just more vulnerable and emotionally fragile in conversations. By focusing on the process of conversation and not just the content, you can notice when those triggers surface and provide emotional support in the moment. By your being willing to pause the conversation and notice feelings, these core wounds and traumas receive the care they need to be less active in the background.

Core Issues

Core issues are generally defined as personal triggers we don't handle well that are often tied to childhood traumas or subconscious defenses. Core issues are wired so deeply into our minds and bodies that it is difficult to see them or avoid the behaviors that result from them. They can include negative thoughts about yourself, a sensitivity to feedback, the residual effects of trauma, emotional ne-glect, or abuse, and can show up in repetitive bad habits like ignoring others when you're overwhelmed, avoiding difficult conversations, rising quickly to anger, or getting defensive. Core issues are often unwieldy—once you get trig-gered, it's hard to be reasonable, open-minded, or act relationally.

Tending to process instead of content can help you manage core issues well enough not to threaten each other or the relationship, because you can pivot to offer care when they pop. This approach protects the relationship from the acti-vation and intense feelings we have in such moments and keeps the relationship off thin ice when you hit those spots. Some of the hardest moments occur when two people's core issues get activated at the same time. Both partners become less reasonable, less open-minded, and feel emotionally overwhelmed together. In those situations, there isn't really one partner who can be the bigger person and care for the other. In addition, because core issues often represent things that deeply matter to our sense of well-being, we also lose a sense of security and support in such moments and fear the relationship can't properly take care of us. The connecting cues and skills in this book will help you function securely even when you're both triggered. In those moments, you generally need to rely on nonverbal connection to signal that you still care about each other, and give your nervous systems a chance to reset and feel soothed. Continuing with con-tent will often result in a bad fight where people say things or behave in ways they later regret.

Healing the Root of Your Communication

While we communicate to convey information, the main reason we communicate in close relationships is to feel understood, loved, cared for, and connected. We can tolerate differences of opinion if our interactions feel loving, but when they don't, our words start to try to carry water for the disconnection we feel and our conversations get cumbersome. Our topics of conversation become ambassadors to try to get back to a sense of connection, but they don't get there efficiently.

It happens to most of us: we start arguing about aspects of joint life, like cleanliness, time, money, parenting; and without a healthy process for commu-nication, it's easy to get lost in the weeds of debates about those things and to start feeling negatively about the relationship. The more your process is broken, the more hopeless you get about being cared for and getting back to a positive view of the relationship again. Process over content helps you bring the focus to what matters most—your pattern of interaction, how it feels, and your sense of connection in the moment—rather than the never-ending to-do list of life.

When you have a challenging *pattern* of communication, litigating one topic or issue doesn't improve how you feel about the issue or the relationship, because the overall process of communication is broken and it impacts how you feel with each other. Conversely, improving your *process* of communication facilitates better, more connected interactions across all topics. You'll have a better foundation for the really difficult conversations and can handle lesser issues easily. Focusing on process also sends each other a signal that says, *I care more about you and how you feel than resolving this right away.* You don't forget the core task of relationship—which is to care for each other—in favor of the topic of the day or the issue at hand.

Process over content starts to correct your communication patterns at the root by tending to your sense of connection in the moment and by sweetly addressing the emotions that come up in interactions rather than neglecting them. Sometimes it takes longer to get to what you need to say when you have a process focus because you take care of feelings that show up along the way. As long as topics don't get postponed indefinitely, it's helpful to move slowly through challenging conversations, notice feelings, and care for them in real time before moving forward. This slower and more methodical way of speaking where you track emotions and ask about them is a process of loving each other in the deep stuff that comes up when you're navigating sensitive territory.

How to Practice Process over Content

You can practice process over content in real time in natural conversations, developing an awareness of being in the moment and handling feelings as they arise, or you can set aside time for intentional practice. I recommend both. The steps are the same, but if you're engaging in deliberate practice you can move through the steps more slowly, take turns practicing, and share what you notice about how the process of communication is different. If you're wanting to use it in real conversations to see how those can become healthier and more productive, you can challenge yourself to engage in the following steps anytime you're interacting with someone:

1. Monitor the people you're speaking with closely to catch any signs of frustration, annoyance, hurt feelings, or stress early. Look at their eyes, face, and body language, and listen to their tone of voice to notice signs of distress. You may need to slow your interactions down a bit at first to catch the information you're looking for.

2. Monitor your own mind and body so that you are aware as soon as you begin to feel frustrated, annoyed, or hurt in the conversation. Keep track of your feelings and emotions and ask for a pause and pivot and for care as needed to keep the conversation feeling pleasant and so you can stay relaxed in the interaction and not get overwhelmed.

3. When you start to feel disconnected, be willing to pause and check in. Ask your partner how they're feeling in the conversation, or share how you're feeling, and work together to reset the conversation to be more pleasant in its process before continuing.

4. Remember that resets can take many forms. You can pivot an interaction by changing your environment. For example, if you're indoors, you might move outside. If you're sitting, you might choose to walk and talk. Consider whether you need to eat, get some water, or take a break and come back later. Sometimes just taking a deep breath, making eye contact, and holding hands is enough to reconnect you. Do whatever works.

5. Keep in mind that you don't necessarily need to pause the conversation to reset. If you both need more soothing, give each other an arm or hand massage as you talk. It's a nice way to stay connected while resetting the conversation. If one of you needs reassurance, you can provide it before you continue talking by saying, "I love you and we're discussing this just so we can get stronger and better and love each other even more." Breaks can be helpful at times, but learning to reset and pivot conversations together in the moment so you can keep going gives you a confidence as a couple that you

can manage how interactions feel and don't always have to go away from each other to de-stress and reset.

6. After you pivot, keep monitoring your feelings to make sure it had the intended effect. If not, why not? What else is needed to help you both relax, feel secure, and be able to open your minds, listen, and care for each other? Caring for the process of conversation also helps you understand deeper feelings you have in the relationship and what you may need in conversations to feel more secure.

Process over Content Examples

Example One: Parenting Difference

Not only do Deion and Candice have different communication styles, they also have different approaches to parenting their two little boys. In communication, Deion likes to talk about feelings and share a lot and Candice is more matter-of-fact. In parenting, Candice is organized, detail oriented, and believes order and structure help raise good children. Deion is more carefree and thinks having fun and excitement are what is best for kids' well-being. He's willing to bend rules, especially when the kids ask, which drives Candice nuts. A lot of times when they talk about parenting, they both end up feeling criticized. And because the boys are usually around, their parents' talks are often short and sometimes pressured.

As a couple, Deion and Candice decide to break their bad pattern of communication. They recognize that neither one of them enjoys the interactions they have around their parenting differences. They decide to use process over content to be more aware of how those conversations go south.

"One thing I notice is how stressed we are sometimes when we sit down to talk," says Deion.

"That's true," responds Candice. "It's so hard to talk around the boys, or when we're tired from dealing with them."

"Why don't we try to notice when we're stressed and try to not let it affect our conversations so much?" says Deion.

"Okay," responds Candice. "We can try."

The next time Candice gets upset with Deion for changing the rules, she decides to talk to him about it but also wants to practice a better process of communication. "Hey, sweetie," she says, "can I talk to you about something? But I also think we should try to practice paying attention to our process as we're talking like we discussed."

"Sure thing," says Deion.

"Well, first of all, how relaxed are we?" asks Candice.

"Mmmm, I don't know, maybe a five out of ten?" responds Deion.

"Me too," says Candice. "That should be good for a start. Let's notice if it changes as we talk."

Candice shares that she got frustrated when Deion blew off an important rule about bedtime on a school night without checking with her. "I feel disrespected," she says.

"Well, I feel like you don't trust me as a parent," Deion answers defensively. "I have to be able to spend time with them the way I like to!"

"I know, but kids need structure and you're always changing it when you don't need to!" responds Candice. "Like today, you could have spent more time with them in the afternoon, not at nine thirty pm!"

"But sometimes we're doing fun, bonding stuff at weird times. It's hard to predict. I feel like you're too rigid," Deion returns.

At this point they notice that the conversation is already starting to feel contentious. Candice can hear Deion's frustration in his tone of voice and he can see the tension and annoyance on her face. "Let's practice our new tools," says Candice.

"Good idea," Deion agrees.

"Okay, what would help us be less defensive but each listen to the other?" asks Candice.

"Honestly, we get so tired at the end of the day, maybe, like, a foot rub while we talk about it?" answers Deion.

"Good idea," says Candice. "I love foot rubs." They take a couple minutes to massage each other without words, to remind them of their connection.

Once relaxed, Candice shares, "I guess the bottom line is that I worry about the kids not having structure. I felt like that as a kid and it made me nervous. It's not a huge deal that they go to bed a bit late once in a while, but I want our parenting to be consistent enough where they don't feel a sense of chaos or a lack of direction. I remember that feeling. My dad was often gone, and my mom would be busy, on the phone or with friends. I didn't know what to do or what was right sometimes."

"I don't want you to feel nervous or worried," Deion shares. "I think we're good parents, though, but I worry about not sharing my spontaneous, fun-loving nature with them. They deserve to see that side of me and I love being that with them. They're kids! They should have fun! But I want you to feel respected and not worried. I'll try to do a better job checking with you if you can be willing to be more flexible."

"I think that could work if we stay connected like this," says Candice. They both notice that the pause and pivot helped them connect and made the conversation much more pleasant. Ultimately, the health of their relationship depends more on *how* they talk than what they talk about. If Deion and Candice can track each other's emotions in their interactions and pause when they get stressed to care for each other, they will become better communicators and will feel bonded even if their parenting differences are always a part of their family life.

Example Two: Power Dynamic

Sally and Joe have been married ten years. They consider themselves to have a fairly healthy relationship, but there's something in their communication that has been bothering Sally for years. To her, Joe often sounds condescending and belittling when he speaks to her. She feels hurt by his tone and demeanor. In addition, when she brings it up to him Joe gets defensive and blames her for being overly emotional and sensitive.

Joe doesn't know he's coming across as condescending, and while he doesn't mean to, he also hasn't been open to looking at it. At this point, Sally mostly puts up with it and occasionally just walks away from conversations or rolls her eyes. Joe seems content to not talk about it. They can both feel the disconnect that's there at times, but other times are good, so they've mostly resigned themselves to the dynamic.

If this sounds familiar, it's because many couples choose to live with unhealthy patterns they feel helpless to change. They don't want to break up because the relationship is "good enough," but when they try to tackle certain issues either one or both are not prepared to look at things or they don't have the skills to navigate them constructively. Let's see if process over content can help Sally and Joe (and maybe you as well).

Sally decides to try focusing more on the process of conversation with Joe. "Hi, Joe," she says to him one day. "You know that communication thing we talk about sometimes, where I feel you're being harsh and you say you're just communicating normally? Well, I think it would help us be closer and more relaxed if we worked together to improve that. I'm sure I have my part. Next time we talk, I'd like us to pay closer attention and notice when one of us gets annoyed. Maybe we'll catch something that will deepen our ability to feel more at peace with each other."

"Sounds fine," says Joe, "as long as we don't have to go into the whole thing. You know how I get tired of all that."

The next day, Joe saw Sally putting some things away in the kitchen in a way he didn't like and said, "I thought I told you those things don't go there! Can't you remember? They go over there because we don't use them much!"

Feeling offended and hurt, Sally figured she'd try their new process.

"Joe, can we talk about something?" Sally asks.

"What?" responds Joe.

Sally answers, "I felt really belittled by the way you spoke to me. But I don't think you meant it or that it's your fault—I know your family speaks to one another that way. It makes me feel so unloved, so disconnected from you. I'd like us to work together to be better as partners."

"Well, I don't know what to do," replies Joe. "You're always unhappy with the way I say things."

"I know," says Sally, "but I think we can get better at how we speak to one another. Maybe we can try to slow down in those moments and notice what you feel and what I feel. Like right now, I'm glad that we're able to talk about it."

"That's good," answers Joe, "but in the moment, I often feel criticized. I also don't like these long conversations where we process things that happened. They feel heavy."

"I don't want you to feel criticized," says Sally, "and I don't want you to get stuck in annoying conversations about things, but I do need a way to tell you when something doesn't feel good; otherwise I get resentful and it sticks with me. Is there a way I could tell you I feel hurt that wouldn't feel critical?"

"Yes. If you don't sound so negative, or just focus on the bad things, it would be easier for me. Like maybe you can say, 'You're a great husband and I really appreciate everything you do, but the way you said that hurt my feelings.' Just that little appreciation would help me take in what you're saying," Joe responds.

"That's a good point," says Sally. "Sometimes I just focus on the negative and don't remind you that I also appreciate you. I can practice that more. How is this conversation going so far for you?"

"It feels fine," Joe notes, "not as unpleasant as some of them. It's the longer ones that go on and on I don't like."

"Well, let's keep it brief, then," says Sally, "but I think it's great that we can talk about moments like that when I felt hurt; it's an improvement over our usual way of neglecting it. How about if we spend five minutes discussing what happened and how we can do better and feel more loved, and then I'll leave you alone and we can relax?"

"Sure," Joe agrees. "Honestly, putting a time limit on these conversations does help me relax and listen better."

Placing a timer on sensitive or emotional conversations often helps those who are less comfortable in such interactions relax, as they don't feel trapped in a conversation that feels stressful to them and never-ending. Because Joe and Sally are focusing on how their process of communication feels and not just what they have to say, this conversation is going better than usual.

"Can I make some tea while we talk?" asks Joe. "Having something to do with my hands might help me focus on the conversation."

Sally agrees, then says, "I think what happens to me in those moments when you speak to me in those ways is that I feel belittled, like you don't feel I deserve your respect. I don't think you mean to come off that way, but that's how it feels. I feel horrible, hurt, like I'm not your equal, and then I don't want to connect with you the rest of the day."

"Of course you're my equal! What are you talking about!" says Joe, elevating his voice. "You should know I respect you by now."

Sally pauses and notices that Joe's shoulders are hunched forward and that he seems more tense.

"It seems like you're feeling defensive or angry," she says, noticing the moment and curious about what's happening for Joe.

"Well, yeah," Joe says. "Every time you say this, all I hear is that the way me and my family talk is bad and aggressive and mean and that I'm always the problem. I don't like that."

Sally nods and passes him the teacups.

"I guess I get a little defensive when you point out how I say things," he continues. "My mother was always so critical of everything I did when I was little; I could do nothing right in her eyes." Joe pours the water over the tea. "I really don't want you to feel the way you described," he says, showing care in the moment. He touches her hand, a signal of connection. "I now get defensive when you give me that feedback, but I also know I need to be better in how I say things to you." His acknowledgment means a lot to Sally.

"That's a good insight about your mom," says Sally. "I hadn't made that connection, but it makes sense in terms of why these conversations are difficult and why you don't like it when I give you feedback."

"I'll try to work on how I speak to you," says Joe.

"That's good," says Sally. "The other thing is that in these conversations about those moments, I often don't feel like you care about me and my experience because sometimes you get defensive and it feels dismissive."

"Well, you may be right, but it's also how I feel when you're constantly giving me feedback and making it sound like I'm doing something wrong all the time," answers Joe.

They then join hands, which helps them feel a little more connected in this tense part. "I think if you can make it clear that I'm not just in trouble or that you think I'm a good person, it would be easier to hear," he says.

"I'd be willing to practice that," Sally replies. "I think you're a good person, and I know it's just a bad habit."

"And I want you to feel loved when you bring something to me, not dismissed. I know I'm not great at that. How is this conversation feeling to you?" he asks.

"Pretty good. I appreciate you asking. I think the fact that we're checking in periodically is helping. I feel more cared for. I can help you by being a little less critical and more reassuring that I still think you're a good person when those things happen," says Sally. "Why don't we practice a bit? What would you say to me if I told you I felt hurt by something you said?"

"Well, if I wasn't defensive, I might say, 'I'm really sorry you feel that way; I will watch my tone,' and then I could come give you a hug," Joe answers.

"I would like that very much," Sally replies. "I think this was a productive conversation and I feel better. And I want to keep it short so you don't feel stuck in a long processing of feelings. The next time I get my feelings hurt, I'd like to be able to talk about it again and I'll be mindful to be a little more positive toward you as well."

"That would be great," says Joe, "and I'll be open to talking about it and being more caring."

They practice their new sequence of him listening better and caring for her hurt feelings and Sally being more affirming a few times to make sure they're comfortable with it. Joe practices saying he's sorry she feels hurt and coming over to give her a hug, and Sally practices being less negative and reminding him he's still a good person. By bringing some attention to their process of communication—how he gets defensive and feels criticized and how she feels frustrated and dismissed—and practicing a better way to handle those moments, they're beginning to have hope that they can have better communication around this issue. And their conversation about it actually went pretty well because they checked in with each other every few minutes and stayed connected.

By rehearsing a better process of communication, Sally and Joe are prepared for moments of disconnection and have rehearsed some ways of responding to them. Sally can practice ways to bring things up that don't elicit as much defensiveness, and Joe can practice sounding caring rather than dismissive until Sally gives him a thumbs-up that it's working. They may need more time to feel confident that they can reconnect smoothly, but they're on the right track and both are now showing enough team spirit and willingness to tackle the issue together that they can make forward traction.

A Process Focus and Advanced Couples

Research literature on healthy relationships sometimes refers to "master couples," whom I call advanced couples. These pairs tend to their connection, monitor their process of interaction and pivot as needed, track each other's needs in real time, and clean up mistakes quickly so resentments don't linger. They are willing to be honest with each other, but in a way that is connecting and caring, and they navigate the balance well of being authentically themselves and giving the relationship what it needs to feel secure.[5]

Process over content is a key part of learning how to be an advanced couple. We all get self-absorbed at times, especially when we're upset or hurt. Advanced couples defend against self-centeredness and keep the focus on taking care of both people at the same time and on what the relationship needs.[6] If one person is upset, they help them, but not by sacrificing their own core requirements. Rather than present their own needs selfishly, they keep track of their partner's needs and can champion those as well. It takes some practice, skill building, psychological flexibility, and emotional resilience to care for two people at once and function as a team even when upset, but it can be done. When you practice process over content, you are building those skills that teach you how to care for yourself and each other simultaneously so that the relationship does not suffer when one or both partners are having a hard time.

Process over content embodies the skill set of the advanced couple because it requires combining many of the skills that promote connection. Tending to feelings, tracking emotional changes, staying in touch with our own needs, and connecting nonverbally are important to developing a process of interaction that fosters closeness.[7] Process over content, and the emotional awareness it takes, is emblematic of one of the most important skills advanced couples have: the ability to go slow, track emotion, and care for each person in real time.

Focusing on the process of your connection can heal bad communication habits and past emotional wounds because it asks you to show up in real time. It connects the care you can offer each other in the moment to the triggers and wounds that surface in your interactions, allowing you to eventually forge a more secure relationship.

Exercise to Develop a Process Focus

Select a topic you talk about often in which the conversation gets difficult. You're going to practice shifting the focus of your conversation from the content to the process of talking. It helps to have a partner for this exercise. If you're in a primary romantic relationship, I recommend practicing with your partner, but you can pick a friend or family member as well.

Start to talk about the issue and notice how the default focus is often on the topic itself more than on how each person feels. Keep going for a couple minutes, the way you normally might in such a conversation. You want to get far enough along where your differences start to show, where you debate your different perspectives or even begin to get annoyed or frustrated.

At that point, pause and take a moment to notice how you feel. How would you describe it? How does your partner seem to feel? Are they smiling and relaxed? Are you? Or does talking feel annoying or stressful? Share with each other and notice if you accurately read how the other was feeling at that point in the conversation. Don't be afraid to say, "Yeah, it was starting to feel a little stressful." Or, "I guess I was starting to get a little frustrated or annoyed." It's better to be honest and pivot than hide a feeling of annoyance that might escalate into an argument.

Collaborate on ways to make the conversation feel easier to relax into. Come up with some ideas, and try them. Notice if they work. Be creative. Try taking a moment of silence or rededicating yourselves to notice each other's state and stress level in the conversation with an activity like massaging each other's hands or taking a walk and talking. Look into each other's eyes and state your intent in the conversation and say something you love and appreciate about the other to reassure each other.

Before you return to the content, notice if you have succeeded in changing your mood in the conversation to feel more connected. Once you've pivoted to make the discussion feel more relaxing, you can go back to the topic again. Notice how you can maintain awareness of both how you're feeling in the conversation as well as the topic, tracking those two aspects of your interactions at the same time. Be willing to comment on how the process feels at any time if either of you needs a reset or some support to feel secure and relax.

You can continue to monitor your feelings as you go to make sure the process of interaction feels good. Some content will always be challenging and bring up anxiety, fear, stress, or core differences, but the way you care for those feelings, signal friendliness and security, and show respect to your values or perspectives is what allows you to stay connected. That closeness and trust balance out your differences, helping you communicate smoothly and make decisions collaboratively, bringing you one step closer to deep connection.

Notes

1. John Mordechai Gottman and Julie Schwartz Gottman, "Gottman Method Couple Therapy," in *Clinical Handbook of Couple Therapy*, 4th ed., ed. Alan S. Gurman (New York: Guilford, 2008), 138–164.

2. John M. Gottman, Julie S. Gottman, Andy Greendorfer, and Mirabai Wahbe, "An Empirically Based Approach to Couples' Conflict," in *The Handbook of Conflict Resolution: Theory and Practice*, ed. P. T. Coleman, M. Deutsch, and E. C. Marcus (San Francisco: Jossey-Bass/Wiley, 2014), 898–920.

3. Daniel J. Siegel, "Mindfulness Training and Neural Integration: Differentiation of Distinct Streams of Awareness and the Cultivation of Well-Being," *Social Cognitive and Affective Neuroscience* 2, no. 4 (2007): 259–263.

4. Stephen W. Porges, "Neuroception: A Subconscious System for Detecting Threats and Safety," *Zero to Three (J)* 24, no. 5 (2004): 19–24.

5. John M. Gottman and Julie S. Gottman, "Difficulties with Clients in Gottman Method Couples Therapy," in *Transforming Negative Reactions to Clients: From Frustration to Compassion*, ed. A. W. Wolf, M. R. Goldfried, and J. C. Muran (Washington, DC: American Psychological Association, 2013), 91–112.

6. Sue Johnson and M. Kerman, "Emotionally Focused Couple Therapy: It's All about Emotion and Connection," in *Clinical Pearls of Wisdom: 21 Leading Therapists Offer Their Key Insights*, ed. Michael Kerman (New York: W. W. Norton, 2009), 133.

7. Sue Johnson and Brent Bradley, "Emotionally Focused Couple Therapy: Creating Loving Relationships," in *The Wiley-Blackwell Handbook of Family Psychology*, ed. H. Bray and M. Stanton (Hoboken: Wiley-Blackwell, 2009).

7.

Inviting Care

Staying vulnerable is a risk we have to take if we want to experience connection.

—Brené Brown

Most of us are a little shy about inviting care: we're not used to directly asking for our needs to be met. Inviting care is asking for support and attention when you want or need it, especially emotional care. As you learn to use inviting care, you'll find that it's a connecting superpower. It's an efficient way to get back to connection when we get off track, and it helps build strong relationship bonds that support you in life's ups and downs.

Inviting care is a mature, direct, and sweet way to be vulnerable and attract support. For some, especially in more self-reliant societies, welcoming compassion can feel like an admission of weakness or a burdening of others. But the act brings the listener to an action point and often compliments our partners by making them feel important. For example, when others ask us to help them with something, we are often inclined to say yes, if we can. If we can't, we often still find a way to be considerate. It is the same with inviting care. Rather than staying silent when we're upset or want to connect, we can ask for what we need in a positive way that makes others feel great. Rather than hoping others will figure it out when we are hurt or have an issue, or using passive-aggressive strategies, we ask for support directly and make it easy for others to provide it by setting it up in a way that is clear. It's a fast, effective, proactive way to handle hurts and misattunements, and promotes confidence in the security of your relationship.

Inviting care has two parts: Do you expect care, and can you invite it? We sometimes struggle with the first part. Unless we grew up with a lot of emotional support, many of us don't expect care from others when we're struggling. But this is a problem that impacts secure functioning in relationships. To approach our partners or friends with a sweet request for help, we have to believe that care is available for us and that others don't mind providing it. That's a tall order for someone who grew up without it. Being aware that we may not even expect care is an important part of learning how to better invite it. And when you expect it's there for you, your invitations are more positive and work better to elicit the support you need.

Inviting care requires several prerequisite skills to pull off smoothly:

1. **Identifying Your Feelings.** To describe your emotions to others, you must first be able to identify them.
2. **Being Vulnerable.** "Vulnerability" is sometimes used as a synonym for weakness, but in close, trusted relationships being vulnerable enhances connection by disclosing tender feelings and creating opportunities for deeper bonding.
3. **Strong Emotional Skills and Practice.** Inviting care is a culture shift for some that requires a willingness to talk to your partner about hurt feelings, make eye contact, and face your partner when upset and try new ways of asking for support until that approach becomes more natural.

How to Invite Care

While we are typically not used to asking for attention or support, inviting care is one of the most effective methods I've encountered for improving connection and communication in relationships. The way you invite care can make the difference between your partner feeling criticized and getting defensive, and stepping in to understand and care for you in the way you want. Inviting care is a powerful way to get your needs met in relationship and to clean up errors and hurt feelings quickly. You need to see your partner as a resource when you're upset and humbly ask for support with whatever feeling or issue you're experiencing. Often, when something is wrong, we make our partners feel bad because we're hurt or angry and we get critical or imply wrongdoing on their part. While other people definitely have their role in disconnecting interactions, inviting care is a way to make our partners feel good while also giving them feedback and requesting a different way of doing things. Inviting care sees our partner as a caring resource and honors them by signaling that their love and care make a positive difference to us. In that way, we can attract care efficiently while building up the relationship.

The way we invite care illustrates the difference between our intentions in relationships and our default habits. In our intent, we desire to be able to share our feelings and have our partner move toward us to listen, be empathic, and show care. But in our default habits, we often engage in behavior that disables that care. While we want the loving response, we limit it with how we seek (or don't seek) support.

To add to our annoyance, we often don't know we're limiting the care we want. Default habits often move from the subconscious habits developed in childhood and behaviors that live in our blind spots. Almost all of us project past relationship experiences onto our partners even when the current relationship doesn't merit those projections. It's just what the mind does. The mind perceives through memory and assigns intent in others from both conscious and unconscious impressions from earlier in our lives.[1] For example, we may not trust others to emotionally care for us because our parents did not offer such nurture. In the moment, that past experience may be subconscious but still moves us to assume that our partners lack empathy. Because we don't expect compassion to be there or believe it is available, we often get frustrated and critical, feeling hopeless when upset. These perceptions, projections, and unconscious memories are often invisible to us; we only experience the failure of the love we want. And because we're missing the self-awareness to understand our part in the failure, we often attribute the failure to our partners.

When emotional care is lacking in a relationship, a couples therapist may be curious to notice if it's getting disabled on the ask or on the supply side, or both. Often, both the asking and the responding are problematic and involved in the dynamic, but it is often easier to pin the failure on the response. Too often, when we don't receive the care we want we perceive our partners as failing in their support, but we don't stop to think about how we may have asked for that help and if we made it clear that we needed them. In many cases, we may not have asked directly or nicely. Other times, we actively disable it by being critical or blaming, causing others to become defensive and withdrawn. In secure relationships, partners tend to ask clearly for support and set their partners up for success, meaning they make it easy for others to supply care, and then they reinforce by being appreciative. Partners in such relationships also tend to have more skill in providing support, but the ask side is what can make the biggest difference. In insecure relationships, the asking for and supply of care are often obscured, making it difficult for emotional support to happen.

If you include yourself in how the care cycle plays out in your relationship rather than assign blame to your partner, you reclaim your power to have healthier interactions that elicit the love you want. You have more control over your own behavior than that of others, and it's empowering to know that inviting care can attract the care and understanding you deserve. Reducing blame and recognizing that you can shape interactions to be more connecting is self-responsible and makes for healthier relationships.

Of course, relationship is a two-way street and a team effort, so your partner will have to show up and actually deliver care when invited. If they match your effort in reshaping the relationship's culture around emotional support, it makes changing individual habits easier. Notice how you may occasionally disable connecting opportunities when what you really want is love and support. That awareness makes it easier to work together to improve.

Inviting care can be verbal, nonverbal, or a combination of the two. A verbal request for care with matching expression and tone is effective at attracting support. The key is recruiting help from your partner rather than blaming them for failing you. Inviting care nonverbally can be extending your arms for a hug, leaning your head on someone's shoulder, or holding someone's hand. In terms of how it might sound in words, the chart on the following page illustrates how to transform disabling statements into inviting ones.

Inviting care identifies an issue and asks for help with it. It doesn't blame, criticize, or assign judgment. It's a vulnerable request for assistance, and because partners in relationship exist to help each other, it's hard to turn down a request for help when it is sincere and sweet.

Inviting care frames the need as a positive for the relationship, showing what is possible if you get better at something together. For example, "Why do you never listen to me?!" becomes, "I'm feeling hurt in some ways by how we talk. I think we could do better in how we listen to each other. Would you be willing to practice that with me? I think that would help me a lot." Instead of pointing out a negative, it points to the positive. Inviting care also appreciates and thanks our partners for showing up, encouraging that behavior and letting our partners know that they can be successful at supporting us.

Bad Habit	Inviting Care
I hate it when you do that!	Can we work together to improve this?
You never listen!	Would you be willing to listen to me? It would mean a lot to me.
This always happens. You're so frustrating!	I need your help with something. I've been getting really frustrated and I need your support.
You just don't care!	I'm wondering if you would help me with something. Sometimes I feel like you don't care, but I don't know if that's true. Can we work together to figure out how to better support each other?
You're just really bad at caring for me.	I know we can do better, and I know I have my part. Would you be willing to practice ways we can do it better?

Our bad habits can cause us to sound negative and highlight others' behavior when we're needing support. It's important to present our needs in the form of a positive vision for the future that partners can collaborate toward. That reduces defensiveness and creates a shared intent to grow toward the goal together. We tend to have more energy and bandwidth for care if we're moving toward a positive, clearly defined outcome. This doesn't mean we neglect negative emotions or fail to express anger; it means we know how to share those feelings authentically in a way that invites others rather than in a way that pushes them away.

Inviting Care around Anger

Anger deserves care, as it often represents important information about how we feel, but when poorly directed it can disable others' ability to listen and care for our experience. One of the best ways to handle anger is to take a few minutes to discover the vulnerable emotions underneath the anger, which is typically sponsored by more tender emotions like hopelessness, frustration, and disappointment. Those initial emotions can be harder to detect as they move quickly through the subconscious before turning into anger, but once we locate the disappointment, frustration, or helplessness underneath we can share and invite care without the anger guarding the gates.

The best way to express anger is by sharing how you experience it rather than throwing it at others in rage. When we act loud and aggressive, it's often intimidating and disables any care and understanding we could receive. While we may think we're being effective when making our point with anger, we're often compromising the ability of others' brains and nervous systems to listen and to take an interest in their part of the issue. You don't need to hide anger or bury it to be polite. It often contains very important information about your relationship. But don't throw it at people unless you're intentionally trying to start a fight. Others listen better when we can describe our anger and what we're angry about and explain why it's important.

Inviting Care with Kids

Some people worry that inviting care from your kids may cause an inappropriate burden for them. Of course, everything requires balance and moderation—some people do overburden their kids with their need for emotional care or ask their kids to take on adult support roles they're not suited for. But most of the time, involving your kids in your emotional life in an age-appropriate way helps them become more emotionally intelligent and gives them opportunities to practice caring skills like empathy and supporting people in their feelings.

Opening up to your kids within reason helps them avoid a one-person or self-centered psychology, since they get to perceive you as a real human being, rather than just an authority figure, giving you common ground to talk about feelings, including theirs. It is also a less stressful way for your kids to be aware that you're having a hard day, instead of the usual ways moodiness and irritation can come out, like argumentativeness or combativeness.

Expecting Care

Many of us did not grow up in emotionally supportive households and therefore didn't receive much emotional care or see examples of emotional care between others. As a result, inviting care is unfamiliar, in part because we may not even believe we deserve it. That part may be unconscious, but it keeps us from asking for care before we get outwardly angry at our partners for not providing it. When we train ourselves to expect care, we start to see our partners as a resource and ask for support in ways that are more inviting. We also tend to be clearer about what we need and show more gratitude to others for providing it, which reinforces the cycle of providing emotional support.

Inviting care is a practice in sending others a clean signal rather than a muddled one. To make that runway for care as wide and clear as possible, you don't want a conflicted signal. A mixed signal happens when we ask for care but mix it up with subtle jabs, undermining comments, condescension, criticism, or just too many distracting words, or when we throw others off the scent by relaying random anecdotes or saying what we're feeling is not a big deal. Mixed signals are hard to read and distract others from what we need. Relating a painful experience with a smile makes it confusing for others to know what we need.

A clean signal is an invitation that is clear and obvious as to its purpose—in this case, to attract love, understanding, empathy, and support toward us and our experience. A sign of truly expecting care is that you can issue invitations that are clean, obvious, and inviting. To extend a clean signal, it helps to expect care, not just consciously, but all the way through your being, so that your nonverbal invitation is consistent with your words.

When we extend invitations, it's helpful to expect others to meet our needs. It's better to expect care and suffer the disappointment of it not being there than to lose hope that it's there. At least with the first problem, you can work on the relationship's response to need and how to better engage in emotional support. But with the second problem, the request for love and care itself gets disabled and there is little chance for the relationship to work on its failures in responding. When we expect care, we don't feel hopeless. It won't necessarily be there every time, because our partners have bad days, but positive requests for support start to improve your relationship culture and cause partners to be available and responsive more often. When the care isn't there, I recommend making your need more obvious with increased vulnerability and persistence. Sometimes we have to recognize it's not a good time, but in most cases we can get our partner's attention on what we need even if they don't respond well right away.

If you find yourself arguing a lot in relationship, consider whether you are inviting care on the issues that matter to you in an attractive manner. If not, you may have a part in the negative communication pattern. You might reflect a little on past relationships you've had, including those in early childhood, and consider if those experiences gave you confidence that emotional care is available. Did you feel reassured that others would be empathic and support you if you asked? That the support would be attuned and sensitive? Early relationship experiences can shape how clean our signal is when we ask for help and support and how easy we make it for others to provide what we need.

There are other reasons why we may have negative tendencies in inviting care: Personality traits, culture, neurodiversity, or being stoic or independent in our feelings can play a role. Trauma can impact how comfortable we feel being vulnerable and asking for help, including inequity-based trauma such as oppression, racism, and social marginalization. The chronic nature of systemic oppression can leave many feeling distrustful. Despite difficulties we may begin with when it comes to inviting care, we can more readily believe it is available from our close relationships, learn to be more direct, vulnerable, and positive in asking for it, and develop the ability to attract it from others on demand.

Inviting Care in an Integrated Manner

Inviting care is a full-body activity. When our words, facial expressions, tone, and body language are all aligned and communicating need, others get the message to move toward us and support. If others need guidance on the right way to support, you can help them understand how to care for you, and from that vulnerable place it won't sound controlling. Sometimes we try to guide our partners around the care we need, but we do it in a bossy or critical way. That can alienate others or cause them to feel like failures in caring for us. Asking in that way undermines connection in relationship—better to keep things positive. A habit of asking for care with criticism sometimes hides under the radar to those who exhibit that tendency. It benefits from awareness so it does not negatively impact relationships.

Be willing to ask for care in the moment you need it, not later or when others happen to have the time. Few things are more important in relationships than providing love when someone is in emotional need. You may feel like you're burdening your partner to approach them while they're in the middle of something, but we're always in the middle of something and it starts to make the relationship feel special to be able to interrupt each other when we need love and care.

To better integrate your requests for support and have more success attracting care, try to match your nonverbals and your words. For example, if you use positive words while glaring, your partner may respond to your facial expression rather than your language. If you ask your partner to help you with the right words, but in an angry, judgmental way, you probably won't get the response you're looking for. Your requests for help don't need to be perfect—you can feel angry or frustrated or sad and still invite care. But they do need to be sincere so your partner can move toward you with an open heart.

For those who are not accustomed to showing vulnerability, demonstrating that need in your facial expression and tone can be even more difficult than finding the words to ask for support but helps communicate your need in an effective manner. Being too stoic can cause our hurts and struggles to fly under the radar and go unnoticed, or get glossed over by daily life or others' needs. Asking for care with our whole being, perhaps with open body language, and "placing our heart in our partner's hands" creates a clear opportunity.

When others begin to show care, it's good to reinforce it by appreciating them and letting them know they're helping. We might say, "Thank you so much for supporting me; it feels really good." Or, "I really appreciate you caring for me; that's really hitting the spot." Your appreciation lets them know they're on the right track and helps them feel confident in their care of you. There's room for all couples to polish their care skills with time and practice, but appreciating effort keeps you moving in the right direction.

Changing Your Care Culture

Many of us tend to be critical or blaming when relationships upset and frustrate us. We get disappointed, angry, and sometimes even go after our partners verbally, pointing out their flaws and bad habits, or using guilt and shame to try to achieve different behavior from them. Those approaches don't work and tend to make thing worse. It's important to learn how to kindly ask for the attention, empathy, and support we need, especially from our partners.

Learning how to invite care changes the culture of your relationship and how you communicate, but that culture won't necessarily turn on a dime. As you start practicing inviting care, you'll need to give your partner some time to adjust to the new approach and learn how to respond. Many cultural shifts in partnership require time to reinforce a new behavior and establish it as a norm. When one person deepens in vulnerability, it gives the other partner a nudge to go deeper themselves. Relationship culture, like company culture, is strong and tends to pull partners back into familiar, yet negative, habits. It takes some effort to break it and develop a new culture moving forward.

If you're the one implementing the new behavior—in this case, inviting care—and you don't get a good response, you may be tempted to return to old behaviors or take your partner's poor response as evidence that the new approach doesn't work. Rather than take their rejection or failure too personally, help them learn what they can do to match the new approach you're using. Use the tools in chapter 4—"we" language and teamwork—to work together to practice how to respond to requests for care. By practicing such scenarios over and over, both of you will be more familiar with how you can respond when one of you invites care.

Sometimes inviting care doesn't work. Your partner doesn't get it or just doesn't have the skills to provide emotional support in the way you need. Rather than giving up or going backward, double down on the strategy and keep giving the relationship opportunities to learn how to adapt. Asking for care is a step in the right direction and being consistently vulnerable creates a demand pressure for your partner to learn how to respond in a sensitive way. If you revert to old habits, the relationship loses that demand signal for growth and it may take longer to adopt the new pattern.

Receiving Care

For the cycle to work, we must be open to receiving care when our loved ones offer it, meaning that we let others' efforts to soothe us in and we allow ourselves to feel relief through the comfort others give us. Receiving care entails letting your guard down and letting yourself be emotional. It's letting others hug you or hold you, not just pat you on the back. It's allowing your grief to show, crying with others, and letting them help put you back together. It's letting others compliment us and drinking in their admiration, or asking for attention and appreciation when we need it. When we were babies, we had no choice but to surrender into someone's arms and cry it out when upset. As we get older, we develop more independent strategies for self-soothing, but it can still be nice at times to fold into someone's arms and let out the stress and frustration. Letting ourselves be held, soothed, admired, and loved by our partners also helps them feel successful in how they love us and reinforces the care cycle.

If we find it difficult to offer care to others, we may need to learn how to better support others emotionally, which I cover in the next chapter. Emotional care works both ways: if it's difficult to receive it, it's often difficult to give it as well. Learning how to receive care improves our ability to offer it, and vice versa. When our partners complain that we don't offer enough emotional support, it's sometimes because we don't allow ourselves to receive it. Tuning your availability to receive love will help you be more natural in how you offer it when others need support.

While it's fine to self-soothe at times, research has generally shown that allowing ourselves to connect to others when we're upset allows for faster recovery and boosts our relationships.[2] Many people are socialized to be self-reliant, even in distress. While this can be a useful coping mechanism growing up in a family that didn't offer much emotional support, the downside of being too self-reliant in adult relationships is a loss of the value of bonding around tender feelings and moments. Receiving care enhances the connection and meaning of relationships, while being overly self-reliant can disable the care we secretly want. Processing emotions with others is typically a more efficient way for the brain and mind to feel better.[3]

Part of receiving care is being willing to make eye contact with others when we're struggling in order to see the care and empathy in their expressions. The nervous system is very visual, and while words can be comforting, there is no substitute for seeing a loving, caring look in someone else's eyes. Part of the reason we avoid eye contact when in need is the shame we sometimes feel when vulnerable. It can be hard to look at others in those moments, but it can help receive the care into our nervous system.

To improve how you receive care, ask for it in a way that invites it, then be ready to receive others' empathic responses. I see many people ask for care and then keep on talking, not allowing themselves to actually receive what they are asking for in the moment. Or we express a feeling that begins to invite the care of others, yet follow it with a criticism or judgment that disables it. It's best to be concise when asking for care and then pause, giving your listener a chance to give to you in that moment. Think of creating a lull for them to step into after making a clear invitation. It may take others a minute to figure out that you want to be soothed and how they can offer support. If you stay too busy in the conversation, they'll need to respond to the next three or four things you say and caring for you in what you shared can get lost. That pause to receive care is a critical moment you want to create in interactions so that you have a chance to move toward each other when in need and show your stuff.

Example of Inviting Care

Jana tends to come home late from work, often tired and stressed. Her partner, Emily, has been getting irritated at Jana working late a lot and how she often isn't home for dinner. To make things worse for Emily, Jana tends to leave her phone off while at work and doesn't check messages, so Emily doesn't know when she plans to be home. In their current pattern of communication, Jana often comes home tired and stressed, Emily expresses frustration at her being home so late and not communicating, and Jana accuses Emily of not appreciating everything she's doing and always being negative. Emily feels unheard and unsupported and they both either feel angry and ignore each other for the rest of the evening or get into an argument about it.

When they argue, Jana gets defensive about her work and schedule ("Other people would be grateful I work this hard! Cut me a break already!") and Emily complains that Jana doesn't care about her or about the relationship and has her priorities backward ("You just don't get it! Most people have partners that come home for dinner; you act like you're single most of the time!"). Let's see how inviting care might change their way of communicating on this issue.

It's a typical night: Jana comes home late and exhausted, and Emily expresses how frustrated she feels after a day with no communication from her. Here's where inviting care can make a big difference. Instead of being defensive, Jana says, "You know, I'm sorry I've been working hard and am not easy to reach during the day, but I just had a really long day and I really need your love and support." By asking for the care she needs in a direct but kind manner, Jana is likely to get it, and it softens the dialogue between them.

On an ordinary day, Emily might be able to switch gears and care for Jana after she apologized, shared how hard her day had been, and asked for support, but this is not a normal day. Emily is pissed, because this issue has been going on for a while, and she's not in a mood to be so forgiving. Sometimes, when you invite care, your partner may not respond well right away. That's okay; Jana is prepared for times like this.

"You always prioritize yourself," Emily responds. "Never us. You come home late, with no communication about when, and then you ask that I support you in your workaholic habit. What about me and us having time together?!"

Jana feels hurt because she asked for support and instead got more criticism and anger, but she doubles down on inviting care. She looks up at Emily with pleading eyes and says, "I'm really sorry you're so hurt, I'm willing to talk about it and work to make it better, but honestly, I'm so spent from a really stressful day and overwhelmed. I really need you right now. I promise, we'll talk about this issue tomorrow and explore how to improve it." Emily softens after hearing Jana ask for help a second time, and this time with a greater sense of need. After years together, Emily knows that Jana means it when she says they'll work on the issue. Emily's still frustrated, but she's willing to deal with it for now and be there for her partner, who did a great job asking for what she needed emotionally in a nice, respectful way.

The next day, Emily has a chance to ask for her needs to be better met in the relationship. "I don't want to be pissed at you all the time and when you come home, but I care about our relationship and want it to mean something, and most of the time I just feel alone and forgotten," she shares. "I really need your attention on this issue. We need to find a better way to solve it so we're not feeling so hurt." Emily pauses there, giving Jana room to step in and care. "I really do care about you, Emily," she says. "I'm so sorry I've been so busy. You're right; we need a different way. I care about our relationship and you deserve better." By asking for care with kindness and some vulnerability, Emily headed off much of the defensiveness that often happens when she criticizes Jana for her work habits. Jana was responsive because she didn't feel attacked and because her partner was simply asking in a kind way for the love and care she wants to feel in the relationship.

Inviting Care Exercise

This exercise will help you to invite and receive care. You may want a partner—whether a friend or primary partner.

1. Identify a tender or difficult emotion you have felt in the last two days or maybe feel in the moment. It could be a way you're feeling disappointed or a desire you have for more closeness, respect, or love in the relationship.

2. Frame the issue in terms of positive goals for the relationship, not just pointing out what's not working. For example, you might say, "If we get better at this, I would feel much closer—I think we can do it!"

3. Next, practice inviting care around the feeling you just identified, and work to make your request clear, concise, and obvious. Beware of blame and criticism—use your vulnerability to elicit care and interest, and ask your partner to support you in the specific ways you need.

4. As your partner cares for you, practice receiving their support. Don't talk over them or distract the conversation with something else. Stay present, expect comfort, and let your partner seek ways to help you feel better. If what they're doing isn't working, then ask for something specific and tell them how much it would help you if they did that particular thing. Our partners want to feel successful in caring for us but not bossed around or controlled, so be sweet in your requests. Then switch!

Inviting care is a productive way to meet needs in relationship. It's direct, kind, and clear and helps others know how to support us. That clarity makes relationships easier and makes providing care more efficient. Do you feel you need more appreciation? Acknowledgment of all the hard work you're doing? More romance or sex? Tenderness and emotional support? Friendship and fun? Reassurance that your partner is dedicated to you? Whatever it is you need and that would help you feel better in the relationship you can ask your partner for their help with. Be sweet, humble, and ask nicely, but expect their care and believe the relationship can show up for you.

Notes

1. Marie Vandekerckhove, Luis Carlo Bulnes, and Jaak Panksepp, "The Emergence of Primary Anoetic Consciousness in Episodic Memory," *Frontiers in Behavioral Neuroscience* 7 (January 2014): 210.

2. Judith R. Schore and Allan N. Schore, "Modern Attachment Theory: The Central Role of Affect Regulation in Development and Treatment," *Clinical Social Work Journal* 36, no. 1 (2008): 9–20.

3. Allan N. Schore, *Affect Regulation and the Repair of the Self*, Norton Series on Interpersonal Neurobiology, vol. 2 (New York: W. W. Norton, 2003).

8.

The World of Emotions

I've learned that people will forget what you said, people will forget what you did, but people will never forget how you made them feel.

—Maya Angelou

Why Emotions Matter

Emotions are the lifeblood of relationship. They are often misunderstood because they don't conform to the rules of logic, sometimes getting dismissed as irrational, but they have more connecting power than thoughts. Emotions are an incredibly important aspect of life and human experience, and by increasing our emotional intelligence we can create much stronger connections with others.[1] Emotions are how we feel and appreciate life. They help us understand what matters and where our passion lies. They represent the pain of failure and the excitement of our triumphs and, when shared, create deep bonding opportunities.

In addition, emotions track our life's ups and downs and give us insight into our subconscious experience.[2] By being with others in their emotions, we get to know them at a deep level and can support them in impactful internal experiences. Our emotions point to what excites us and give us important information about what needs to change. We love through emotion. Emotions are interest, which is why good art and music get us to *feel* something. Emotion is also romance and desire, grief and loss. If we neglect or dismiss emotional experience, our relationships can start to feel flat.

I'll be honest. Emotions are one of the hardest areas of relationship life for me to feel skillful in. I didn't grow up sharing them and often feel stressed in emotion-laden interactions. But precisely because of my growth curve in this area, I have taken a special interest in gaining competency in the world of emotions. I understand how beautiful and powerful and bonding sharing feelings can be, and I have to continually challenge myself to open up and rise to meet those occasions. Those of you who didn't grow up sharing emotions and are less comfortable with them will relate to my struggle. People who are analytically gifted are sometimes not as smooth or capable in the emotional arena. They may struggle to feel and identify their own emotions and to support others in theirs. They may be more accustomed to intellectual conversation and problem solving than extending empathy and emotional care. While it has taken me a long time to understand how to connect emotionally, I have found that it is one of the best and most direct ways to create a strong connection with others.

Emotional connection is one of the cornerstones of bonding. We don't care much without emotion—it points to what has meaning. We can share thoughts in relationship, discuss world events, politics, and the weather, but such conversations may not be bonding enough. Emotions give others a window into what we're feeling inside and the experience of our hearts. They show our need and hopefully attract the interest and care of others. If you are too inhibited, relationships lose their juice and lack a compass to know where and how to deepen. We can't choose or control emotions—they just happen—and we deal with them productively or not.

There's one group of professionals who certainly don't neglect emotions: advertisers. Sometimes described as the smartest people in the room because they have to sell stuff to the rest of us, advertisers know that emotions form a much stronger bond than information alone.[3] Before they give us factual data about a product, advertisers pull on our heartstrings, showing us babies, dogs, aging parents, weddings, and the epic lifestyle we could be living. If they can get us to *feel* something, we'll care. Before telling us the car has a V6 3.0-liter engine, they show us the California coast where we can drive to take our kids surfing. Those who sell things always seek an emotional bond because such bonds create relevance in our minds and trigger desire. We do well to make use of these same forces in our relationships.

What Are Emotions?

Emotions are generally believed to have developed in the brain as an evolutionary mechanism to keep us safe.[4] They help us evaluate our environment and, using fast, primitive circuits, can create impressions and reactions faster than thought. The basic emotions are ways we mobilize brain and body quickly in response to stimuli, and serve as a motivational system for our behavior and how we adapt to our environment.[5] While thought allows us to reflect on our reactions, emotions contain key information about our subconscious experience and how the brain is measuring connection in real time.[6]

Fields like psychology, neuroscience, evolutionary biology, and primatology study emotions as distinct events in the mind and brain that correlate to survival and other life functions. Technically, emotions consist of chemical and electrical events in the brain that communicate information to other parts of the body, mobilizing hormones, neurotransmitters, and other chemical messengers. Practically, however, emotions are simply how we feel, and can connect our internal experience to others. They represent important information about the relational space that we can share to broker more secure bonds with others.

Neuroscientists and psychologists sometimes like to be specific in their definition of emotions, distinguishing them from general feelings and sensations.[7] That specificity is helpful when conducting research, but in everyday life it's fine to use the terms and concepts of "feelings" and "emotions" interchangeably. As therapists, we champion emotions, ask about them, and care for them, but they can be mysterious even to us at times. Emotions don't always make sense, but they do often point to important aspects of our experience. It's useless to argue with emotions, as they are not ambassadors of our logical minds but rather bring their message from a deeper place within us. Without having grown up with good examples or specific training, it's hard to know how to dance with emotions in a caring way, but when you can identify them in yourself, in others, and share that level of experience you can offer next-level care that is highly valuable.

While the nervous system may read physical cues such as touch, proximity, and eye contact when first assessing connection, emotions run close behind and also play an important role in helping our nervous system evaluate our connections.[8] Emotions are wired into early evolutionary regions of the brain and feed our bodies information about safety and security.[9] By being more aware of our emotions, and those of others, we can catch issues before they escalate, gather important data about how someone feels in real time, and efficiently create deeper connection in our relationships.[10]

While there is no singular agreed-upon list of the important emotions that humans feel,[11] the following list represents some of the more common emotions discussed in neuroscience and psychology.[12] Look at this list and ask yourself how you feel some of the emotions described. Your ability to identify these aspects of experience in yourself and in others will make you a better connector.

Seven Common Emotions
- Joy
- Sadness
- Anger
- Fear
- Disgust
- Surprise
- Contempt

Additional Emotions Explored by Science
- Lust
- Shame
- Love
- Embarrassment
- Pride
- Interest
- Excitement
- Relief

Other Feelings That Can Be Helpful to Identify
- Loneliness or Isolation
- Safety and Security
- Closeness (sometimes described as feeling "warmly" toward someone)
- Trust
- Annoyance
- Frustration
- Jealousy or Envy
- Hopelessness, Helplessness, or Despair
- Protectiveness
- Being Overwhelmed

How to Identify Feelings

Some people find it easy to identify, feel, and share emotions, and some find it difficult. Whether or not identifying emotions comes naturally to you, here are a few principles you can use to notice your feelings more easily and share them with others:

1. **Be grounded and present in your body.** Take a couple deep breaths and sink into your body. Relax your belly and spine and try to locate your awareness in your lower body, such as in the heart and belly. Some of us are used to being in our heads and operating from our logical minds and that can make it harder to notice feelings.

2. **Start with physical sensations.** Body sensations can act as a doorway to getting more emotional information about how you feel. Begin by being aware of the sensations in your body in the moment. For example, do you feel tension anywhere in your body? Stress? Tightness? Coolness or warmth? Heaviness or lightness? When we pay attention, we may notice that our jaw is tight or our shoulders are raised. Now imagine what feelings those physical sensations might represent.

3. **Use an emotions chart.** By working with an emotions chart,[13] you can try to remember when you've personally experienced each feeling, either past or current. Making connections between the emotions on the list and your experience helps your brain begin to identify those feelings with the emotion key word associated with that feeling.

Emotions and the Subconscious

Emotions are an important part of our subconscious experience. Sometimes we're not fully conscious of how we feel with others but have an underlying feeling about them. We become aware of some of our emotions, but others hide below the surface, forming part of the 90 percent of information that flows between people. Sometimes other people know what we're feeling before we do, because they can see it on our faces or hear it in our tone.

In neuroscience terms, the unconscious mind represents signals created by the body's sensory perception before the brain codes them with emotion.[14] Some of those sensory inputs are sent up to the brain, and some circulate throughout the body as signals for various unconscious activities. Once the amygdala encodes the signals it receives with emotion, we start to have some sense of what we're feeling, even if that experience is not fully conscious yet. If we tune in to our subtle experience, we might feel some of it, but we may not be able to make full sense of it. The brain filters a lot of that information out before it reaches the thinking parts, but once those parts engage our experience, we become conscious of how we feel. The brain collects too much information to bother the high-resource thinking areas with all of it, so much of what we perceive never becomes conscious.[15] We still use the data, however, in the background, to make determinations about how connected we feel to someone.[16] Those impressions also generate responses in the body.

As part of our nonconscious awareness, emotions can also fuel some of the automatic behaviors we have in relationships.[17] Emotions are registered by the brain between twenty-seven and thirty-three milliseconds after we sense an experience, while the conscious mind engages at about forty-seven milliseconds.[18] Studies have shown that while an experience and its related emotions may be nonconscious, the impression is enough to affect our behavior.[19] In fact, much learning that shapes our impressions and behavior happens in this manner throughout the day, outside of our conscious awareness.[20]

If we pay attention to our emotions, they give us an important picture of how the body and nervous system are experiencing someone we're connecting with. Because the subconscious has access to much more data about our experience than what is allowed into our awareness, the more we can tune in to our gut sense, what our heart feels, and other impressions, the more information we can capture about how we're feeling with others. Emotions are not just artifacts of drama or exaggeration, and they aren't just part of a person's psychology: they represent important information the body and nervous system are communicating to the brain.[21] If we are present in our bodies, and tuning in to our feelings, we may have a chance to notice those inputs before they become fully conscious. We may not know exactly what those feelings mean, but we can sense something brewing underneath the surface.

Sharing Emotions

Since much of connection is determined nonverbally and emotions are part of the primitive system that determines security, it is important to allow emotions to be a part of your daily experience of relationship, to honor them, celebrate them, and care for them, and give them room to express themselves so that your love can grow. It's helpful to be able to share your feelings with some specificity. Instead of replying "I'm fine," or "I don't feel that great," you might say, "I feel sad this afternoon because I was thinking about my parents getting older, and on top of that, I had a frustrating meeting with my boss, who wasn't happy with a project I spent a lot of time on."

Emotions create the opportunity for compassion, and compassion generates love. While we sometimes see negative emotions as interrupters of connection, they offer a chance to deepen care and can elicit valuable empathy in relationships. As self-compassion expert Dr. Chris Germer likes to say, suffering is the *occasion* for compassion, a concept borrowed from ancient Buddhist teachings about how to deepen love and peace in emotional pain.[22]

Emotional sharing can be stressful for some, so it helps to be concise and create space often for others to enter the conversation. Partners with attention deficit disorder (ADD), anxiety, or a lack of emotional resilience may get impatient or uncomfortable in emotional conversations and sometimes seek to end those conversations quickly, solve the problem intellectually, or dismiss the need for the feeling. Those moves can feel rejecting to others. If both partners in an interaction tend to the conversation, it makes it easier to share feelings and have your partner be present and responsive. For example, you might give your partner some context: "I've been feeling sad and frustrated today and it would help me if you could sit with me and talk for a bit. Could you do that for me?" Such context gives our partners a clear focus and mandate for how to support us and limits their fear of what the emotions might represent.

If you're someone who doesn't share emotions often, it may help your relationship to share little things you feel throughout the day, even if they don't seem significant. That allows your partner to know you better and feel more connected to the inner workings of your mind. If you're the type of person who sometimes shares a lot, you may overwhelm or tire your partner at times. A healthy balance of not keeping things in but also not overwhelming our partners with too much talk and emotion allows both partners to feel safe and relaxed together. A basic rule of thumb is to share anything that's been on your mind for more than a couple days, as that is a sign that the feeling represents something important.

Some people wait to share their feelings until they know what they are and what they want to say about them, while others find out how they feel by sharing with others, examining their experience out loud. Exploring feelings with others can help us understand ourselves with greater clarity, as another person can help illuminate what they mean and provide a sounding board. For those who prefer to make sense of their internal experience before sharing it, I recommend trying out sharing your feelings before you fully understand them. That makes it a joint bonding activity, helping provide additional insight, compared with working things out just in our own minds. You can start a feelings-based conversation by saying, "I'm not quite sure what this means, but I've been feeling [x, y, or z]." Sometimes if we wait to share only when we fully understand our feelings and have some prepared comments, it comes across as intellectual or analytical, not as connecting.

Advanced couples often share their emotions in real time, helping each other remain aware of how the other is feeling. If you get into this habit of sharing emotions more often, then it feels less awkward to share an emotion in the moment and you can keep better track of how to care for each other throughout the day. It takes a little practice, so use the list of emotions provided and try talking about one or two per day to others so you get more comfortable identifying and revealing your inner experiences.

Deepening Connection through Emotion

Ideally, you want your relationship and yourselves to have enough emotional resilience to tolerate and welcome the full range of feelings. If you limit the relationship's willingness to embrace all emotions including anger, sadness, disappointment, and frustration, you may inadvertently limit the flow of positive emotions as well, such as love, passion, interest, and desire. Holding and sharing difficult feelings can be stressful, but as you develop tools for their care, they become more manageable and offer points of connection.

Emotions are the occasion for care: they pull forth the natural dependency we have as humans to lean on each other when things get tough. The need we have for support from others when we're upset is something to celebrate, not hide.

Western society's focus on independence sometimes suggests that we shouldn't need anyone—that we should feel complete and whole as individuals—and that if we choose to bring someone into our life, it's just to share life as two healthy, complete individuals, but not because we need each other. As we have explored before, sometimes pop ideas in Western society (which is highly individualistic and self-reliant) don't match up with the science of attachment and healthy relationships. Need is a key motivator of connection in relationships. If you don't need each other, you're replaceable, which means you're not very important to each other.

Western culture's emphasis on logic and rationality tends to marginalize and diminish the important role emotions play in relationships and bonding. Our emotional need for others is a healthy expression of our attachment tendencies as people and of how we collaborate with others to sustain ourselves and build greater security into our lives.[23] While it's tempting to think that we are so independent and resilient that we don't need others to feel whole, primary relationships don't operate on an "I could take it or leave it" principle. Attachment relationships are defined by need, and we seek them out in order to feel more secure as social beings who are built to live in connection with others.

Being independent while maintaining strong connections with others is healthy, but being overly self-reliant can cause people to feel emotionally disconnected or isolated. Feeling alone is correlated with higher rates of depression, health issues, and reduced life-span, while creating and maintaining strong, secure bonds with others is a health booster.[24] Need and healthy dependency are qualities to be celebrated, not avoided. Needing each other makes your relationships richer, and the seeking of emotional care can strengthen those bonds.[25]

In the attachment spectrum of bonding, there is independence on one end, co-dependence on the other, and a healthy interdependence in the middle. Both extremes are generally unhealthy. Those who don't feel comfortable by themselves and need constant connection to feel regulated, sometimes to the point of overburdening or controlling others, create problems for themselves and in relationships. In a similar manner, those who become overly independent often neglect important emotional and bonding needs in themselves and their relationships.

The right balance to strike is interdependence: a healthy need for others and a relational life that allows us to feel strong and whole in ourselves; secure bonds that celebrate our individuality while also offering mutual care. Interdependence offers emotional support to both connecting needs and individual desires, so that each partner can work toward their goals and dreams without sacrificing a strong sense of home. Interdependence doesn't seek to limit individuals but rather champions the needs of partners in ways that are good for everyone.

To deepen connection through emotion, be willing to share how you feel on a daily basis so it becomes more of a habit. Learn to convey when you feel sad, angry, or disappointed instead of holding it in until you feel resentful. You need to be careful to disclose feelings in a respectful, relational way so as to not disrupt the sense of security in your relationship. Sharing feelings of helplessness or hopelessness can help you stay ahead of anger and make for more constructive interactions about change and need. And make sure to share your positive emotions too. Conveying appreciation, love, admiration, and desire is important!

When someone shares an emotion, or expresses feelings without explicitly naming them, it is helpful to focus on them. Follow up on the feeling, ask about it, and show interest, because it likely represents the greatest meaning in what that person was sharing. In a sea of words, thoughts, ideas, and insights, emotions capture meaning and convey it in its raw form. If you listen for emotional information, you can get to know others more deeply and they will experience you as more supportive. You'll start noticing feelings even before others know they're feeling them. This radar for emotions increases attunement and helps you become a source of care for yourself and others.

Connection is also about knowing when to give yourselves a break from emotional conversation and just go have fun, rest, or talk about more concrete matters. Intentionally mixing it up so you're not always on one channel in your communication style gives you important relief from difficult conversations, emotional heaviness, and builds your bond by allowing you to relax together. It's important to negotiate those transitions, so that no one feels rejected in their emotions, dismissed by a quick change, or neglected in their internal experience. But part of connecting is knowing when you need to switch to something easier and a way of being that gives you a change of pace and a chance to create some positive memories together.

Amplifying Positive Emotions

In the same way that caring for tender feelings can deepen connection, amplifying positive emotions offers great opportunities to deepen your bond. Therapists call this upregulating, and it's a key marker of healthy connection in relationships.[26] Essentially, when someone gets excited or is celebrating a win, you join them in that emotion, getting excited with them, letting your energy go up to match them, and sharing the moment together. Upregulating allows you to share higher states of joy, excitement, passion, and euphoria and amplify those feelings by feeding them in a joint space. When your partner, kids, or a friend is excited about something, let yourself show your excitement as well. That honors their positive moments in life and those joint celebrations constitute an important part of a couple's memory. If our partners get excited and we stay too low or calm, they may experience us as distant from the emotion they are feeling, which can be disconnecting.

When your loved ones are excited, you can elevate your voice, let your face show the excitement, jump around, wave your hands, smile, laugh, and enjoy the moment with them. Their energy may be infectious and rub off on you, lifting your spirits as well. You might say, "That's so awesome! Yay! Congratulations! I'm so excited for you!" Let your tone and facial expression mirror your emotional excitement. While emotional support often focuses on helping to comfort negative emotions like sadness and grief, sharing positive emotions is an important part of supporting our partners emotionally. Seize those opportunities for bonding and practice expressing and feeling the high range of emotions with others!

Providing Emotional Support

One of the most important reasons to understand and respect emotions is to be able to provide support to our partners, kids, and friends that deepens our relationships. If we overlook emotions that are shared with us, explicitly or implicitly, or we don't know how to respond to them, we miss the opportunity to offer love, care, and build trust with others.

Emotional support is the way you verbally and nonverbally respond to others when they're feeling something, allowing your empathy and care to flow. Let yourself sink into the moment and be present with others. Breathe to relax your body and reduce stress. Maintain eye contact if appropriate, and use your body language to show interest. Use the Language of the Nervous System to convey connection and security, and offer care to feelings, even if they don't make sense or you disagree with them.

Don't be too wordy or try to offer logical solutions. The part of the brain that experiences emotion generally just needs care. Some words of encouragement can be helpful, like indicating you care, are present, and want to help. For example, you might say, "I'm so sorry you feel that way; I'm here with you. Tell me more." Letting people know you care about their feelings and asking a few questions that encourage them to share more is generally experienced as supportive.

In emotional conversations, the best follow-up questions ask about the emotion itself, rather than the situation or the context. Logical suggestions often fall flat, because they don't contain the empathy and emotional care that signal nervous system support. Emotions are like waves—they rise and fall. Sometimes your relationship needs to understand feelings to adapt to what you each need. Other times, with the right support, emotions often run their course, resolve, and return to baseline. In that sense, your presence, empathy, and care are all the solution that is needed, and typically the best "solution."[27]

Relationships Can Help Heal Emotional Wounds

Connection is the healing ingredient that allows partners to feel safe enough to open up, consider new approaches, receive love into painful experiences from the past, and relax into more secure ways of being.[28] Primary attachment relationships offer the opportunity to heal old emotional and psychological wounds. As emotional triggers come up, they can be seen, understood, and worked with, and eventually healed. Opening up to someone who gets to know those wounds and can care for you when they arise serves as a built-in healing mechanism in your life. Healing can take place more quickly if you're vulnerable, willing to share feelings, and if you develop a culture that cares for each other's tender spots. Neuroscience has shown that change happens most under conditions of safety and security, where people feel safe enough to let down their guard and try new things, rather than as a product of criticism or pressure.[29] The consistent security of a healthy bond helps to relax the nervous system and allows us to let go of anxieties and defenses we developed in the past.

Because many of our issues originate from our childhood, primary attachment relationships create unique access to those issues. The healing process can then make use of the brain's plasticity and ability to improve neuronal connections throughout adult life, resulting in greater mental and emotional peace and well-being.[30] Different phases of life will elicit different traumas from the past and different levels of those traumas. When old emotional wounds get triggered and "pop," creating turbulent territory, those traumas are then also more available and can make use of the relationship's security to be revised. In that sense, resurfacing triggers are sometimes an indication of a deepening level of safety in relationship rather than a step back. A secure relationship allows individuals to feel safe enough to open up and take greater risks in their personal growth work.

In my case, I didn't live with my parents until I was twelve, lost my primary caregiver at nine, didn't have support to talk about feelings, left home at fifteen, and bounced around, yet being in a secure relationship has helped me to heal many of those wounds and artifacts from trauma that were getting in my way in life. By working together with others, I was able to accelerate my healing beyond what I could accomplish on my own. Relationship life still sometimes causes my traumas and triggers to come up. When that happens, I double down on connecting strategies and vulnerability to try to bring collective love and care to those places within me.

Creating Opportunities for Emotional Care

The best way to use the connecting power of emotion is to create opportunities for care and to be aware of such opportunities as they naturally arise. If you're feeling something, seek out other people and ask if they would support you while you share and explore it. We often don't know the full extent of an emotion until we begin exploring it, and sharing with someone supportive is a great way to do that and make a relationship more meaningful.

If your partner is not that great at providing emotional care, ask them to sit, focus, listen, be supportive, and ask questions. Put a time limit on the exchange so they don't feel trapped in a conversation they feel uncomfortable in. Ten minutes is reasonable if someone is new at this; twenty minutes is more adequate if someone has experience and feels comfortable. Offering support and care doesn't need to take a long time. Often, the right kind of empathic support can help people feel better quickly. When it's a serious situation, then you'll want to take more time to hold your partner, support them, and let them cry with you.

When moments organically arise in the course of daily life that involve feelings, don't overlook them or blow past them—make good use of them. That includes noticing positive emotions and amplifying them, and being aware of when someone may be feeling something they're not overtly mentioning. When someone has a feeling, take some time to ask them about it, offer some kindness, and let them discuss it with you. That kind of support goes a long way to creating valuable and meaningful bonds.

Metabolizing Emotional Experience

There are three primary ways the human nervous system regulates feeling and activation to find calm, feel better, and connect. We typically use a combination of these strategies to work through our emotions or support others in theirs. *Autoregulation* involves the automatic things our bodies do to calm our nervous systems, like taking big breaths to relax and moving blood flow around the body. *Self-regulation* includes conscious ways we calm ourselves down, like meditation, exercise, and visualization, or shifting our posture and modifying eye contact when we're with others. *Interactive regulation* is considered the gold standard, as it tends to be the most efficient from a brain standpoint. Sometimes known as co-regulation, it involves actively engaging to relax and receive comfort, connecting to others' brains, bodies, and nervous systems as a resource for our own.

According to Dr. Stephen Porges, the body and brain are built to regulate more efficiently in concert with others.[31] Interactive regulation makes use of the nervous system's ability to receive care from others and can increase recovery speed from a traumatic event.[32] Receiving emotional support from others allows us to use the body's natural efficiencies to soothe and de-stress by being held, receiving empathy, crying with someone, or doing something fun and relaxing together. Others can also reassure us in ways we can't do for ourselves. By connecting to another nervous system that is available to offer help, our wiring makes use of the interaction to benefit from the human care and support being offered.[33]

If we stay grounded in our bodies and connected to our inner experience, we sometimes have a chance to regulate our nervous systems before our experience becomes fully conscious. This is, in part, how meditation works to develop a calmer mind. By sitting with an experience and bringing a calming resource to it—whether that's another person or an exercise—we can connect our emotions and a sense of being resourced together, which increases our resilience and inner peace.[34] Since we can sense the subconscious, especially if we slow down and pay attention, we can metabolize some of that nervous system activity without needing to interpret it.[35] While the field of psychology has typically believed that conscious reflection and cognitive insight are needed for significant behavioral and mental change, there is growing evidence that subconscious regulation of states and automated learning at that level are enough for the mind to learn new tricks, develop a stronger ability to manage feelings, and shape new behaviors.[36] But while all regulating strategies are important and helpful, learning to interactively manage our states and emotions with other people speeds up our ability to reconnect and feel secure again, helps us feel less isolated in our feelings, and creates a sense of security in our relationships.[37]

What to Do with Differences of Emotional Style

Different emotional styles between people need to be bridged well so they don't frustrate partners or leave individuals feeling alone and unsupported. Diverging approaches to emotional processing can create significant disconnection. In fact, relationship researcher John Gottman found that partners with very different emotional processing styles tend to struggle unless they learn to handle the difference effectively.[38]

In general, the acts of sharing emotions and caring for feelings both strengthen and enhance relationships and make them more satisfying and viable over the long term.[39] But another important factor is balancing different needs and preferences between partners in how emotions are processed. While increasing our comfort with emotions is important, some people are more circumspect with their feelings, and their style also deserves respect and care within their relationship. For example, a person who is comfortable sharing emotions can usually make their needs known, while a partner who is less habituated to engage emotion may find them stressful and may share less about how they're feeling. Relationships should seek to be sensitive to the needs of different styles.

An outwardly emotional person may need to be heard, understood, validated, and cared for in order to feel connected. But a partner who is less comfortable with the world of emotions may need less stress, less drama, less emotional intensity, and more calm to feel secure. These different styles are both legitimate, and caring for both is important to a relationship's connection. If these different styles are not equally supported, the relationship can start to feel out of balance.

To bridge emotional differences, it is first important to validate each side. A more emotional partner might say, "It would mean a lot to me if you would listen to me share and offer your care for how I'm feeling. I know emotions can be stressful for you, so we can keep it short and I promise not to blame or criticize you; I just need your love and support." The partner who is more uncomfortable with emotion might say, "I know how important it is for you to receive care and support, but emotions are stressful for me. I need a sense of calm and to be able to relax and just enjoy ourselves. If we talk for ten minutes about how you're feeling and I give you my full attention and care, can we then spend some time just relaxing and having fun? I want to practice caring for you without getting overwhelmed, and I also need times when we're not processing feelings and can just have a good time together." Bridging between these styles rather than trying to bend one to the other's approach strengthens your bond.

All this requires some skill building. The more emotional partner needs to learn how to imagine the stress and feeling of being overwhelmed their partner might experience in emotional situations, and help care for them by offering support and less stress and intensity. The partner who is more dismissive of emotion or withdrawn needs to practice reaching out, asking questions about feelings, and providing care, as well as sharing their own feelings.

With a little practice and willingness, partners with different emotional styles can get less hurt and stressed by the other, and the different styles can then function like assets, protecting each partner from the tendency to live at either extreme. Learning to bridge emotional styles also helps each person become wiser and more empathic to a diversity of personalities and communication styles, which is helpful to connection in all relationships, including at work and with kids. If you can remain open to how another's experience of emotion differs from yours, you're well on your way to bridging such differences.

Example of Emotional Care

Deion and Lanelle are sometimes so busy, they don't pause much to sink into the moment with each other and ask how they each feel. When they do have downtime, they tend to watch TV. Sometimes they even eat in front of the TV. But other times, Lanelle wants to connect around how she feels, and it's hard to get Deion's attention for that. He's very intellectual, and when she brings up feelings he tends to just offer logistical solutions that leave her feeling emotionally invalidated and unsupported. This is a common issue between partners in relationship.

We all want to help but sometimes don't have the emotional skills or habits to support them in the right way. Let's see if some of the emotional principles we have discussed in this chapter can help them connect better in their emotional experience.

Deion asks, "Want to watch TV?"

Lanelle responds, "Yeah. But first, can we talk for a second? I had a hard run-in with my boss today, and it left me feeling kind of shook up."

"Oh yeah? What kind of run-in?" questions Deion.

Lanelle replies, "Well, it's just I've been working on a project and I thought I had this week to finish it, but he wanted it today, and implied I should have had it done by today. The way he spoke to me left me feeling uneasy."

Deion counters with, "Oh, don't worry about that, baby; that's just bosses being bosses. I'm sure he likes you. Just brush it off, no sweat."

Lanelle exasperates, "That doesn't really help me feel better. I guess I was hoping you would care a little more about how it felt for me." We often offer intellectual solutions or pat reassurance to comfort others emotionally, but those responses can feel dismissive and distant. Let's see how Deion might better support Lanelle.

Deion replies, "I'm sorry. You're right; I was kind of dismissive. I love you and care about your experience. Tell me more about what happened."

Lanelle continues, "Well, I felt nervous, and also kind of disrespected. I felt like he was pulling his authority card and kind of shaming me around not having done it faster. It just didn't feel good."

"I'm so sorry. That sucks. You really don't deserve that. Come here, let me hug you." Deion offers her a hug and holds her a good thirty seconds. Lanelle starts to relax and feel better. "How does it feel now? It sounds like the bad feeling kind of stuck with you," he asks.

Lanelle answers, "Definitely. I still feel stressed by it. I don't even want to interact with him now, and going in tomorrow is going to feel different."

"Man, that's rough. I'm really sorry. Come here, sit closer to me. [He holds her hand and is looking at her in a kind, bolstering way.] Anything I can do to help you feel better?" Deion is doing a good job being supportive. He's resisting the tendency to offer logical solutions to get rid of the emotion, and he's asking good questions, giving her a chance to share more about how she feels, which is helping her feel seen and also process what happened. He's making good use of the *spotlight principle*, which means he's keeping the spotlight on Lanelle and not switching it to himself. He's not saying, "When I had a run-in with my boss twenty years ago here's what I did. . . ." He's staying focused on her and her experience.

When people are sharing their experience, you can imagine them on a stage with the spotlight on them and you in the audience. Sometimes we insert our thoughts and experiences too soon when others' are sharing and it can disable their ability to rely on us emotionally.

"I think it's going to be hard to see him tomorrow and interact with him this week, but I appreciate you being here for me and talking to you about it helps. I don't need to process it all night. Let's go watch TV," Lanelle concludes. By being available and supportive and not rushing his care, Lanelle felt regulated by Deion and her emotions returned more to baseline. When emotional support is there, recovery doesn't need to take a long time, but when we dismiss emotions to "move on," we may prolong the process of repair.

Exercise to Deepen Emotional Skill

You'll need a partner for this exercise. It can be a friend, family member, or primary partner. Use an emotions chart, like the one on the PRESENCE wellness center website, or the list of feelings earlier. Sit across from each other at close range, facing each other. Pick an emotion off the chart or list, and tell your partner how you're experiencing that emotion in your life right now. Give them some detail. The partner's job is to ask questions, be curious, show empathy and care, and be genuinely interested. Then switch! Each sharing can take just a few minutes.

After you've each gone once, pick another emotion from the list or chart, and again describe how it's showing up in your experience. Take some time to feel that emotion in your body, and describe to your partner how you feel it. The listener can practice sharing supportive words, such as, "I'm really sorry you feel that way; that sucks. Tell me more about it." Or, "Yay! I'm so happy you feel excited about that; that's awesome! Tell me more about how it feels!"

When you're the listener, practice keeping the spotlight on your partner and the feeling they're sharing, and keep showing interest so they can really flesh out their experience for you. If you're the sharer, don't just be in your head describing the feeling; try to feel it physically and express how it feels in your heart and body. Are there any physical sensations connected to that feeling? How often do you feel it? You might use this practice a few times a week, so you can eventually cover all the emotions on the chart or list. That will help you talk about feelings you might otherwise neglect to notice or share. When we're in touch with our feelings, we can usually locate how we feel every single emotion on the chart at any one time. This exercise makes it easier for you to identify your emotions faster and helps you get more comfortable with sharing them and caring for others.

Emotions offer important bonding opportunities in relationship. Our sense of self and self-esteem is largely based in the quality of our relationships,[40] and our confidence can be shaped by how supported we feel by others. Getting in touch with emotions helps us understand ourselves and gives us a much deeper knowledge of our partners and others. Emotional support confers resilience that helps you manage shame and embarrassment, so we can be more compassionate with ourselves when we make mistakes, and emotional care helps us lick our wounds after failure, so we can get up and move toward our life dreams and goals again.

Notes

1. Daniel Goleman, *Emotional Intelligence: Why It Can Matter More than IQ* (New York: Bantam, 2012).

2. A. R. Damasio, "The Somatic Marker Hypothesis and the Possible Functions of the Prefrontal Cortex," *Philosophical Transactions of the Royal Society of London, Series B: Biological Sciences* 351 (October 1996): 1413–1420.

3. Gerald Zaltman, *How Customers Think: Essential Insights into the Mind of the Market* (Cambridge, MA: Harvard Business School Press, 2003).

4. Jaak Panksepp and Lucy Biven, *The Archaeology of Mind: Neuroevolutionary Origins of Human Emotions*, Norton Series on Interpersonal Neurobiology (New York: W. W. Norton, 2012).

5. Carroll E. Izard, *Human Emotions* (Berlin: Springer Science+Business Media, 2013).

6. Ibid.

7. Jaak Panksepp, *Affective Neuroscience: The Foundations of Human and Animal Emotions* (Oxford: Oxford University Press, 2004).

8. Jonathan H. Turner, *Human Emotions: A Sociological Theory* (Abingdon, UK: Taylor & Francis, 2007).

9. Ralph Adolphs, "Neural Systems for Recognizing Emotion," *Current Opinion in Neurobiology* 12, no. 2 (April 2002): 169–177.

10. Don R. Catherall, *Emotional Safety: Viewing Couples through the Lens of Affect* (Abingdon-on-Thames, UK: Routledge, 2006).

11. Paul Ekman, "Basic Emotions," in *Handbook of Cognition and Emotion*, ed. Tim Dalgleish and Mick J. Power (New York: Wiley, 1999), 16.

12. Magda Kowalska and Monika Wróbel, "Basic Emotions," in *Encyclopedia of Personality and Individual Differences*, ed. Virgil Zeigler-Hill and Todd K. Shackelford (Cham, Switzerland: Springer International, 2017), 1–6.

13. You're welcome to use the emotions chart at presencewellness.co/emotions -chart.

14. Allan N. Schore, *The Development of the Unconscious Mind*, Norton Series on Interpersonal Neurobiology (New York: W. W. Norton, 2019).

15. Heather A. Berlin, "The Neural Basis of the Dynamic Unconscious," *Neuropsychoanalysis* 13, no. 1 (2011): 5–31.

16. Elisabeth A. Murray, "The Amygdala, Reward and Emotion," *Trends in Cognitive Sciences* 11, no. 11 (November 2007): 489–497.

17. David H. Zald, "The Human Amygdala and the Emotional Evaluation of Sensory Stimuli," *Brain Research Reviews* 41, no. 1 (January 2003): 88–123.

18. Noriya Watanabe and Masahiko Haruno, "Effects of Subconscious and Conscious Emotions on Human Cue-Reward Association Learning," *Scientific Reports* 5 (February 2015).

19. Ibid.

20. Damasio, "The Somatic Marker Hypothesis," 1413–1420.

21. Carroll E. Izard, "Basic Emotions, Relations among Emotions, and Emotion-Cognition Relations," *Psychological Review* 99, no. 3 (July 1992): 561–565, https://doi.org/10.1037/0033-295X.99.3.561.

22. Christopher Germer, *The Mindful Path to Self-Compassion: Freeing Yourself from Destructive Thoughts and Emotions* (New York: Guilford, 2009).

23. Phillip R. Shaver and Mario Mikulincer, "Adult Attachment Strategies and the Regulation of Emotion," in *Handbook of Emotion Regulation*, ed. James J. Gross (New York: Guilford, 2007), 465.

24. John T. Cacioppo and Stephanie Cacioppo, "Social Relationships and Health: The Toxic Effects of Perceived Social Isolation," *Social and Personality Psychology Compass* 8, no. 2 (February 2014): 58–72.

25. Diana Fosha, Daniel J. Siegel, and Marion F. Solomon, eds., *The Healing Power of Emotion: Affective Neuroscience, Development & Clinical Practice* (New York: W. W. Norton, 2009).

26. Claudia M. Haase, "Emotion Regulation in Intimate Relationships," *Society for the Study of Behavioral Development* 1, no. 65 (2014): 17–21.

27. Peter A. Levine, *In an Unspoken Voice: How the Body Releases Trauma and Restores Goodness* (Berkeley: North Atlantic Books, 2010).

28. Bonnie Badenoch, *The Heart of Trauma: Healing the Embodied Brain in the Context of Relationships*, Norton Series on Interpersonal Neurobiology (New York: W. W. Norton, 2017).

29. Louis Cozolino and Susan Sprokay, "Neuroscience and Adult Learning," *The Neuroscience of Adult Learning: New Directions for Adult and Continuing Education* 81, no. 110 (Summer 2006): 11.

30. Louis Cozolino, *The Neuroscience of Human Relationships: Attachment and the Developing Social Brain*, Norton Series on Interpersonal Neurobiology (New York: W. W. Norton, 2014.)

31. Stephen W. Porges, *The Polyvagal Theory: Neurophysiological Foundations of Emotions, Attachment, Communication, and Self-Regulation*, Norton Series on Interpersonal Neurobiology (New York: W. W. Norton, 2011).

32. Tara Boer, review of *Neurobiology for Clinical Social Work: Theory and Practice*, by Janet Shapiro and Jeffrey S. Applegate, *Journal of Evidence-Based Social Work* 17, no. 3 (2020): 368–369.

33. Levine, *In an Unspoken Voice*.

34. Daniel J. Siegel, "Mindful Awareness, Mindsight, and Neural Integration," *The Humanistic Psychologist* 37, no. 2 (2009): 137.

35. Allan N. Schore, "Paradigm Shift: The Right Brain and the Relational Unconscious," *Psychologist-Psychoanalyst* 28, no. 3 (2008): 20–25.

36. Efrat Ginot, *The Neuropsychology of the Unconscious: Integrating Brain and Mind in Psychotherapy*, Norton Series on Interpersonal Neurobiology (New York: W. W. Norton, 2015).

37. Shaver and Mikulincer, "Adult Attachment Strategies and the Regulation of Emotion."

38. John M. Gottman and Robert W. Levenson, "A Two-Factor Model for Predicting When a Couple Will Divorce: Exploratory Analyses Using 14-Year Longitudinal Data," *Family Process* 41, no. 1 (Spring 2002): 83–96.

39. John M. Gottman, *What Predicts Divorce?: The Relationship between Marital Processes and Marital Outcomes* (London: Psychology Press, 2014).

40. John P. Hewitt, "The Social Construction of Self-Esteem," in *The Oxford Handbook of Positive Psychology*, (New York: Oxford University Press, 2009), 309.

9.

Words That Connect

To fulfill our biological imperative of connectedness, our personal agenda needs to be directed toward making individuals feel safe.

—Stephen Porges

While nonverbal communication speaks directly to the primitive parts of the brain that evaluate safety and connection, words have their place in human interactions and can support establishing secure bonds. The trick with words is to not let them interfere with establishing a sense of security with others but rather use them to add to our overall connecting message. Ideally, our words are consistent with our nonverbal communication and don't clutter our connecting cues. When conversation supports relating, it can be helpful, such as when we say sweet, loving things that increase security. And when connection is strong, talking can be fun, playful, and interesting. But words alone can't change the feeling someone may get from our overall approach to connection, so our language needs to rest in the larger context of how we show up with others.

We want our words to enhance our interactions and not interfere with what matters most to connection. Words recruit higher-order processes in the brain, so when we begin speaking it often stimulates thinking, which can take us out of our hearts and into our heads. Words convey ideas that require interpretation and response, which takes energy, focus, and can pull other people into their analytic minds. Interpreting language is resource heavy for the brain, one reason why we may sometimes find conversation annoying when we're tired. Language exists in the realm of concepts and ideas, which opens up room for diverse interpretations of words and concepts. Conversation can highlight differences of personality and perspective that more primitive ways of connecting like touch may not.

We want to capture the beauty of words without the stress of them. We want our words to send a clear signal that is consistent with our intent to create a sense of security and connection. And we want to speak those words alongside nonverbal connection so they work harmoniously with the more primitive cues that speak security to the nervous system.

Remember the Nonverbals First

You want your words to emphasize what others can read in your tone and eyes as connecting cues. Think of your nonverbal communication as the foundation of a house and your words as the finishing touches. If the foundation isn't sound, the finishing touches won't be able to mask that issue forever. But if the foundation is strong, then the finishing touches can give that strong house more color, nuance, and complexity. When your relationship feels secure, the words sitting on top of that security can add flair and detail.

When your words match your nonverbals, you can amplify your communication to send a powerful message of connection. When they are congruent, you are believable and can effectively communicate connection. If you can combine both nonverbal cues and connecting words, you have a deep and strong skill set for connecting with others.

After working with couples for over a decade, I've noticed four primary ways that partners make errors of connection in how they use language. Western society is a verbal and intellectual culture, so it makes sense that most of us would seek to connect through ideas and words. But we are not taught in the same degree how to connect emotionally and how to communicate safety to others' nervous systems, so unfortunately, our use of words sometimes gets in the way of the connection we seek. Here are four errors often made with words you can identify and begin to correct.

Four Common Mistakes We Make with Words
1. We *say too much* without saying anything meaningful.
2. We use words that *create mistrust and disconnection*, such as those that create insecurity or confusion.
3. We *don't say enough* to create a feeling of value and connection.
4. We *clutter the beautiful messages* from our hearts with additional words that detract from the ones that count.

Let's look at these four common errors:

1. **We say too much without saying anything meaningful.**
   Some people talk a lot but don't say much that moves the needle of connection. The classic example is someone who talks your ear off about the weather or politics but doesn't check to see if the conversation is interesting to you. People with this tendency can connect better by practicing being more concise, speaking in complete sentences with periods, and pausing more frequently to let others contribute to the conversation. They also need to practice tracking others' facial expressions, eyes, and body language more closely to know when their listener is getting bored or tired and to stop and change the interaction.

   Another example is when we come home and tell our partners all the details about what we did that day but never say things that matter more to connection, like "I love you" or "It's really nice to see you." If we're going to spend so much energy on words and conversation, at least some of it should directly build the relationship at its core. It's fine to chat about the day, but at some point we might want to move in close, make meaningful eye contact, kiss, and say, "I feel so lucky to have you in my life." Combining superficial talk with the occasional phrase that is more connecting satisfies diverse aspects of what we need from our relationships.

2. **We use words that create mistrust and disconnection, such as those that create insecurity or confusion.**
   Some people use words and language in a way that immediately decreases the sense of security and connection with others. When it's intentional, it's usually because we're angry, fed up, or feel mistreated. Sometimes a person may use words and language to bully others, try to exert power or control over others, retaliate for feeling hurt, or make others feel small. Sometimes we choose to use passive-aggressive or condescending language when we're frustrated with the same negative effect.

   When our words degrade connection, but it's unintended,

it's typically because of bad habits in how we communicate, and we may be unaware that we're sabotaging others' ability to trust us. *It's helpful to keep in mind that if our words are not proactively creating a sense of security, they are likely doing the opposite.* That's just how the brain works—it scans for negatives first, determines security, then opens up to play into the nuance of interactions. In the absence of positive cues, the brain often assumes the connection is not secure.

Even worse, if your words actively cause others to become afraid, recoil, feel like they have to defend themselves, or shut down, your connections with others are likely to be fragile. In such situations, it's important to take responsibility for a toxic communication style and get help to remedy it before it destroys relationships you care about. If your use of disconnecting words is intentional, it is also helpful to seek support to learn and practice how to communicate more effectively.

People with a tendency to create disconnection with words need to become more aware of their pattern and what it would sound like to shift their style. They need to listen respectfully to others' feedback, especially that of close loved ones, and understand the deeper psychological roots behind their communication style. With intention, dedication, and practice, people can shift from language that arouses suspicion to using words that create security and a sense of ease; from communication that is vague and hard to read to interactions that signal friendliness in obvious ways.

3. **We don't say enough to create a feeling of value and connection.**
   Some people just don't say much at all. That can be perfectly fine if you're good at nonverbal connecting behaviors and if others report feeling close to you despite your few words. Most partners, however, need a little conversation to feel fulfilled in relationships. You don't necessarily need to talk at length if you can connect in other ways, but never saying how you feel, not professing your love, and not engaging enough in conversation will cause some partners to lose a sense of the relationship's value and their sense of connection to you.

If your partner typically wants more engagement, you might challenge yourself to tell them one thing a day you appreciate about them, or one thing you felt during your day. Communication like that enhances your bond and strengthens relationships. Just talking about chores and logistics and transactional items throughout the day doesn't count as much toward connection, so even though you may be talking, it's not connecting you. Make sure to single out moments for conversations that have more connecting value.

Notes can be a less intimidating way to communicate from your heart and share how you feel while still getting the message across. If words don't come easy or you're not sure how to share connecting sentiments with others, you might consider writing a love letter to your partner or kids from time to time, or trying your best effort at a sappy poem. We don't have to be eloquent—our loved ones just like hearing how we feel about them and if we appreciate them.

If your partner is asking for more interaction, don't just come up with superficial discussion topics—push yourself to say the sorts of things people say on their wedding day or on Valentine's Day. A useful but emotional exercise is to imagine what you might say to someone on their deathbed leaving this world. Sometimes we don't appreciate what we have until it's gone. A sense of urgency can help you communicate your love, desire, and affection in meaningful ways that deepen connection.

4. **We clutter the beautiful messages from our hearts with additional words that detract from the ones that count.**
    Even people who connect well with words tend to obscure the loveliest things they say with other clutter that doesn't belong in the same communication. When you say something sweet and meaningful, let it stand on its own, even if it feels awkward. Shining the light on your sweet, connecting message gives your partner a chance to take it in and often makes your nonverbals better aligned with your words. A helpful challenge that strengthens connection is to get close to a loved one, look them in the eye, and say beautiful things

about what they mean to you without any additional words that clutter the message. Let your words sink in, and see how connection can deepen in the moment when you're willing to be bold and show your love in a clear way.

The person listening to us, whether it's our partner, kids, or a friend, often has their own challenges with the awkwardness of emotional intimacy. If we give them too many verbal targets, they may focus on the easier but less-connecting ones that are more intellectual or logistical. For example, if we say, "Can you pick up the kids? Thanks, I appreciate all you've been doing for us lately. Oh, can you also pick up my prescription on the way home?" while our partner might have heard the appreciation we voiced, the opportunity to enjoy it got swept away by the talk about the other chores. Rather than bury connecting statements in a conversation about chores, you might look that person in the eye and say, "I appreciate everything you've been doing for us lately. You're the best," and let that message stand on its own.

Keep Words Focused

In moments of emotional intimacy, our bodies, eyes, and nonverbal cues can communicate closeness, as can our words, if they're focused on that purpose. Because emotional intimacy is awkward for many, we often use words to lighten the moment, make a joke, or start a random conversation. Instead, we can take the opportunity to say less or say more meaningful things that deepen love, and allow connection to happen.

A rule of thumb when using words to bond is to keep it short, sweet, and to the point. "I love you," "I care about you," and "I'm here for you" are all concise, important messages that connect well. They don't take a lot of brainpower to interpret unless they are surprising or unwelcome. In contrast, a long diatribe about legal affairs or your latest model toy hobby is unlikely to help much unless you're both into the same thing. Check that you're bringing others along with you in conversation, and if you're wanting to feel more connected keep in mind that you may need to deepen the conversation into more emotionally intimate territory.

Generally, the most connecting conversations are ones in which people talk about the things that are meaningful to them, that they feel deeply, and in which they get to experience genuine interest from others in who they are. You might ask people what has them feeling most excited lately, what they feel most proud of, or what they're looking forward to in this phase of life.

The concept of "date night rules" refers to topics that are to be avoided when you're on a romantic date with your partner. Date night rules often suggest avoiding any talk about your kids, money, responsibilities, or chores and instead focusing on flirting, connecting, appreciating the relationship in the moment, and speaking as friends do, about hobbies and common points of interest that are fun. We spend so much time talking about the logistical aspects of life, this concept highlights the importance of having time when you're simply acting as friends and tending to your romantic partnership, not negotiating chores.

Words can detract from a beautiful evening together, a romantic moment, or an opportunity to relax with each other, or they can enhance those moments. Be aware to not let your language distract from the joy of what is possible, and use words strategically with your other connecting cues to send consistent, coherent messages of connection to others.

Speak from the Heart

Almost everyone appreciates concise declarations of love, interest, desire, affection, admiration, appreciation, and commitment. Words that connect the most tend to be concise statements of love and security spoken straight from the heart. Speaking sweet words such as "I love you," "You mean a lot to me," and "You're the most important thing in my life" directly to others can feel unfamiliar and awkward but enhances your connection. It is important to practice saying what we mean from our hearts so there is no doubt and so that others can hear the outward expression of our feelings.

Communication that shows consistency between our words and our true feelings—between what we say and how we say it—has the most emotional impact. If speaking from your heart is unfamiliar to you, take some time to contemplate how you feel about your partner and what your heart would say if it could speak. **When you know how to communicate safety to others' nervous systems** *and* speak your feelings from your heart, you have a powerful combination for creating a strong sense of connection in relationships.

Casual Chitchat

You don't always have to be deep and serious with your words to connect! Engaging in light, relaxing, and mutually enjoyable small talk can be a nice way to de-stress from the day or connect in a light manner over a meal. You need to read the mood of your relationship to know what it needs. Some people get tired of light banter and don't enjoy the superficial nature of it. Others like it but still have deeper feelings to share sometimes. As with all things, track yourself and your partner to gauge if the relationship is responding well to your habits.

Sometimes partners who engage in small talk often don't go deeper to speak eye-to-eye and heart-to-heart, in ways that convey love directly. The nervous system needs ongoing reassurance that our dedication to a relationship is still intact, plus reassurance is nice to hear. If you don't feel positively about the relationship and it would be disingenuous to say kind, reassuring words, then it's helpful to identify what needs to happen for the relationship to rekindle those feelings. Challenging yourself to either declare love and commitment to others or acknowledge that the relationship needs attention gives you a chance to deepen connection either way. If there are some wounds in the relationship, they may need joint attention to repair to elicit close feelings again.

Relationship Tune-Ups

Sometimes the busyness of life makes it difficult to sink into deeper or challenging conversations that require more thought and time. Every now and then it's helpful to engage in a relationship retreat to set goals and process issues or just to celebrate your connection and love free of distractions. These retreats offer a chance to take a meta-perspective on how things are going, talk about your relationship in greater depth than daily life may allow, hopefully relax and have some fun together, and set goals for continual improvement. If you can get away for a weekend, that's great; if not, a few hours at a park on a weekend still give you focused time to discuss how you're doing.

Relationships take continual tending and maintenance—a tune-up is where you take stock of where you are and what needs to occur for connection to deepen. You might need to process hurts, or talk about feelings you've been neglecting to bring up. If you feel you have slipped in some areas as a couple, it can be a good occasion to get to know each other better in those areas and get even stronger. Relationships go through phases, and down phases create an opportunity to pivot, fix some things, and continue as an improved union.

You can take relationship retreats by attending couples workshops led by experts, but these sometimes have busy schedules and can be emotionally tiring, which may not allow a lot of room for you to guide your own conversations. Decide ahead of time if you want a guided process and a training structure or if you just need some time with each other to share and talk in your own way. I recommend you take downtime with each other once per quarter or so to share more deeply and discuss how to keep improving. A close, connected relationship typically doesn't happen all by itself—it takes dedication, perseverance, effort, and attention.

Honesty versus Authenticity

Honesty is thought by many to be the most helpful policy in relationships, but authentic communication is far more important. Honesty is conveying whatever thoughts or feelings you have in a given moment, but it doesn't always take into account the purpose of communication. Honesty may be accurate, but accuracy may not serve the goal of connection. Couples who worry too much about accuracy end up litigating who said what, when, and how and can get into annoying arguments. Memory is based in perception and perception of the same situations varies by person, so it's better to use that energy to respect each other's feelings and try to bridge between different viewpoints.

Authenticity captures the *purpose* of your communication. It seeks to find words that move along that purpose rather than just being honest. Honesty isn't always connecting and, at times, can be disconnecting. We all have random thoughts and judgments about others that would not be nice or polite to say out loud. The key thing is to find an authentic way to express how you feel and what you need that honors the goal of your communication. Most of the time, your goal will be to connect, be heard, respected, validated in how you feel, and understood. Authentic communication that helps you connect gets you there more than pure honesty.

I've heard people justify crass and misaligned remarks by saying, "I was just being honest!" as if being honest is a pass for hurting someone's feelings, and as if others should be immune to reactions to us when we're being honest. It may be honest to scream your anger at your partner because it's how you feel in the moment, but it's not authentic unless your true intent is to scare or hurt your partner or for the relationship to end on bad terms.

If you ask people who pride themselves on honesty and who tend to rub others the wrong way if their authentic purpose is to put others on edge or make others uncomfortable, they might say no. But their raw and sometimes harsh honesty does exactly that. Their claimed "authenticity" is really about being an individual who acts in ways that are true to just themselves but is not an authenticity that champions relationship goals or learning how to deepen love and security with others. In this way, "authenticity" has become a buzzword that represents independence and a radical honesty of being. But if your purpose is to live life in close connection and harmony with others, then being "authentic" needs to take on a different sense and be more defined by genuinely relational goals.

Relationships are team events: they are circular in that one person's feelings alter the context and therefore the "truth" of a situation, so there typically is not an objective truth outside of our subjective individual experience. Relationships need mutual care to succeed in developing security, so validating each person's truth is important and helps that individual feel cared for. Simply being honest and conveying your own thoughts and feelings does not always represent joint truth or care and therefore may not actually enhance your relationship—it could take it backward.

Many people get confused as to why conversations with others, especially partners, often don't work out well, and the secret is sometimes in the disconnect between the chosen words and the authentic purpose. To communicate authentically, ask yourself: *Why am I communicating this?* Are you interacting to feel closer, to fall in love, to support someone, to create a sense of trust, or to just be yourself and see if you fit with someone else? Or are you communicating to express anger, hurt, to criticize someone's actions, to demean someone, or to harm the relationship in some way? Getting clear on your purpose organizes your words and helps you determine what authentic communication means for that moment. If your intent is to connect, you might measure connection before, during, and after a conversation to see if your way of communicating is accomplishing the goal.

Before you speak honestly, ask yourself what your intent is with the person you're relating to. I would recommend even stating that intent before sharing anything else, because the intent helps set the context, which shapes how people hear words and the meaning they assign to them. No one wants to hear "We need to talk" without knowing what the conversation might be about. By clearly stating, "I'd like to feel closer and have more fun with you, and there's something I want to discuss that I think will help us get there," we're signaling an authentic intent and our partner knows why we want to talk about an issue, which is to improve and get closer, not to judge, criticize, or break up. Setting a positive context like that helps disable defensiveness and makes conversations about issues easier.

What Not to Say

While every relationship is unique, there are some things that are generally inadvisable to say that may decrease connection and take your relationships backward. Since connection is usually deepened by growing the sense of safety and security in relationships, it's typically good to avoid words that convey a sense of unease and doubt. You don't want to keep people guessing as to your intent to create safety and connection; in the absence of obvious positive cues for secure interaction and relationship, the mind will often assume a negative. And, of course, overt aggressive or threatening words can do serious damage to the security system of relationships.

Even if your aim is to dissolve a relationship, such a goal is better achieved within as secure a context as possible. Communicating in a way that is defensive, belligerent, hostile, or mean makes breakups worse and more complicated. Toxic breakups leave a legacy of emotional stress and trauma for all individuals, reduce empathy between people, make co-parenting harder, and obscure helpful data you may need so you can understand what happened and try to have healthier relationships going forward. More-secure breakups help protect children from the negative fallout of a divorce or separation, allow you to move on more easily with future partners, and reduce anxiety if you maintain connections in a common friend group or live in the same town. Under almost all conditions, it is best to use words that create a sense of security in the interaction because it helps others listen better to what you're saying and what you need.

Words That Can Harm Connection

1. **Don't threaten the relationship itself (unless you mean it).**
    In general, you don't want to threaten a relationship unless you actually intend for it to end. Many partners use threats of breaking up as a way to express frustration, hopelessness, anger, and a need for things to change. These kinds of threats typically backfire. First, they don't securely communicate the issue and invite a partner into a positive, collaborative process of teamwork for change. Second, the threats diminish the sense of security and commitment in the relationship, both of which are important foundational forces that help you move toward change. Keep in mind that learning and change are difficult for most and breaking bad habits requires much support, reinforcement, and practice. Without the support of a strong foundation, it's hard for people to practice and learn the positive changes they need to step into better habits and to have healthier relationships.

2. **Don't demean or belittle your partner.**
    Condescension is not tolerated well in relationships. Smugness is in the "contempt and disgust" range of emotions, which is dangerous to your bond and commitment. If you have an issue with your partner and you have built up strong resentments over years, you still may want to find a productive way to talk about those feelings without damaging the relationship or your future prospects with someone. You certainly don't want to overtly talk down to someone, pretend you know better in any general sense, or imply they are not your equal in some way. Everyone deserves the dignity and respect of being understood for who they are and how they think, even if you disagree with them, feel annoyed by some of their habits, or think they have some things to learn in certain areas.

3. **Don't insult others.**

    Insults are sometimes exasperated comments of last resort when our anger and frustration turn to helplessness, but they also often convey a sense of superiority and belie strong character judgments in a way that harms the core of your bond. If you're tempted to insult your partner, instead find the deeper feeling in yourself that is spurring that, then find a respectful way to share that feeling and bridge differences. Insults come off as mean, and no one wants to be in relationship with someone mean. While this type of communication is normalized or common in some families and you may have been around it growing up, being insulting is sure to degrade the sense of emotional security you need to trust each other and have a healthy relationship.

4. **Be cautious questioning your love.**

    Love is a subjective feeling. It can come and go at times, get stronger or weaker, and sometimes it's hard to connect to when you're in a distressing cycle, but that doesn't mean your love isn't alive in the background. If you question your love with your partner out loud to them, it can sound like you're questioning the relationship itself or saying it's over. That can set your sense of security back, making it harder to work on issues together.

    Love is helpful as a force of attraction and care, but it is not enough in itself to make relationships healthy or sustain them. You still need relationship skills, the ability to share diverse perspectives, and compatible lifestyles to be on solid territory. Sometimes, when your feeling of love wavers in a relationship, it's because other things aren't working well. You're getting frustrated with your partner, parenting isn't smooth, you disagree about money, you're not making enough headway on critical issues, or you have structural stressors at home like health problems or caring for difficult family members. Sometimes, once those issues get resolved, the feeling of love returns from the background.

5. **Don't act aggressively.**

When you yell at others, get loud, act aggressive, or talk insensitively over them, you are degrading the security quotient of your relationship and deeply harming it. Healthy relationships are built on a sense of safety and security, care and mutuality, and acting aggressively violates all of those. If you're elevating your voice and using insults when addressing your partner, that starts veering toward verbal abuse. Your partner may feel physically unsafe, even though you may not act physically aggressive. Many people have prior experiences with abusive parents or traumatic experiences and those feelings get triggered when others are aggressive with them. You or your partner will likely feel emotionally unsafe in those conditions, degrading the sense of trust and security that is essential for healthy bonds.

When you can't rely on the emotional security of a relationship, the relationship elicits chronic stress, increasing allostatic load.[1] Allostatic load is a measure of cumulative stress that is linked to genetic degradation and susceptibility to disease, both mental and physical. Acting aggressive also violates the pact to take care of each other, turning a teammate into an enemy you have to be wary of. And acting aggressively violates mutuality, the "good for you, good for me" rubric of heathy interactions.

Anger problems destroy relationships quickly. If you have anger problems, it is important to handle them by seeking psychotherapy to understand stressors, traumas, and to create a plan to improve the issue. That plan could include anger management classes, a psychiatry consult to rule out depression, anxiety, or other factors, and lifestyle changes such as modifications to diet and exercise. The bottom line is that if you want your relationships to succeed, be willing to work on yourself, learn, and get help from others to move toward positive goals. If you have toxic habits in relationships and want those relationships to survive and to keep your family intact, I recommend you do everything you possibly can to quickly clean up how you communicate when upset.

I have seen too many relationships fail because people with
bad habits take too long to clean up their tendencies.

Your Relationship Is Unique

Every relationship is different. Individuals are unique, with distinct personal back-
grounds, culture, and experiences, and each relationship is a new coming together of two or more unique individuals that has its own culture and develops
its own history. The advice in this book is broadly applicable because it considers
what helps brains and nervous systems feel secure, and because humans have a
lot of overlap in terms of how our security systems and bodily responses to connection and threat tend to work. But there is still great variety in our psychological
and neural makeups as people, cultural diversity in how we perceive and interpret
threat and stressors, and certainly much uniqueness to each relationship, so any
advice given needs to be tested in your relationship to determine its effectiveness and applicability.

Respecting the diversity of your relationship is important when considering
what type of communication and interactions benefit your connection the most.
Some relationships thrive by speaking less, touching more, or with partners engaging in quiet, parallel activities with each other. Some need more stimulation,
engagement, and direct conversation to thrive and feel satisfying. Some partners
need to get outside their bubble and play more with other people by engaging
with friends or participating actively in the community. Some need to spend more
time with just each other, socializing less and giving their relationship focused
attention. Some couples benefit from getting outside their usual day-to-day routine, and some do well in their usual routine, with familiar things and activities.

While all relationships benefit from increasing the sense of safety and security with each other, tracking emotions, using connecting cues, and strengthening
the foundation of mutual care, couples and individuals are different in the kinds of
lifestyles they enjoy and pursue. I encourage you to notice what helps you enjoy
each other and your lives as you implement the concepts in this book, and to be
aware of what deepens connection in your specific relationship.

When it comes to the phrases I've used as examples of words that connect,
they are generally phrases that deepen connection, but feel free to modify them

to fit your style. If you understand the concept those phrases convey—the appreciation, sense of commitment, dedication to security, interest, desire, and empathy—then you can say them in your own words and in a way that fits you and your relationship's culture.

Notes

1. Bruce S. McEwen, "Stressed or Stressed Out: What Is the Difference?," *Journal of Psychiatry & Neuroscience: JPN* 30, no. 5 (October 2005): 315–318.

Conclusion

Alone we can do so little; together we can do so much.

—Helen Keller

onnection is what life is all about. While relationships come with expectations, demands on your time and attention, and ask you to learn and grow, they can also offer increased security, emotional support, romance, love, and tighter family bonds. By applying the principles in this book, you can experience the positive side of living as humans have evolved to live—in a tribe and in close teamwork, emotionally and physically, with others—without the drawbacks of problematic relationship patterns. When functioning well, relationships seem well worth the energy it takes to maintain them, but we have to develop the skills to connect and practice forging secure bonds to reap the most benefit.

When I reflect on my journey toward a healthy partnership and family life, I see my progress has been due to learning the concepts in this book and being willing to practice them, even if awkwardly. My relational skills have come from setting clear goals that represent where I need to grow every year and having a clear plan of action for reaching them. It helps to have healthy companions to practice with, so if you're in a partnership and don't feel it's ready to pursue such growth, you might begin by developing closer and healthier dynamics in your friendships and other relationships. When partners are ready, I always recommend that they work to grow together when possible and take on a practice culture to develop skills for greater ease and deeper love.

A sense of security is the foundation that allows your relationship to be bold and take risks, knowing you have a strong base on which to process your experiences and the connection to track and pivot your interactions as needed. You can also explore dimensions of your individual selves as you grow, knowing the relationship can handle changing perspectives and maturing individuals exploring themselves throughout life. In a strong relationship, you can be weak, imperfect, and vulnerable, knowing that those close to you will love you and have your back. When your connections are strong, you can focus your energy on the full spectrum of life, feeling supported in your individual dreams and goals.

The Rock Star Relationship

Research helps us understand what allows advanced couples to reach a high level of closeness and satisfaction. In John Gottman and Robert Levenson's early research observing the patterns that separate "masters" from "disasters," happy, long-term partnerships were correlated with key relationship behaviors. Gottman and Levenson found that when such partners place a similar value on emotional sharing, they can reflect on their interactions and ease each other into difficult topics rather than surprise each other. Advanced partners fight fair, even complimenting each other in conflict, and repair misattunements and arguments quickly. And these skilled partners tend to their friendship, using it as a source of goodwill to buffer against toxic behavior, even when upset.[1] Connection gives you the foundation to build and enhance in all areas of life. By focusing on developing a more secure connection, you can strengthen the other major dimensions of primary relationships.

Friendship

While other aspects of relationship life (like sex, youth, attractiveness, health, and an active lifestyle) may come and go, friendship can endure all the way to the end—it is the bedrock of your existence as a couple. Tend to it, care for it, and nurture it, because without a friendship, relationships feel flat. When your friendship is strong, you tell each other things, you open up, you can rely on each other emotionally, you keep challenging the relationship to grow because you care, and you trust the other has your back. A strong friendship includes the sense that your partner cares just as much about your happiness and well-being as you do and will place what's good for you above their own interests at times. A friend defends you with others, protects you, and helps you when you need support.

Romance

If romance is part of your relationship, it's important to continue nurturing it throughout. A strong connection can help maintain desire and attraction and creates a sense of security that allows you to explore new things, communicate about sex, and deepen your romantic life.[2] Keep in mind that romance is not always tied to sex. You can flirt, and create romantic moods and interactions without them needing to be focused on sex or designed to lead to it. But if you like being open to that possibility, then creating romantic opportunities is a great way to kindle desire and warm up to physical contact.

Romantic interactions can include a date to a quiet restaurant, drawing a bath with lighted candles and great music, or a deep conversation at close range. Romance can be making your partner their favorite breakfast while giving them a sweet card you wrote, a walk in nature holding hands, or just complimenting and appreciating your partner. Being romantic tends to increase your connection as long as your romantic interactions are mutually appreciated.

While a strong emotional connection often supports romance and sex, some people like a sense of surprise, spontaneity, and novelty in their romantic lives and find a little distance or "strangerness" stimulating. For some, focusing too much on a close, safe emotional connection in romance can inhibit sexual interest at times. Being a secure couple allows you to play with erotic tension as you wish without actually being unsafe or with someone unfamiliar. Intimacy expert Esther Perel has discussed how sexual interest is sometimes kindled by a sense of strangerness, distance, and novelty and how couples can incorporate such stimulation within a secure base.[3]

Those who enjoy kink—the practice of non-conventional sexual practices and fantasies—play in this realm of primal instinct, sometimes acting dominant and at other times submissive, as well as exploring the relationship between pain and pleasure. Kink can enhance connection in secure relationships, because it requires vulnerability, honesty, and good communication to pursue safely and pleasurably and has a strong element of play.[4] But care needs to be taken in sexual play to establish consent for all aspects of an encounter, to practice honesty about partners' sexual health, intentions, and boundaries, and to track each person's experience carefully throughout an encounter, looking for signs that might indicate a need to stop, pause, or check in. A secure couple can engage in these forms of play without worrying that the aggression or uncertainty in the interaction is real. With a sense of security and based on consent, adults can enhance their sex lives by exploring their fantasies and turn-ons with creativity and curiosity.

Companionship

Companionship refers to whether you enjoy a shared lifestyle, move through life together with shared values and activities, agree on home life, work/relationship balance, travel, and hobbies, and can also coordinate well emotionally and logistically in your activities. Couples who are strong in their companionship typically have common goals and values for how they want to live, how they keep their home, and play well together in joint activities. A strong sense of connection allows you to broker a shared lifestyle, try new things together, coordinate your values and priorities, support each other in your respective activities, and negotiate a joint life you enjoy together.

Business Partnership

Primary partner relationships often involve a business partnership as part of sharing life with each other. Marriage and life partnership joins you financially in significant ways. Regardless of whether you maintain separate or joint money, you are still emotionally and often financially tied at the hip on issues related to your home, saving for retirement, spending and budgeting, family planning, parenting and school choices, funding a desired lifestyle, healthcare options, and many more shared aspects. Managing money is one of the most challenging aspects of partnership. It's easy to get scared, angry, and frustrated by the different habits you may have from each other. Differences in money management are a leading cause of divorce, so tending to your business partnership is a vital way of securing your relationship health.

Brokering a joint financial life is as much about tending to emotions about security and money as it is about financial planning and making smart decisions. If you can successfully care for and signal protection of each other's need to feel safe in life, to have resources, and to plan well for the future and you trust your partner has your back emotionally, it's much easier to be open-minded and consider ways of handling money that may be different from your own default style. A strong connection helps you bridge your differences with greater ease and to make room for individual preferences while still moving together.

Play

Play is crucial to strong relationships. It instills a sense of goodwill, which you need to buffer against conflict and disagreements. A strong connection makes you want to play together. It allows you to open up emotionally and physically. Play relaxes you together, allowing you to share a joint space of fun and laughter, which is bonding. It builds your emotional bank account, protecting you from frustration or resentment in more challenging aspects of relationship. And play helps you keep joy alive in your sharing of life with each other.

Play is also vulnerable. We have to let loose, let our guard down, and show expressions or emotions that might not be our norm when we're more defended. If you're generally a serious person, allowing yourself to play broadens the way you connect with others.

Play can extend into the bedroom, keeping your sex life fun and interesting. Play helps you bond with your kids, learning what they're into, engaging in activities with them, and entering into their world of fun so you can play together. Play helps you bond with infants, stimulating their social and emotional development, and it offers opportunities to connect with friends and partners that bring variety and different conversations into your life. Play also helps you meet new people, stimulates your mind, and can expand your social community so you have a greater sense of belonging. Most everyone loves to play, so it's not difficult to attract others to fun activities that elicit excitement, joy, and laughter.

Parenting

Parenting is difficult enough on its own, but it is doubly hard when you don't have a strong connection with your partner or co-parent. So many decisions need to be made, big and small, and it's easy to feel like the security and well-being of your kids is at stake, which increases parents' anxiety and defensiveness. A strong connection allows you to get on the same page and support each other when kids act out, offering each other care and compassion as adults for the challenges of parenting. When adult partners are doing well and have a strong, secure bond, it helps kids feel at ease, reducing their anxiety, stress, and moodiness.

Putting It All Together

We've covered a lot of ideas in this book, but one you'll constantly need to refer to going forward is the markers of secure functioning in relationships. These five questions offer a simple guide:

1. Does the relationship exhibit mutuality (do your interactions feel good for all parties)?
2. Do you track each other's emotional cues and states in the moment (noticing stress on the face, tension in the eyes, or more explicit displays of emotion) and adapt your interactions as needed?
3. Do you feel physically relaxed around each other as partners, including when looking into each other's eyes? (This gives you a sense of your nervous system activity around others, including if you feel stressed due to a lack of emotional security).
4. Can you see the world from each other's point of view and appreciate and validate different perspectives?
5. Do you empathize, invite care, offer emotional support to each other, and can you be emotionally vulnerable with each other?

These five aspects give you a basic way of measuring the security of your relationship and noting where growth areas may lie. You can reflect on these components to explore how your relationships are doing in their ability to connect and feel secure.

Another shorthand to evaluate connection is whether you are able to land in real time with others and comfortably give and receive love. That simple test captures much of what connection is about. As one of my clients once said, "We know we love each other, but I don't *feel* loved." Connection is the distinction between having the knowledge of commitment and dedication and being able to richly feel loved all the way through your being.

The Microcosm Is the Macrocosm:
How Healthy Relationships Can Change the World

If you want to know why we find personal relationships difficult, just look to the greater society. When groups that disagree politically or culturally can't get along, we see the same dynamics that make our most intimate personal human relationships challenging. You might think that by choosing someone, you can avoid some of those difficult differences, but you can't. Not only do opposites attract, but over a lifetime people change and develop different perspectives and habits from the ones they had twenty years before. (And if you have kids who become teenagers, well, good luck to you.)

To succeed in relationships, it is important to be ready to embrace differences of perspective, habit, and culture and to see the wisdom and benefit in opening your mind to such differences. The skills we need to succeed at home in connection are the same skills we need as citizens to bridge differences among groups and individuals in society, to offer compassion and support to those who do not receive treatment equal to that of others, and to help heal divisions. As they say, it all begins at home, and when our primary relationships are loving, resilient, and places of embraced diversity, we can emerge into society healthier, kinder, more compassionate and empathic, emotionally intelligent, and understanding of why it is critical to individual and collective happiness to treat others with love and respect despite our differences.

Relationships and community health operate on a principle of mutuality—good for you and good for me. And yet mutuality cannot be practiced if we don't even see how we fail to create equality at home in our personal relationships, and in the culture and society at large. If we miss the oppressions, condescension, judgments, and holier-than-thou domestic interactions we sometimes engage in, how can we see the way we oppress and condescend to and judge others and groups in our lives outside our four walls? But if we embrace the challenge to love more deeply in our personal relationships, we find that same skill and ability in us in society.

Personal relationships have an uncanny ability to fill in our blind spots as they seek deeper connection. The question is, do we listen? Sometimes what we are not able to see keeps us from acknowledging that what others raise awareness about may be true. If we choose humility and curiosity, we can see how to improve our home life and how to improve equality and fairness in our society as well.

The microcosm of home mirrors the macrocosm of life on the planet. Our struggles to fully embrace those within our own homes show up in our deficiencies to embrace those within our larger community who are different from ourselves. Learning to live a more relational life is not just about having a better partner relationship, better friendships, or being a better parent to our kids—it's also a spiritual practice of digging deep and discovering the depth of who we are, going beyond a limited self, and embracing a collective reality. Learning to have healthy relationships puts us up against our preferences, biases, judgments, and fears, and we have to look them all in the eye and grow in order to have the most success.

Relationship is ultimately a process of finding unity in multiplicity. It's the same challenge we face more generally in life. It seems everywhere we look in our own lives and in the world there is triumph and tragedy, ease and difficulty—a mixed combination of emotions and experience. Being in relationship asks us to question our essential purpose in life: Is it to have fun, to learn, to grow, to help others? Is it to self-actualize, to raise the next generation of humans, or to leave a legacy? As we sort through our essential purpose for living, we also seek peace, love, and a sense of home. Close, connected relationships can help us find that peace within ourselves and sense of home that transcends our limited individual existence, helping us to realize that we can live for something greater.

Relationship is a path of personal growth. If we use our relationships as opportunities to reflect the macrocosm of life's challenge into the microcosm of our home life, we see a close, personal playground in which to test our ability and skill to navigate diversity, and the ups and downs of human emotional experience.

The essential task of relationship life is managing the friction between individuality and a shared existence. This attempt to find unity in the multiplicity of thoughts, habits, preferences, and cultural differences is the balance we seek in stable relationships. Navigating the complexity of shared life well results in a secure partnership that forms a solid foundation for life. In the same way that individuals may wrestle within themselves to find peace in a chaotic world, partners seek a shared unity amid the chaos of their diverse preferences and habits. Understood in this way, relationship becomes a kind of spiritual practice—a way to seek harmony and togetherness without diminishing the important, vibrant, and valuable diversity of people and of our world.

Embracing diversity leads to increased tolerance of complexity, psychological flexibility, and emotional resilience, all of which impart a sense of depth and peace to the relationship and the individuals in it. The amount of energy we use in relationships trying to avoid uncomfortable and annoying differences is better spent developing and flexing the muscles of open-mindedness, acceptance of diversity, resilience, and empathy. By letting our relationships with others act as our teachers in that respect, we can develop important individual qualities of maturity and improve our collective society as well.

Relationship is everything, and connection is at its core. Without connection, our individual bodies begin to fail, our minds suffer, our relationships fade, and society becomes a less secure place to live. Connection is love, connection is peace, and connection is the excitement and passion that drives us in life. Connection allows us to embrace differences, develop greater maturity of self, and begin to heal some of the inequities and divisions we face as societies. Connection helps us to heal ourselves, our relationships, our society, and the world, while enriching our lives with love, support, and freedom. My hope is that by learning to live in deeper love with others and training ourselves to form more secure bonds, we can extend those resources and skills into the world to help our communities heal and be more at peace, in our home, and between all our homes.

If you want to feel the love that is available to you with others, practice creating nervous system security at the core of your relationships and sharing that secure base with those in your life. In connecting deeply and securely, nervous system to nervous system, a whole world of safety, love, and peace is available to you, just in *how* you show up with yourself and others. Connection offers an efficient path to both individual and relational healing and fulfillment. If you embrace that path, I wish you success and that you come to enjoy its benefits. **To more love!**

Notes

1. John Gottman and Robert Levenson, "Why Marriages Fail: Affective and Physiological Patterns in Marital Interaction," in *Boundary Areas in Social and Developmental Psychology*, ed. John Masters (New York: Academic Press, 1984), 67–107.

2. Emily Nagoski, *Come As You Are: The Surprising New Science That Will Transform Your Sex Life* (New York: Simon & Schuster, 2015).

3. Esther Perel, *Mating in Captivity: Unlocking Erotic Intelligence* (New York: Harper, 2007), 272.

4. Sabitha Pillai-Friedman, J. L. Pollitt, and Annalisa Castaldo, "Becoming Kink-Aware—a Necessity for Sexuality Professionals," *Sexual and Relationship Therapy* 30, no. 2 (2015): 196–210.

Next Steps

If you've enjoyed this book and you want to know more about how to achieve relationship security in your life, optimize your partnership, and develop some of the skills we have described, I encourage you to head over to readysetlove. com/toolkit. There you'll find a bonus chapter on adult attachment, my myth-busting guide, and a cheat sheet to connecting more deeply in everyday life.

For those who wish to go deeper and engage in the practice of connection with their partners, our twelve-week Ready Set Love® course is a focused, online program that guides you through the exercises that facilitate connection. You can learn more information about the program on the toolkit page, and we have an audio course for individual learners. As always, I'm committed to helping you achieve deeper and healthier relationships so you can thrive in life and feel vibrant and happy. There's also a way to contact me at readysetlove.com/toolkit if you'd like to let me know what you thought about the book, and you can hop on our email list for future tips and offers to continue deepening your most important relationships. **Let's stay connected!**

The Big Ideas

A Review of the Book's Key Concepts

Connection Matters More than Communication

Communication has been sold as the golden ticket to a healthy relationship, but how we create safety and security at the nervous system level matters more.

The Language of the Nervous System

Highlights six key ways to speak connection directly to the primitive parts of our brain and nervous system: proximity, touch, tone, eye contact, body language, and speed of response.

The Power of Practice to Reshape Relationship Habits

Our relationship behavior is largely automatic. Retraining these wired-in habits takes procedural practice, not just conversations about issues.

A Strong Relationship Is More about Skill than Compatibility

We often talk about relationship magic as finding the right person, but developing our relational skill set is generally more important. Once baseline compatibility is established, we all need to develop skills to improve the relationships we're in.

Relationship as a Path of Personal Growth

Close relationships are often the greatest opportunity and avenue we have for personal growth—beyond individual pursuits. Relationships challenge us, illuminate our blind spots, and push us to develop new capacity.

Ninety Percent of Connection Happens out of Conscious Awareness

Our nonverbal signals communicate tremendous information to others' brains that feeds the connection calculation. While the brain collects much more information than it can be consciously aware of, we can shape what is communicated in that 90 percent.

Most Relationship Behaviors Are Automatic

We tend to assign personal intent to our partner's bad habits and behaviors, but most of the time they're running a wired-in program, like we are. Understanding how automatic we all are engenders compassion for flaws and mistakes and helps us focus our efforts on how to actually improve rather than relying on pressure, criticism, guilt, or judgment.

Process over Content

The way we talk is more important than what we're talking about. Caring for each other even in difficult conversations is what makes a relationship secure, not resolving specific points of order. Trusting that we will be cared for in present moment interactions over a lifetime of personal change creates strong partnerships.

Landing on the Same Little Patch of Grass

Most of us have an allergy to intimacy. We were trained away from sinking into moments of emotional connection and closeness. Love can happen more deeply when we land in the moment, relax, and are both available for close connection.

"We" versus "I"

Relationships function as a unit—as a team. Sometimes we get too caught up in saying "I feel this," and, "I need this," which, while healthy and a good expression of individuality, can also set up debates that can be disconnecting. In addition to individual experience, it helps to discuss things as a "we," such as, "How do we get better at this?" "Why do we do that?" and "What is our relationship needing more of in this pattern?"

Thermometers

The concept of thermometers is that each partner is the primary judge on the issues that matter most to them and on how improvement is going in those areas. Partners can share their opinion, and score and rate the other on the status of the pattern. This allows you to capture better data about your relationship and provides a more accurate sense of progress as you grow.

Picking Up Each Other's Flag

When caught in a debate of ideas, it helps to either jump onto the same side and look at the overall issue as a team or argue each other's position for the other, in order to improve theory of mind—seeing the world through someone else's eyes. This practice improves understanding, connection, and empathy.

Works Cited

- Acevedo, Bianca P., Arthur Aron, Helen E. Fisher, and Lucy L. Brown. "Neural Correlates of Long-Term Intense Romantic Love." *Social Cognitive and Affective Neuroscience* 7, no. 2 (February 2012): 145–159.

- Adolphs, Ralph. "Neural Systems for Recognizing Emotion." *Current Opinion in Neurobiology* 12, no. 2 (April 2002): 169–177.

- Andersen, Susan M., and Elizabeth Przybylinski. "Shared Reality in Interpersonal Relationships." *Current Opinion in Psychology* 23 (October 2018): 42–46.

- Anielski, Mark. *The Economics of Happiness: Building Genuine Wealth.* Gabriola, BC: New Society, 2007.

- Arnsten, Amy F. T. "Stress Signalling Pathways That Impair Prefrontal Cortex Structure and Function." *Nature Reviews Neuroscience* 10, no. 6 (June 2009): 410–422. https://doi.org/10.1038/nrn2648.

- Arnsten, Amy F. T., Murray A. Raskind, Fletcher B. Taylor, and Daniel F. Connor. "The Effects of Stress Exposure on Prefrontal Cortex: Translating Basic Research into Successful Treatments for Post-traumatic Stress Disorder." *Neurobiology of Stress* 1, no. 1 (January 2015): 89–99.

- Aron, Arthur, Edward Melinat, Elaine N. Aron, Robert Darrin Vallone, and Renee J. Bator. "The Experimental Generation of Interpersonal Closeness: A Procedure and Some Preliminary Findings." *Personality and Social Psychology Bulletin* 23, no. 4 (April 1997): 363–377.

- Atkinson, B. J. *Emotional Intelligence in Couples Therapy: Advances from Neurobiology and the Science of Intimate Relationships.* New York: W. W. Norton, 2005.

- Atkinson, Brent J. "Mindfulness Training and the Cultivation of Secure, Satisfying Couple Relationships." *Couple and Family Psychology: Research and Practice* 2, no. 2 (2013): 73.

- Atkinson, Leslie, Eman Leung, Susan Goldberg, Diane Benoit, Lori Poulton, Natalie Myhal, Kirsten Blokland, and Sheila Kerr. "Attachment and Selective Attention: Disorganization and Emotional Stroop Reaction Time." *Development and Psychopathology* 21, no. 1 (2009): 99–126.

- Badenoch, Bonnie. *The Heart of Trauma: Healing the Embodied Brain in the Context of Relationships.* Norton Series on Interpersonal Neurobiology. New York: W. W. Norton, 2017.

- Bahney, J., and C. S. von Bartheld. "The Cellular Composition and Glia-Neuron Ratio in the Spinal Cord of a Human and a Nonhuman Primate: Comparison with Other Species and Brain Regions." *Anatomical Record* 301, no. 4 (2018): 697–710. https://doi.org/10.1002/ar.23728.

- Barry, Dr. Harry. *Emotional Resilience: How to Safeguard Your Mental Health.* London: Orion, 2018.

- Beauchaine, Theodore. "Vagal Tone, Development, and Gray's Motivational Theory: Toward an Integrated Model of Autonomic Nervous System Functioning in Psychopathology." *Development and Psychopathology* 13, no. 2 (Spring 2001): 183–214.

- Berlin, Heather A. "The Neural Basis of the Dynamic Unconscious." *Neuropsychoanalysis* 13, no. 1 (2011): 5–31.

- Berntson, Gary G., Martin Sarter, and John T. Cacioppo. "Ascending Visceral Regulation of Cortical Affective Information Processing." *European Journal of Neuroscience* 18, no. 8 (October 2003): 2103–2109.

- Boer, Tara. Review of *Neurobiology for Clinical Social Work: Theory and Practice,* by Janet Shapiro and Jeffrey S. Applegate, *Journal of Evidence-Based Social Work* 17, no. 3 (2020): 368–369.

- Bond, Frank W., Steven C. Hayes, and Dermot Barnes-Holmes. "Psychological Flexibility, ACT, and Organizational Behavior." *Journal of Organizational Behavior Management* 26, no. 1-2 (2006): 25–54. https://doi.org/10.1300/J075v26n01_02.

- Bond, Frank W., J. Lloyd, and N. Guenole. "The Work-Related Acceptance and Action Questionnaire: Initial Psychometric Findings and Their Implications for Measuring Psychological Flexibility in Specific Contexts." *Journal of Occupational and Organizational Psychology* 86, no. 3 (September 2013): 331–347. https://doi.org/10.1111/joop.12001.

- Bonnano, George A. "Loss, Trauma and Human Resilience: Have We Underestimated the Human Capacity to Thrive after Extremely Adverse Events?" *American Psychologist* 59, no.1 (January 2004): 20–28.

- Brandon, Marianne. "Monogamy and Nonmonogamy: Evolutionary Considerations and Treatment Challenges." *Sexual Medicine Reviews* 4, no. 4 (October 2016): 343–352.

- Brecht, Michael, and Winrich A. Freiwald. "The Many Facets of Facial Interactions in Mammals." *Current Opinion in Neurobiology* 22, no. 2 (April 2012): 259–266. https://doi.org/10.1016/j.conb.2011.12.003.

- Breit, S., A. Kupferberg, G. Rogler, and G. Hasler. "Vagus Nerve as Modulator of the Brain-Gut Axis in Psychiatric and Inflammatory Disorders." *Frontiers in Psychiatry* 9, no. 44 (March 2018). https://doi.org/10.3389/fpsyt.2018.00044.

- Bretherton, Inge. "The Origins of Attachment Theory: John Bowlby and Mary Ainsworth." *Developmental Psychology* 28, no. 5 (1992): 759.

- Brooks, Kathryn P., Tara Gruenewald, Arun Karlamangla, Peifung Hu, Brandon Koretz, and Teresa E. Seeman. "Social Relationships and Allostatic Load in the MIDUS Study." *Health Psychology* 33, no. 11 (November 2014): 1373–1381.

- Bruce, Liana DesHarnais, Joshua S. Wu, Stuart L. Lustig, Daniel W. Russell, and Douglas A. Nemecek. "Loneliness in the United States: A 2018 National Panel Survey of Demographic, Structural, Cognitive, and Behavioral Characteristics." *American Journal of Health Promotion* 33, no. 8 (June 2019): 1123–1133.

- Buchheim, Anna, Markus Heinrichs, Carol George, Dan Pokorny, Eva Koops, Peter Henningsen, Mary-Frances O'Connor, and Harald Gündel. "Oxytocin Enhances the Experience of Attachment Security." *Psychoneuroendocrinology* 34, no. 9 (October 2009): 1417–1422.

- Burgoon, Judee K., David B. Buller, Jerold L. Hale, and Mark A. de Turck. "Relational Messages Associated with Nonverbal Behaviors." *Human Communication Research* 10, no. 3 (March 1984): 351–378.

- Burgoon, Judee K., Laura K. Guerrero, and Valerie Manusov. *Nonverbal Communication.* New York: Routledge, 2016.

- Burkett, J. P., and L. J. Young. "The Behavioral, Anatomical and Pharmacological Parallels between Social Attachment, Love and Addiction." *Psychopharmacology* 224, no. 1 (August 2012): 1–26. https://doi.org/10.1007/s00213-012-2794-x.

- Byock, I. *The Four Things That Matter Most: A Book about Living.* 2nd ed. New York: Atria Books, 2014.

- Cacioppo, John T., and Stephanie Cacioppo. "Social Relationships and Health: The Toxic Effects of Perceived Social Isolation." *Social and Personality Psychology Compass* 8, no. 2 (February 2014): 58–72.

- Camfield, Laura, Kaneta Choudhury, and Joe Devine. "Well-Being, Happiness and Why Relationships Matter: Evidence from Bangladesh." *Journal of Happiness Studies* 10, no. 1 (February 2009): 71–91.

- Carter, C. Sue. "The Oxytocin–Vasopressin Pathway in the Context of Love and Fear." *Frontiers in Endocrinology* 8 (December 2017): 356.

- Catherall, Don R. *Emotional Safety: Viewing Couples through the Lens of Affect.* Abingdon-on-Thames, UK: Routledge, 2006.

- Catron, Mandy Len. *How to Fall in Love with Anyone: A Memoir in Essays.* New York: Simon & Schuster, 2017.

- ———. "To Fall in Love with Anyone, Do This." *New York Times*, January 9, 2015. https://www.nytimes.com/2015/01/11/style/modern-love-to-fall-in-love-with-anyone-do-this.html.

- Cho, Sumi, Kimberlé Williams Crenshaw, and Leslie McCall. "Toward a Field of Intersectionality Studies: Theory, Applications, and Praxis." *Signs: Journal of Women in Culture and Society* 38, no. 4 (Summer 2013): 785–810.

- Chow, Daryl L., Scott D. Miller, Jason A. Seidel, Robert T. Kane, Jennifer A. Thornton, and William P. Andrews. "The Role of Deliberate Practice in the Development of Highly Effective Psychotherapists." *Psychotherapy* 52, no. 3 (2015): 337.

- Cozolino, Louis J. *The Neuroscience of Human Relationships: Attachment and the Developing Social Brain.* Norton Series on Interpersonal Neurobiology. New York: W. W. Norton, 2014.

- Cozolino, Louis J., and Erin N. Santos. "Why We Need Therapy—and Why It Works: A Neuroscientific Perspective." *Smith College Studies in Social Work* 84, no. 2-3 (August 2014): 157–177.

- Cozolino, Louis J., and Susan Sprokay. "Neuroscience and Adult Learning." *The Neuroscience of Adult Learning: New Directions for Adult and Continuing Education* 81, no. 110 (Summer 2006): 11.

- Culpeper, Jonathan. "'It's Not What You Said, It's How You Said It!': Prosody and Impoliteness." *Discursive Approaches to Politeness* 8 (2011): 57–83.

- Damasio, A. R. "The Somatic Marker Hypothesis and the Possible Functions of the Prefrontal Cortex." *Philosophical Transactions of the Royal Society of London, Series B: Biological Sciences* 351 (October 1996): 1413–1420.

- de Gelder, Beatrice. "Towards the Neurobiology of Emotional Body Language." *Nature Reviews Neuroscience* 7, no. 3 (March 2006): 242–249.

- Demarinis, Susie. "Loneliness at Epidemic Levels in America." *Explore* 16, no. 5 (September–October 2020): 278–279. https://doi.org/10.1016/j.explore.2020.06.008.

- Diego, Miguel A., and Tiffany Field. "Moderate Pressure Massage Elicits a Parasympathetic Nervous System Response." *International Journal of Neuroscience* 119, no. 5 (2009): 630–638.

- Drescher, Jack, and Kenneth J. Zucker. *Ex-gay Research: Analyzing the Spitzer Study and Its Relation to Science, Religion, Politics, and Culture.* New York: Routledge, 2013.

- Editors of Harvard Health Publishing in Consultation with Robert Schreiber, MD. *Living Better, Living Longer.* Boston: Harvard Health, 2017.

- Ekman, Paul. "Basic Emotions." In *Handbook of Cognition and Emotion,* edited by Tim Dalgleish and Mick J. Power, 16. New York: Wiley, 1999.

- Ellingsen, Dan-Mikael, Johan Wessberg, Olga Chelnokova, Håkan Olausson, Bruno Laeng, and Siri Leknes. "In Touch with Your Emotions: Oxytocin and Touch Change Social Impressions While Others' Facial Expressions Can Alter Touch." *Psychoneuroendocrinology* 39 (January 2014): 11–20.

- Emery, Nathan J. "The Eyes Have It: The Neuroethology, Function and Evolution of Social Gaze." *Neuroscience & Biobehavioral Reviews* 24, no. 6 (September 2000): 581–604.

- Ericsson, K. Anders. "The Differential Influence of Experience, Practice, and Deliberate Practice on the Development of Superior Individual Performance of Experts." In *The Cambridge Handbook of Expertise and Expert Performance,* edited by K. A. Ericsson, R. R. Hoffman, A. Kozbelt, and A. M. Williams, Cambridge Handbooks in Psychology, 745–769. Cambridge: Cambridge University Press, 2018.

- Ericsson, K. Anders, Ralf T. Krampe, and Clemens Tesch-Römer. "The Role of Deliberate Practice in the Acquisition of Expert Performance." *Psychological Review* 100, no. 3 (1993): 363.

- Fegert, Jörg M., Benedetto Vitiello, Paul L. Plener, and Vera Clemens. "Challenges and Burden of the Coronavirus 2019 (COVID-19) Pandemic for Child and Adolescent Mental Health: A Narrative Review to Highlight Clinical and Research Needs in the Acute Phase and the Long Return to Normality." *Child and Adolescent Psychiatry and Mental Health* 14 (May 2020): 1–11.

- Fern, Jessica. *Polysecure: Attachment, Trauma and Consensual Nonmonogamy.* Portland, OR: Thorntree Press, 2020.

- Field, Tiffany. "Touch for Socioemotional and Physical Well-Being: A Review." *Developmental Review* 30, no. 4 (December 2010): 367–383.

- Fishbane, Mona DeKoven. *Loving with the Brain in Mind: Neurobiology and Couple Therapy.* Norton Series on Interpersonal Neurobiology. New York: W. W. Norton, 2013.

- Fonagy, Peter, and Mary Target. "Attachment and Reflective Function: Their Role in Self-Organization." *Development and Psychopathology* 9, no. 4 (1997): 679–700.

- Fosha, Diana. *The Transforming Power of Affect: A Model for Accelerated Change.* New York: Basic Books, 2000.

- Fosha, Diana, Daniel J. Siegel, and Marion F. Solomon, eds. *The Healing Power of Emotion: Affective Neuroscience, Development & Clinical Practice.* New York: W. W. Norton, 2009.

- Gardenswartz, Lee, Jorge Cherbosque, and Anita Rowe. "Emotional Intelligence and Diversity: A Model for Differences in the Workplace." *Journal of Psychological Issues in Organizational Culture* 1, no. 1 (April 2010): 74–84.

- Germer, Christopher. *The Mindful Path to Self-Compassion: Freeing Yourself from Destructive Thoughts and Emotions*, New York: Guilford, 2009.

- Gimpl, Gerald, and Falk Fahrenholz. "The Oxytocin Receptor System: Structure, Function, and Regulation." *Physiological Reviews* 81, no. 2 (April 2001): 629–683.

- Ginot, Efrat. *The Neuropsychology of the Unconscious: Integrating Brain and Mind in Psychotherapy*. Norton Series on Interpersonal Neurobiology. New York: W. W. Norton, 2015.

- Goldstein, D. S. "Adrenal Responses to Stress." *Cellular and Molecular Neurobiology* 30, no. 8 (November 2010): 1433–1440. https://doi.org/10.1007/s10571-010-9606-9.

- Goldstein, Sondra, and Susan Thau. "Integrating Attachment Theory and Neuroscience in Couple Therapy." *International Journal of Applied Psychoanalytic Studies* 1, no. 3 (September 2004): 214–223.

- Goleman, Daniel. *Emotional Intelligence: Why It Can Matter More than IQ*. New York: Bantam, 2012.

- Gottman, John M. "New View of Mind Gives Unconscious an Expanded Role." *New York Times*, February 7, 1984, 1.

- ———. *What Predicts Divorce?: The Relationship between Marital Processes and Marital Outcomes*. London: Psychology Press, 2014.

- ———. "Why Marriages Fail: Affective and Physiological Patterns in Marital Interaction." In *Boundary Areas in Social and Developmental Psychology*, edited by John Masters, 67–107. New York: Academic Press, 1984.

- Gottman, John M., and Julie S. Gottman. "Difficulties with Clients in Gottman Method Couples Therapy." In *Transforming Negative Reactions to Clients: From Frustration to Compassion*, edited by A. W. Wolf, M. R. Goldfried, and J. C. Muran, 91–112. Washington, DC: American Psychological Association, 2013.

- Gottman, John M., Julie S. Gottman, Andy Greendorfer, and Mirabai Wahbe. "An Empirically Based Approach to Couples' Conflict." In *The Handbook of Conflict Resolution: Theory and Practice*, edited by P. T. Coleman, M. Deutsch, and E. C. Marcus, 898–920. San Francisco: Jossey-Bass/Wiley, 2014.

- Gottman, John M., and Robert W. Levenson. "A Two-Factor Model for Predicting When a Couple Will Divorce: Exploratory Analyses Using 14-Year Longitudinal Data." *Family Process* 41, no. 1 (Spring 2002): 83–96.

- Gottman, John M., and Nan Silver. *The Seven Principles for Making Marriage Work: A Practical Guide from the Country's Foremost Relationship Expert*. New York: Harmony, 2015.

- Gottman, John Mordechai, and Julie Schwartz Gottman. "Gottman Method Couple Therapy." In *Clinical Handbook of Couple Therapy*, 4th ed., edited by Alan S. Gurman, 138–164. New York: Guilford, 2008.

- Guilliams, Thomas G., and Lena Edwards. "Chronic Stress and the HPA Axis." *The Standard* 9, no. 2 (2010): 1–12.

- Haase, Claudia M. "Emotion Regulation in Intimate Relationships. *Society for the Study of Behavioral Development* 1, no. 65 (2014): 17–21.

- Hartling, Linda M., PhD. "Strengthening Resilience in a Risky World: It's All about Relationships." *Women & Therapy* 31 (2008): 2–4, 51–70. https://doi.org/10.1080/02703140802145870.

- Hazan, Cindy, and Phillip Shaver. "Romantic Love Conceptualized as an Attachment Process." *Journal of Personality and Social Psychology* 52, no. 3 (March 1987): 511.

- Heath, Melanie. *One Marriage under God: The Campaign to Promote Marriage in America*. Vol. 16. New York: NYU Press, 2012.

- Helms, Janet E., Nicolas Guerda, and Carlton E. Green. "Racism and Ethnoviolence as Trauma: Enhancing Professional and Research Training." *Traumatology* 18, no. 1 (2012): 65–74.

- Hesse, Erik. "The Adult Attachment Interview: Protocol, Method of Analysis, and Selected Empirical Studies: 1985–2015." In *Handbook of Attachment: Theory, Research, and Clinical Applications*, 3rd ed., edited by J. Cassidy and P. R. Shaver, 553–597. New York: Guilford, 2016.

- Hewitt, John P. "The Social Construction of Self-Esteem." In *The Oxford Handbook of Positive Psychology*. New York: Oxford University Press, 2009: 309.

- Holt-Lunstad, Julianne, Timothy B. Smith, Mark Baker, Tyler Harris, and David Stephenson. "Loneliness and Social Isolation as Risk Factors for Mortality: A Meta-Analytic Review." *Perspectives on Psychological Science* 10, no. 2 (March 2015): 227–237. https://doi.org/10.1177/1745691614568352.

- Howard, John. "Emotions Chart." http://www.presencewellness.co/emotions-chart.

- Imada, Andrew S., and Milton D. Hakel. "Influence of Nonverbal Communication and Rater Proximity on Impressions and Decisions in Simulated Employment Interviews." *Journal of Applied Psychology* 62, no. 3 (1977): 295.

- Imran, Nazish, Muhammad Zeshan, and Zainab Pervaiz. "Mental Health Considerations for Children & Adolescents in COVID-19 Pandemic." *Pakistan Journal of Medical Sciences* 36, no. COVID19-S4 (May 2020): S67.

- Izard, Carroll E. "Basic Emotions, Relations among Emotions, and Emotion-Cognition Relations." *Psychological Review* 99, no. 3 (July 1992): 561–565. https://doi.org/10.1037/0033-295X.99.3.561.

- ———. *Human Emotions.* Berlin: Springer Science+Business Media, 2013.

- Johnson, Addie. "Procedural Memory and Skill Acquisition. In *Handbook of Psychology*, 2nd ed., vol. 4, *Experimental Psychology*, edited by Alice F. Healey and Robert W. Proctor. Hoboken: Wiley, 2012.

- Johnson, Sue. *Love Sense: The Revolutionary New Science of Romantic Relationships.* New York: Little, Brown Spark, 2013.

- Johnson, Sue, and Brent Bradley. "Emotionally Focused Couple Therapy: Creating Loving Relationships." In *The Wiley-Blackwell Handbook of Family Psychology*, edited by H. Bray and M. Stanton. Hoboken: Wiley-Blackwell, 2009.

- Johnson, Sue, and M. Kerman. "Emotionally Focused Couple Therapy: It's All about Emotion and Connection." In *Clinical Pearls of Wisdom: 21 Leading Therapists Offer Their Key Insights*, edited by Michael Kerman, 133. New York: W. W. Norton, 2009.

- Kashdan, Todd B., and Jonathan Rottenberg. "Psychological Flexibility as a Fundamental Aspect of Health." *Clinical Psychology Review* 30, no. 7 (2010): 865–878. https://doi.org/10.1016/j.cpr.2010.03.001.

- Keleher, Alison, and Eric R. A. N. Smith. "Growing Support for Gay and Lesbian Equality since 1990." *Journal of Homosexuality* 59, no. 9 (2012): 1307–1326.

- Kohl, James V., Michaela Atzmueller, Bernhard Fink, and Karl Grammer. "Human Pheromones: Integrating Neuroendocrinology and Ethology." *Neuroendocrinology Letters* 22, no. 5 (2001): 309–321.

- Kok, Bethany E., Kimberly A. Coffey, Michael A. Cohn, Lahnna I. Catalino, Tanya Vacharkulksemsuk, Sara B. Algoe, Mary Brantley, and Barbara L. Fredrickson. "How Positive Emotions Build Physical Health: Perceived Positive Social Connections Account for the Upward Spiral between Positive Emotions and Vagal Tone." *Psychological Science* 24, no. 7 (July 2013): 1123–1132.

- Kowalska, Magda, and Monika Wróbel. "Basic Emotions." In *Encyclopedia of Personality and Individual Differences*, edited by Virgil Zeigler-Hill and Todd K. Shackelford, 1–6. Cham, Switzerland: Springer International, 2017.

- Lapides, Francine. "The Implicit Realm in Couples Therapy: Improving Right Hemisphere Affect-Regulating Capabilities." *Clinical Social Work Journal* 39, no. 2 (June 2011): 161–169.

- LeDoux, Joseph. "The Amygdala." *Current Biology* 17, no. 20 (October 2007): R868–R874.

- ———. *The Emotional Brain: The Mysterious Underpinnings of Emotional Life.* New York: Simon & Schuster, 2015.

- ———. *Synaptic Self: How Our Brains Become Who We Are.* New York: Viking, 2002.

- Lee, David S., Oscar Ybarra, Richard Gonzalez, and Phoebe Ellsworth. "I-through-We: How Supportive Social Relationships Facilitate Personal Growth." *Personality and Social Psychology Bulletin* 44, no. 1 (January 2018): 37–48.

- Levine, Amir, and Rachel Heller. *Attached: The New Science of Adult Attachment and How It Can Help You Find—and Keep—Love.* London: Penguin, 2010.

- Levine, Peter A. *In an Unspoken Voice: How the Body Releases Trauma and Restores Goodness.* Berkeley: North Atlantic Books, 2010.

- Lewandowski, Gary W., Jr. "AsktheBrains: What Physiological Changes Can Explain the Honeymoon Phase of a Relationship?" *Scientific American Mind* 24, no. 4 (September/October 2013). https://doi.com/10.1038/scientificamericanmind 0913-72a.

- Liu, Frederick, and Stephen Macedo. "The Federal Marriage Amendment and the Strange Evolution of the Conservative Case against Gay Marriage." *PS: Political Science and Politics* 38, no. 2 (2005): 211–215.

- Locke, Joseph, and Ben Wright. "The Politics of Love, Sex and Gender." In *American Yawp: A Massively Collaborative Open U.S. History Textbook.* Stanford: Stanford University Press, 2014 (2020–2021 Updates). http://www.americanyawp.com/.

- Mandal, Fatik Baran. "Nonverbal Communication in Humans." *Journal of Human Behavior in the Social Environment* 24, no. 4 (2014): 417–421.

- Marques de Miranda, Debora, Bruno da Silva Athanasio, Ana Cecília de Sena Oliveira, and Ana Cristina Simoes Silva. "How Is COVID-19 Pandemic Impacting Mental Health of Children and Adolescents?" *International Journal of Disaster Risk Reduction* 51 (December 2020): 101845.

- Mayer, Emeran A. "Gut Feelings: The Emerging Biology of Gut–Brain Communication." *Nature Reviews Neuroscience* 12, no. 8 (2011): 453–466.

- McEwen, Bruce S. "Stressed or Stressed Out: What Is the Difference?" *Journal of Psychiatry & Neuroscience* 30, no. 5 (September 2005): 315–318.

- McEwen, Bruce S., and Peter J. Gianaros. "Central Role of the Brain in Stress and Adaptation: Links to Socioeconomic Status, Health, and Disease." *Annals of the New York Academy of Sciences* 1186 (February 2010): 190–222.

- Melkonian, Tessa, and Thierry Picq. "Opening the 'Black Box' of Collective Competence in Extreme Projects: Lessons from the French Special Forces." *Project Management Journal* 41, no. 3 (June 2010): 79–90.

- Menakem, Resmaa. *My Grandmother's Hands: Racialized Trauma and the Pathway to Mending Our Hearts and Bodies.* Las Vegas: Central Recovery Press, 2017.

- Mesman, Judi, Marinus H. Van Ijzendoorn, and Abraham Sagi-Schwartz. "Cross-cultural Patterns of Attachment." *Handbook of Attachment: Theory, Research, and Clinical Applications* (2016): 852–877.

- Meunier, Vagdevi, and Wayne Baker. "Positive Couple Relationships: The Evidence for Long-Lasting Relationship Satisfaction and Happiness." In *Positive Relationships*, edited by S. Roffey, 73–89. Berlin: Springer, Dordrecht, 2012.

- Mikulincer, Mario. "Attachment, Caregiving, and Sex within Romantic Relationships." In *Dynamics of Romantic Love: Attachment, Caregiving, and Sex*, edited by Mario Mikulincer and Gail S. Goodman, 23–44. New York: Guilford, 2006.

- Mikulincer, Mario, and Phillip R. Shaver. "The Attachment Behavioral System in Adulthood: Activation, Psychodynamics, and Interpersonal Processes." In *Advances in Experimental Social Psychology*, vol. 35, edited by M. P. Zanna, 53–152. New York: Academic Press, 2003.

- Moors, Amy C., Amanda N. Gesselman, and Justin R. Garcia. "Desire, Familiarity, and Engagement in Polyamory: Results from a National Sample of Single Adults in the United States." *Frontiers in Psychology* 12 (March 2021): 811.

- Mujica-Parodi, Lilianne R., Helmut H. Strey, Blaise Frederick, Robert Savoy, David Cox, Yevgeny Botanov, Denis Tolkunov, Denis Rubin, and Jochen Weber. "Chemosensory Cues to Conspecific Emotional Stress Activate Amygdala in Humans." *PloS ONE* 4, no. 7 (July 2009): e6415.

- Mund, Marcus, Christine Finn, Birk Hagemeyer, Julia Zimmermann, and Franz J. Neyer. "The Dynamics of Self–Esteem in Partner Relationships." *European Journal of Personality* 29, no. 2 (March/April 2015): 235–249.

- Murray, Elisabeth A. "The Amygdala, Reward and Emotion." *Trends in Cognitive Sciences* 11, no. 11 (November 2007): 489–497.

- Nagoski, Emily. *Come As You Are: The Surprising New Science That Will Transform Your Sex Life.* New York: Simon & Schuster, 2015.

- Nash, Carolyn Rose. *Monogamists and Consensual Nonmonogamists: Comparing Attachment Styles, Use of Relationship Therapy, Satisfaction with Therapeutic Services, and Overall Relationship Satisfaction.* Fullerton: California State University, Fullerton, 2018.

- Neff, Kristin D. "Self-Compassion, Self-Esteem, and Well-Being." *Social and Personality Psychology Compass* 5, no. 1 (January 2011): 1–12.

- Nygaard, Lynne C., Debora S. Herold, and Laura L. Namy. "The Semantics of Prosody: Acoustic and Perceptual Evidence of Prosodic Correlates to Word Meaning." *Cognitive Science* 33, no. 1 (2009): 127–146.

- Ogden, Pat, Kekuni Minton, and Clare Pain. *Trauma and the Body: A Sensorimotor Approach to Psychotherapy*. Norton Series on Interpersonal Neurobiology. New York: W. W. Norton, 2006.

- Osher, David, Pamela Cantor, Juliette Berg, Lily Steyer, and Todd Rose. "Drivers of Human Development: How Relationships and Context Shape Learning and Development." *Applied Developmental Science* 24, no. 1 (2020): 6–36.

- Özkarar-Gradwohl, Fatma Gökçe. "Cross-cultural Affective Neuroscience." *Frontiers in Psychology* 10 (2019): 794.

- Panksepp, Jaak. *Affective Neuroscience: The Foundations of Human and Animal Emotions*. Oxford: Oxford University Press, 2004.

- Panksepp, Jaak, and Lucy Biven. *The Archaeology of Mind: Neuroevolutionary Origins of Human Emotions*. Norton Series on Interpersonal Neurobiology. New York: W. W. Norton, 2012.

- Pearson, J. L., D. A. Cohn, P. A. Cowan, and C. P. Cowan. "Earned- and Continuous-Security in Adult Attachment: Relation to Depressive Symptomatology and Parenting Style." *Development and Psychopathology* 6, no. 2 (March 1994): 359–73.

- Peck, M. Scott. *The Different Drum: Community Making and Peace*. New York: Simon & Schuster, 2010.

- Perel, Esther. *Mating in Captivity: Unlocking Erotic Intelligence*. New York: Harper, 2007.

- Phutela, Deepika. "The Importance of Non-verbal Communication." *IUP Journal of Soft Skills* 9, no. 4 (December 2015): 43.

- Pillai-Friedman, Sabitha, J. L. Pollitt, and Annalisa Castaldo. "Becoming Kink-Aware—a Necessity for Sexuality Professionals." *Sexual and Relationship Therapy* 30, no. 2 (2015): 196–210.

- Porges, Stephen W. "Love: An Emergent Property of the Mammalian Autonomic Nervous System." *Psychoneuroendocrinology* 23, no. 8 (November 1998): 837–861.

- ———. "Making the World Safe for Our Children: Down-regulating Defence and Up-regulating Social Engagement to 'Optimise' the Human Experience." *Children Australia* 40, no. 2 (June 2015): 114.

- ———. "Neuroception: A Subconscious System for Detecting Threats and Safety." *Zero to Three (J)* 24, no. 5 (2004): 19–24.

- ———. "The Polyvagal Perspective." *Biological Psychology* 74, no. 2 (February 2007): 116–123. https://doi.org/10.1016/j.biopsycho.2006.06.009.

- ———. *The Polyvagal Theory: Neurophysiological Foundations of Emotions, Attachment, Communication, and Self-Regulation.* The Norton Series on Interpersonal Neurobiology. New York: W. W. Norton, 2011.

- ———. "The Polyvagal Theory: New Insights into Adaptive Reactions of the Autonomic Nervous System." *Cleveland Clinic Journal of Medicine* 76, Suppl. 2 (April 2009): S86.

- ———. "The Role of Social Engagement in Attachment and Bonding." *Attachment and Bonding* 3 (2005): 33–54.

- ———. "Social Engagement and Attachment: A Phylogenetic Perspective." *Annals of the New York Academy of Sciences* 1008 (2003): 31–47.

- Porges, Stephen W., and C. Sue Carter. "Polyvagal Theory and the Social Engagement System." In *Complementary and Integrative Treatments in Psychiatric Practice*, edited by Patricia L. Gerbarg, M.D., Philip R. Muskin, M.D., M.A., and Richard P. Brown, M.D., 221–241. Washington, DC: American Psychiatric Association, 2017.

- Porges, Stephen W., Jane A. Doussard-Roosevelt, and Ajit K. Maiti. "Vagal Tone and the Physiological Regulation of Emotion." *Monographs of the Society for Research in Child Development* 59, no. 2-3 (February 1994): 167–186.

- Prieto, Pilar, and Núria Esteve-Gibert, eds. *The Development of Prosody in First Language Acquisition*, vol. 23. Amsterdam: John Benjamins, 2018.

- Qian, Zhenchao, and Daniel T. Lichter. "Changing Patterns of Interracial Marriage in a Multiracial Society." *Journal of Marriage and Family* 73, no. 5 (October 2011): 1065–1084.

- Rajan-Rankin, Sweta. "Self-Identity, Embodiment and the Development of Emotional Resilience." *British Journal of Social Work* 44, no. 8 (December 2014): 2426–2442. https://doi.org/10.1093/bjsw/bct083.

- Ready Set Love®, a twelve-week, science-based relationship improvement program. www.readysetlove.com.

- Rock, David. *Your Brain at Work, Revised and Updated: Strategies for Overcoming Distraction, Regaining Focus, and Working Smarter All Day Long.* New York: HarperBusiness, 2020.

- Rosenblatt, Allan. "Insight, Working Through, and Practice: The Role of Procedural Knowledge." *Journal of the American Psychoanalytic Association* 52, no. 1 (March 2004): 189–207.

- Rossignac-Milon, Maya, Niall Bolger, Katherine S. Zee, Erica J. Boothby, and E. Tory Higgins. "Merged Minds: Generalized Shared Reality in Dyadic Relationships." *Journal of Personality and Social Psychology* 120, no. 4 (July 2020).

- Rossignac-Milon, Maya, and E. Tory Higgins. "Epistemic Companions: Shared Reality Development in Close Relationships." *Current Opinion in Psychology* 23 (October 2018): 66–71.

- Sable, Pat. "What Is Adult Attachment?" *Clinical Social Work Journal* 36, no. 1 (March 2008): 21–30.

- Salas, Eduardo, Nancy J. Cooke, and Michael A. Rosen. "On Teams, Teamwork, and Team Performance: Discoveries and Developments." *Human Factors* 50, no. 3 (June 2008): 540–547.

- Salter Ainsworth, Mary D., Mary C. Blehar, Everett Waters, and Sally N. Wall. *Patterns of Attachment: A Psychological Study of the Strange Situation*. London: Psychology Press, 2015.

- Sapolsky, Robert M. *Behave: The Biology of Humans at Our Best and Worst*. London: Penguin, 2017.

- Schore, Allan N. *Affect Regulation and the Origin of the Self: The Neurobiology of Emotional Development*. New York: Routledge, 2016.

- ———. *Affect Regulation and the Repair of the Self*. Norton Series on Interpersonal Neurobiology, vol. 2. New York: W. W. Norton, 2003.

- ———. "Attachment, Affect Regulation, and the Developing Right Brain: Linking Developmental Neuroscience to Pediatrics." *Pediatrics in Review* 26, no. 6 (June 2005): 204–217.

- ———. "Attachment and the Regulation of the Right Brain." *Attachment & Human Development* 2, no. 1 (April 2000): 23–47.

- ———. *The Development of the Unconscious Mind*. Norton Series on Interpersonal Neurobiology. New York: W. W. Norton, 2019.

- ———. "Paradigm Shift: The Right Brain and the Relational Unconscious." *Psychologist-Psychoanalyst* 28, no. 3 (2008): 20–25.

- ———. "Playing on the Right Side of the Brain: An Interview with Allan N. Schore." *American Journal of Play* 9, no. 2 (Winter 2017): 105–142.

- ———. "The Right Brain Implicit Self Lies at the Core of Psychoanalysis." *Psychoanalytic Dialogues* 21, no. 1 (February 2011): 75–100.

- Schore, Judith R., and Allan N. Schore. "Modern Attachment Theory: The Central Role of Affect Regulation in Development and Treatment." *Clinical Social Work Journal* 36, no. 1 (2008): 9–20.

- Shapiro, J. R., and J. S. Applegate. "Cognitive Neuroscience, Neurobiology and Affect Regulation: Implications for Clinical Social Work." *Clinical Social Work Journal* 28 (March 2000).

- Shashwati, Sudha, and Preksha Kansal. "Is There a Right Way to Love?: Mindset in Romantic Relationships." *International Journal of Innovative Studies in Sociology and Humanities (IJISSH)* (February 2019).

- Shaver, Phillip R., and Mario Mikulincer. "Adult Attachment Strategies and the Regulation of Emotion." In *Handbook of Emotion Regulation*, edited by James J. Gross, 465. New York: Guilford, 2007.

- Sherkat, Darren E., Melissa Powell-Williams, Gregory Maddox, and Kylan Mattias De Vries. "Religion, Politics, and Support for Same-Sex Marriage in the United States, 1988–2008." *Social Science Research* 40, no. 1 (January 2011): 167–180.

- Siegel, Daniel J. *The Developing Mind: How Relationships and the Brain Interact to Shape Who We Are.* New York: Guilford, 2020.

- ——. *The Developing Mind: Toward a Neurobiology of Interpersonal Experience.* New York: Guilford, 1999.

- ——. "Mindful Awareness, Mindsight, and Neural Integration. *The Humanistic Psychologist* 37, no. 2 (2009): 137.

- ——. "Mindfulness Training and Neural Integration: Differentiation of Distinct Streams of Awareness and the Cultivation of Well-Being." *Social Cognitive and Affective Neuroscience* 2, no. 4 (2007): 259–263.

- ——. *Pocket Guide to Interpersonal Neurobiology: An Integrative Handbook of the Mind.* New York: W. W. Norton, 2012.

- ——. "Toward an Interpersonal Neurobiology of the Developing Mind: Attachment Relationships, 'Mindsight,' and Neural Integration." *Infant Mental Health Journal: Official Publication of the World Association for Infant Mental Health* 22, no. 1–2 (2001): 67–94.

- Solomon, Marion F., and Daniel J. Siegel, eds. *How People Change: Relationships and Neuroplasticity in Psychotherapy.* Norton Series on Interpersonal Neurobiology. New York: W. W. Norton, 2017.

- Solomon, Marion F., and Stan Tatkin. *Love and War in Intimate Relationships: Connection, Disconnection, and Mutual Regulation in Couple Therapy.* Norton Series on Interpersonal Neurobiology. New York: W. W. Norton, 2011.

- Southwick, Steven M., George A. Bonanno, Ann S. Masten, Catherine Panter-Brick, and Rachel Yehuda. "Resilience Definitions, Theory, and Challenges: Interdisciplinary Perspectives." *European Journal of Psychotraumatology* 5 (October 2014). 10.3402/ejpt.v5.25338. https://doi.org/10.3402/ejpt.v5.25338.

- Speer, Shari R., and Kiwako Ito. "Prosody in First Language Acquisition—Acquiring Intonation as a Tool to Organize Information in Conversation." *Language and Linguistics Compass* 3, no. 1 (February 2009): 90–110.

- Strathearn, Lane. "Maternal Neglect: Oxytocin, Dopamine and the Neurobiology of Attachment." *Journal of Neuroendocrinology* 23, no. 11 (November 2011): 1054–1065.

- Swain, James E., Pilyoung Kim, Julie Spicer, Shao-Hsuan Ho, Carolyn J. Dayton, Alya Elmadih, and Kathryn M. Abel. "Approaching the Biology of Human Parental Attachment: Brain Imaging, Oxytocin and Coordinated Assessments of Mothers and Fathers." *Brain Research* 1580 (September 2014): 78–101.

- Tamietto, Marco, and Beatrice de Gelder. "Neural Bases of the Non-conscious Perception of Emotional Signals." *Nature Reviews Neuroscience* 11, no. 10 (October 2010): 697–709.

- Taormino, Tristan. *Opening Up: A Guide to Creating and Sustaining Open Relationships.* Jersey City: Cleis Press, 2008.

- Tatkin, Stan. "Applying a Psychobiological Approach to the Identification and Treatment of Socialemotional Deficits in Couple Therapy." *Psychotherapy in Australia* 19, no. 4 (August 2013): 14.

- ———. "How Couples Change. A Psychobiological Approach to Couple Therapy (PACT)." In *How People Change: Relationships and Neuroplasticity in Psychotherapy*, edited by Marion F. Solomon and Daniel J. Siegel, Norton Series on Interpersonal Neurobiology, 320. New York: W. W. Norton, 2017.

- ———. "A Psychobiological Approach to Couple Therapy: Integrating Attachment and Personality Theory as Interchangeable Structural Components." *Psychologist-Psychoanalyst: Division 39 of the American Psychological Association* 29, no. 3 (2009): 7–15.

- ———. *Wired for Love: How Understanding Your Partner's Brain and Attachment Style Can Help You Defuse Conflict and Build a Secure Relationship.* Oakland: New Harbinger, 2012.

- Turner, Jonathan H. *Human Emotions: A Sociological Theory.* Abingdon, UK: Taylor & Francis, 2007.

- Umberson, Debra, and Jennifer Karas Montez. "Social Relationships and Health: A Flashpoint for Health Policy." *Journal of Health and Social Behavior* 51 (Suppl.) (2010): S54–S66. https://doi.org/10.1177/0022146510383501.

- Vaillant, George E., Charles C. McArthur, and Arlie Bock. "Grant Study of Adult Development, 1938–2000." Harvard Dataverse V4 (2010). https://hdl.handle.net/1902.1/00290.

- Vandekerckhove, Marie, Luis Carlo Bulnes, and Jaak Panksepp. "The Emergence of Primary Anoetic Consciousness in Episodic Memory." *Frontiers in Behavioral Neuroscience* 7 (January 2014): 2010.

- van der Kolk, Bessel A. "The Body Keeps the Score: Memory and the Evolving Psychobiology of Posttraumatic Stress." *Harvard Review of Psychiatry* 1, no. 5 (January–February 1994): 253–265.

- Veaux, Franklin, and Eve Rickert. *More than Two*. Portland, OR: Thorntree Press, 2014.

- Watanabe, Noriya, and Masahiko Haruno. "Effects of Subconscious and Conscious Emotions on Human Cue-Reward Association Learning." *Scientific Reports* 5 (February 2015).

- Weitzman, Geri, Joy Davidson, R. A. Phillips, James R. Fleckenstein, and C. Morotti-Meeker. "What Psychology Professionals Should Know about Polyamory." *National Coalition on Sexual Freedom* 7 (2009): 1–28.

- West, David, and Scott Dellana. "Diversity of Ability and Cognitive Style for Group Decision Processes." *Information Sciences* 179, no. 5 (February 2009): 542–558.

- West, Richard F., Russell J. Meserve, and Keith E. Stanovich. "Cognitive Sophistication Does Not Attenuate the Bias Blind Spot." *Journal of Personality and Social Psychology* 103, no. 3 (September 2012): 506.

- Willey, Angela. *Undoing Monogamy: The Politics of Science and the Possibilities of Biology*. Durham: Duke University Press, 2016.

- Wilson, Douglas C. *Gay Male Couples and the Issue of Monogamy versus Non-monogamy*. Santa Barbara: Pacifica Graduate Institute, 2012.

- Wilt, Justin, Marissa A. Harrison, and Cobi S. Michael. "Attitudes and Experiences of Swinging Couples." *Psychology & Sexuality* 9, no. 1 (January 2018): 38–53.

- Witteman, Jurriaan, Vincent J. P. Van Heuven, and Niels O. Schiller. "Hearing Feelings: A Quantitative Meta-analysis on the Neuroimaging Literature of Emotional Prosody Perception." *Neuropsychologia* 50, no. 12 (October 2012): 2752–2763.

- Yang, Yang Claire, Courtney Boen, Karen Gerken, Ting Li, Kristen Schorpp, and Kathleen Mullan Harris. "Social Relationships and Physiological Determinants of Longevity across the Human Lifespan." *Proceedings of the National Academy of Sciences* (January 2016). http://www.pnas.org/content/early/2016/01/02/1511085112.

- Yehuda, Rachel. "Risk and Resilience in Posttraumatic Stress Disorder." *Journal of Clinical Psychiatry* 65 (2004): 29–36.

- Young, Emma. "Gut Instincts: The Secrets of Your Second Brain." *New Scientist* 216 (December 2012): 38–42. https://doi.org/10.1016/S0262-4079(12)63204-7.

- Zald, David H. "The Human Amygdala and the Emotional Evaluation of Sensory Stimuli." *Brain Research Reviews* 41, no. 1 (January 2003): 88–123.

- Zaltman, Gerald. *How Customers Think: Essential Insights into the Mind of the Market*. Cambridge, MA: Harvard Business School Press, 2003.

Index

difference between communication
and, xxiv, 2–3
distractions to, xvii–xviii
earliest means of, xi
as facilitating communication, xvii
factors shaping how we connect, 7–8
how to prioritize, 8–13
maintained regularly, 43–44
as more important than
communication, xxiii–xxiv, 189
navigating daily issues of life with, 1–2
need for in-person, xxvi–xxvii
presence and. *See* present/present
moment
prioritizing over communication,
xxiv–xxv
real-world scenarios, 14–16
the science of, xxii–xxiii
sex and, 13–14
in your relationship, evaluating, 183
conversation(s). *See also* verbal
communication; words
connecting, 165–166
date night rules for, 166
example of focusing on connecting
before having, 14–15
feelings-based, 144–145
process over content in. *See* process
over content
relationship retreats allowing for
meaningful, 167–168
superficial, 162
that does not create connection,
163–164
co-regulation, xi–xii, 151
core issues, 109–110
coronavirus pandemic, xxvi–xxvii
cortisol, 5
couples, exercises for. *See* partner
exercises
couples therapy
neuroscience-based, xxxvi
using practice in, xx, 86, 87
couple, working as a. *See* team(s)/
teamwork
Crenshaw, Kimberlé Williams, 69
criticisms/being critical, 75, 116, 117,
118, 125, 130, 131, 136
cultural norms, defining healthy

relationships based on, xxxii–xxxiii,
xxxv
culture(s)
being present and, 40
nonverbal cues and, 11
power imbalances and, 69
relationship, 132, 174
secure functioning and, xxxiii
vocal tone and, 25
culture of growth, 88–90
curiosity, 41, 88, 89, 90

D

"date night rules," 166
dating, xxvii
deception, 64
default habits, inviting care and, 125
defenses and defensiveness, 41–42, 90,
94, 107, 114, 117, 118, 119, 127,
134
demeaning your partner, 171
dependency on others, 146–147
depression, 3, 5, 146
diet and exercise, xxv, 46, 53
differences, managing, 66–67, 77–79
*The Different Drum: Community Making
and Peace* (Peck), 72
differing perspectives, appreciating and
validating, 182
disconnection
differences in emotional processing
styles and, 152
pausing and pivoting when noticing,
108–109
speed of response and, 30
using words that create, 162–163
distractions, 38, 45, 46
diversity, embracing, 67–70, 184–185
dopamine, 6, 72
Drescher, Jack, xxxiii
dysfunctional relationships, impact on
physical health, xxv–xxvi

E

earned security, xxix, xxxviii
emotion(s). *See also* feelings; individual
emotions
about, 140–141
amplifying positive, 147–148

About the Author

John Howard is an internationally recognized therapist, wellness expert, mystic, and educator who uses the latest science to help couples have stronger relationships. He was one of twelve therapists in the world selected to form the founding core faculty of PACT, a leading neuroscience-based approach to couples therapy. He developed the couples and family therapy curriculum for the Dell Medical School in Austin, Texas, where he teaches, and has designed and led a relationship wellness program for Google, Inc.

John is a Licensed Professional Counselor and a Licensed Marriage and Family Therapist. He is the host of the popular *Ready Set Love*® podcast on the new science of relationships (now *The John Howard Show*) and the creator of the Ready Set Love® online program for couples—the first neuroscience-based online relationship course and first of its kind to be inclusive of all couples. John prioritizes diversity and inclusion in his work and draws on multicultural influences from years of traveling and studying ancient and Indigenous traditions. He has presented on the neuroscience of couples therapy at leading psychological conferences and has spoken to organizations such as the Association of Marriage and Family Therapists and Attachment Parenting International.

John is a Cuban American whose first language is Spanish. He grew up in New York City, didn't live with his parents until the age of nine, and experienced trauma and neglect, eventually leaving home at fifteen. He was homeless for a period of time but discovered spirituality and psychology as a means to heal from past attachment wounds. In relationships, he struggled to connect with others until learning how to develop better habits using the new science of relationships. He teaches from experience how to move from disconnection to having close, fulfilling relationships.

John has helped hundreds of couples of all types heal and improve their relationships for over a decade. In 2019, he developed Presence Therapy®, an integrative mind-body approach to therapy that is taught to psychotherapists worldwide, incorporates neuroscience, and helps therapists develop more comprehensive treatment plans. His work aims to help the field of couples therapy be more inclusive and utilize a science-based definition of relationship health. John is also the founder and CEO of PRESENCE, a wellness center in Austin, Texas, helping individuals optimize across the four primary domains of wellness: mental health, physical health, close relationships, and a sense of purpose and meaning. He lives in Austin surrounded by a vibrant community of therapists, healers, entrepreneurs, podcasters, and thought leaders.